PANDEMIC LEGALITIES

D1612570

Law, Society, Policy series

Series Editor: **Rosie Harding**,
University of Birmingham

Law, Society, Policy seeks to offer a new outlet for high quality, socio-legal research monographs and edited collections with the potential for policy impact.

Also available in the series:

*Women, Precarious Work and Care:
The Failure of Family-friendly Rights*
Emily Grabham

Forthcoming in the series:

Deprivation of Liberty in the Shadows of the Institution
Lucy Series

Find out more at
bristoluniversitypress.co.uk/law-society-policy

Law, Society, Policy series

Series Editor: **Rosie Harding**,
University of Birmingham

International advisory board

Lynette Chua, National University of Singapore

Margaret Davies, Flinders University, Australia

Martha Fineman, Emory University, Atlanta, Georgia, USA

Marc Hertogh, University of Groningen, The Netherlands

Fiona Kelly, La Trobe University, Melbourne, Australia

Fiona de Londras, University of Birmingham, UK

Anna Maki-Petaja-Leinonen, University of Eastern Finland

Ambreena Manji, Cardiff University, UK

Linda Mulcahy, University of Oxford, UK

Vanessa Munro, University of Warwick, UK

Debra Parkes, University of British Columbia, Canada

Florence Shako, Riara Law School, Riara University, Kenya

Antu Sorainen, University of Helsinki, Finland

Dee Smythe, University of Cape Town, South Africa

Michael Thomson, Leeds University, UK and UTS, Australia

Bridgette Toy-Cronin, University of Otago, New Zealand

Lisa Vanhala, University College London, UK

Find out more at
bristoluniversitypress.co.uk/law-society-policy

PANDEMIC LEGALITIES

Legal Responses to COVID-19 – Justice
and Social Responsibility

Edited by
Dave Cowan and Ann Mumford

BRISTOL
UNIVERSITY
PRESS

First published in Great Britain in 2021 by

Bristol University Press
University of Bristol
1–9 Old Park Hill
Bristol
BS2 8BB
UK
t: +44 (0)117 954 5940
e: bup-info@bristol.ac.uk

Details of international sales and distribution partners are available at bristoluniversitypress.co.uk

© Bristol University Press 2021

British Library Cataloguing in Publication Data
A catalogue record for this book is available from the British Library

ISBN 978-1-5292-1891-6 hardback
ISBN 978-1-5292-1892-3 paperback
ISBN 978-1-5292-1893-0 ePub
ISBN 978-1-5292-1894-7 ePdf

The right of Dave Cowan and Ann Mumford to be identified as editors of this work has been asserted by them in accordance with the Copyright, Designs and Patents Act 1988.

All rights reserved: no part of this publication may be reproduced, stored in a retrieval system, or transmitted in any form or by any means, electronic, mechanical, photocopying, recording, or otherwise without the prior permission of Bristol University Press.

Every reasonable effort has been made to obtain permission to reproduce copyrighted material. If, however, anyone knows of an oversight, please contact the publisher.

The statements and opinions contained within this publication are solely those of the editors and contributors and not of the University of Bristol or Bristol University Press. The University of Bristol and Bristol University Press disclaim responsibility for any injury to persons or property resulting from any material published in this publication.

Bristol University Press works to counter discrimination on grounds of gender, race, disability, age and sexuality.

Cover design: Andrew Corbett
Front cover image: Witthaya Prasongsin – Getty images
Bristol University Press uses environmentally responsible print partners.
Printed and bound in Great Britain by CPI Group (UK) Ltd, Croydon, CR0 4YY

Contents

List of Figures and Tables

Figures

Tables

Notes on Contributors

Foluke Adebisi is Senior Lecturer in Law at University of Bristol.

Rowan Alcock is a DPhil candidate at Oxford University.

Ivanka Antova is Research Fellow at Queen's University Belfast.

Katie Bales is Senior Lecturer in Law at University of Bristol.

Helen Carr is Professor of Law at the University of Kent.

Dave Cowan is Professor of Law and Policy at University of Bristol.

Mark Flear is Reader in Law at Queen's University Belfast.

Nick Gill is Professor of Human Geography at University of Exeter.

Simon Halliday is Professor of Socio-Legal studies at University of York.

Rosie Harding is Professor of Law and Society at University of Birmingham.

Tamara Hervey is Jean Monnet Professor of EU law at City University of London.

Kathryn Hollingsworth is Professor of Law at Newcastle University.

Suhraiya Jivraj is Reader in Law and Social Justice at University of Kent.

Ed Kirton-Darling is Lecturer in Law at University of Kent.

Kathleen Lahey is Professor of Law at Queen's University, Kingston.

Jed Meers is Lecturer in Law at University of York.

Linda Mulcahy is Professor of Socio-Legal studies at Oxford University.

Ann Mumford is Professor of Law at King's College London.

Albert Sanchez-Graells is Professor of Law at University of Bristol.

Alison Struthers is Assistant Professor of Law at University of Warwick.

Joe Tomlinson is Senior Lecturer in Law at University of York.

Sally Wheeler is Deputy Vice-Chancellor at Australian National University.

Matthew Wood is Research Fellow at University of Sheffield.

Preface

This book was written during the summer and autumn of 2020. The editors asked the authors to consider how austerity had impacted their areas of legal specialism; and, whether this impact had relevance for the challenges likely to be faced as the United Kingdom recovered from the COVID-19 pandemic. The significant cost of initiatives such as the furlough scheme, and the tax incentives offered to employers within the hospitality and tourism industries, were at the heart of the authors' task. The UK seemed poised to incur very significant amounts of debt, which was alarming, given recent history. After the financial crash of 2008, the protections of law had seemed to come a very distant second to economic imperatives. The risk of repeating this pattern was pressing. Thus, the authors were asked to consider what might be fixed, now, before the recovery period began.

As the authors began writing in early summer 2020, it was difficult to anticipate the extent of disruption and trauma that soon was to come. By February 2021, when this book went to press, the death of George Floyd in the US state of Minnesota had led to protests around the world. A second lockdown in the UK had occurred. The pressing concerns about procurement of PPE had not dissipated, but, rather, were exacerbated by concerns over the procurement of vaccines – after months of erratic provision of diagnostic testing. Indeed, 'exacerbated' would appear to be the theme of developments over the course of writing this book – whether concerns over paying for the cost of government borrowing, surprise at tight touch Parliamentary scrutiny, worries over educational disparity, anxieties over inequality in all aspects of law, profound disquiet over the enormous toll of the virus – all of the concerns that drove the inception of this book, tragically, have intensified as it was being written. This makes the calls for action found in these chapters even more pressing. The crisis is too profound for it to make sense for scholars to wait until the crisis ends, and then to reflect upon the choices that were made. There will be a time for that vein of scholarship, and the scholarship will be valuable – this moment, however, is different. As the crisis still rages, our hope is to contribute to the discussion of choices that might be made.

In the short time before this book reaches the reader (and we are enormously grateful to Bristol University Press for their commitment to this not insignificant task), only one thing is certain: there is hope that, in this period of time, the crisis may have improved considerably; and, there is fear that the crisis may have deepened. As we hope for the former, we also nonetheless are not dissuaded by the possibility that an additional intensification of this global crisis might occur in the weeks before this book reaches its readers, and its details are not captured here. This is because the prescriptions found in these chapters were important before the pandemic, and are even more so now. We urge attention to the calls for action offered in this assemblage of leading scholars of law. As the pandemic tragically has affirmed, the structures underpinning law are not secure, and action is needed – as is commitment to optimism for a better future, also offered in the pages of this book.

February 2021

Series Editor's Preface

The Law, Society, Policy series publishes high-quality, socio-legal research monographs and edited collections with the potential for policy impact. Cutting across the traditional divides of legal scholarship, Law, Society, Policy offers an interdisciplinary, policy engaged approach to socio-legal research which explores law in its social and political contexts with a particular focus on the place of law in everyday life.

The series seeks to take an explicitly society-first view of socio-legal studies, with a focus on the ways that law shapes social life, and the constitutive nature of law and society. International in scope, engaging with domestic, international and global legal and regulatory frameworks, texts in the Law, Society, Policy series engage with the full range of socio-legal topics and themes.

Introduction

Dave Cowan and Ann Mumford

It has been reported that the US had bought up the entire stock of a drug, Remdesivir, manufactured by a US company and originally developed to treat Ebola victims, as it had seemed to have a positive impact on those recovering from COVID-19. (Boseley, 2020)

Law and inequality

During troubled times, events that captivate for a minute may quickly be replaced by other, even more troubling developments, and perhaps forgotten. Nonetheless, the quote at the start of this chapter, coupled with Emily Maitlis' now famous Newsnight speech about how COVID-19 is "not a great leveller"[1] offer a metaphor for what the contributors to this book are arguing – the different effects of, and responses to, COVID-19; the fragmentation of the global, and anxieties about the local scale. At heart, we are concerned with the idea of the public, and the presentation of the public as a homogenous community equally affected by COVID-19. Just like the supposed equal effects of the rule of law, we know that the idea and constitution of the public as well as the rule of law are riven with inequalities. We know that class, gender, race and wealth are cleavages in the supposed homogeneity of the public. And we know that the effects of COVID-19 are visited disproportionately on the already disadvantaged.

---

[1] BBC (2020) 'Coronavirus: They tell us it's a great leveller... it's not', https://www.youtube.com/watch?v=L6wIcpdJyCI (accessed 8 April 2021).

Despite – and, perhaps, because of – the economic packages in place to support businesses and others during the pandemic, there are anxieties over how the coming economic crisis caused by the resultant swollen sovereign debt will affect the public. After the last great economic crisis following the bank and market meltdown in 2007–08, austerity measures were put in place. What might be termed 'austerity law' emerged as the need to repay sovereign debt dominated discussions of the economy. It is these questions and anxieties which, virtually, brought us together. We had originally been inspired by the almost naïve questions raised by Dee Cook in her brilliant, innovative book, *Rich Law, Poor Law* (1988), which uncovered not only the differential approaches to tax and social security fraud, but also sought to explain how these differences had come about at a structural level. Even the architecture of the state emphasized this disparity – the majesty of the former London HQ of the HMRC, as opposed to the jobcentres outside which the labour and income poor queue for assistance. The latter, together with the translation of the byzantine rules into everyday life, was captured perfectly by Ken Loach in his film about welfare reform and its effects, *I, Daniel Blake* (2016).[2]

Our work has sought to expand these questions across dimensions of inequalities, and subject areas. Our animating concerns are also positive – what good can come out of the pandemic? What might a fair and just response look like? We are (or try to be) optimists. The past, however, is not a cause for optimism. In this introduction, we seek to set the tone for this collection. We outline the themes and aims, and our collective purpose. Then, we go on to draw attention to our animating concerns around austerity law and its differential effects. We consider the impact of over a decade of austerity on discrete areas of the law. In some areas, severe underfunding has undermined the ability of legal services to deliver advice to vulnerable persons. In other areas, although underfunding is a challenge, the real problem is that the design of law has caused targets to be missed, and the failure of law to deliver on its ambitions.

Contributors to this book understand austerity to have been a wrong turn, and to have placed the rule of law under a burden from which it will be difficult to recover. Legal rights have come to be regarded as an obstacle, as economic growth and sovereign debt management have been prioritized over all else. Existing inequalities have become entrenched and exacerbated. The burdens of the austerity recovery period were borne by the poorest, and the most vulnerable. The book is motivated by a fear of what may come next, but also by optimism that laws, and structures, may be changed.

---

[2]   Ken Loach (2016) *I, Daniel Blake*, Sixteen Films, Why Not Productions and Wild Bunch.

This book is not written for a selective or specialist audience; it is, however, written by academic leaders in their respective fields of law. Each chapter is designed as a think piece, based on the contributors' understandings and appreciations of their field. They reflect on the implications of COVID-19, express their anxieties about the development of policy and practice, and about the overweening, apparently neutral version of law and the economy which has taken root. Contributors draw on diverse resources, from survey evidence to economic rationalities. They are engaging with the current, reflecting on the past, and thinking about how the future response can be positive and productive.

While special advisors and the PM's father seemed oblivious and unaffected by travel restrictions, the ordinary and the relatively poor have had different experiences. Contributors work through the issues that affect particularly vulnerable sectors and populations. Each of these areas was already shot through with almost existential questions about values and purpose, and a recognition of different life-chances. The pandemic and its aftermath require us to think again about these questions in a much sharper way.

The government's programme of austerity law in the period following the global financial crisis did not penalize those who had caused it, but those who were most affected by its consequences. The programme of austerity cuts and reduction in service provision exaggerated the withdrawal of the state from direct provision of services as well as reduced part of the state's revenue-based exposure through social security cuts. Impact assessments expected the cuts to fall on those groups already detrimentally affected by previous cuts. Citizenship became not a right but a tool through which the outsider could be excluded.

Much of the constituent elements of the austerity programme ended up in court, with the government largely admitting (as it had to) that the consequences of its welfare reforms targeted single mothers, large households, disabled people, and Black and minority ethnic households. The government's court-based defences of its various austerity packages – from employment tribunal fees to caps on benefits, from penalizing under occupation of social housing to excluding persons from abroad – have served to create a complex pastiche of the global and local in law, which focused on whether the particular aspect of the programme was proportionate. As a very basic starting point, this demonstrates the real costs of ignoring the law when implementing cuts in governmental spending, or of treating budgeting as a 'neutral' function of government.

The government's vigorous defences of its programme served to reduce its supposed savings, which in some cases were only marginal anyway. The measures could be dismissed as exercises in ideology – creating further conditionality in social security, tightening labour markets, restricting workers' rights and access to justice – but with very real effects. The poor were required to pay disproportionately for the misdemeanours and risks taken on by the wealthy. Areas became segregated on the basis of income. And, it produced, as Blyth (2015: 15) suggested, a polarised and politicized society in which the conditions for a sustainable politics of dealing with more debt and less growth are undermined. Populism, nationalism and calls for the return of 'God and gold' in equal doses are what unequal austerity generates, and no one, not even those at the top, benefits.

If we take the bedroom tax as an exemplar of these issues, we can see how the ideas and ideology of austerity became enmeshed with existing anxieties about the use of what had become, through government intervention, a scarce resource (social housing). The legal technique adopted for the bedroom tax – a bright line rule which restricted the availability of housing-based social security income, depending on a household's composition irrespective of the number of bedrooms in a given property – symbolized the ways in which New Labour and coalition governments re-moulded the law around penalizing households, particularly those with disabilities and those at risk of domestic violence who were recognized to be disproportionately affected, for only limited financial benefit. The resultant court-based challenges to the policy drew on equality law, human rights, and public law, in innovative ways, ending with a partial finding of the government's illogical perversity and breach of human rights. For example, the government had set up sanctuary schemes to assist survivors of domestic violence, but they were subject to the bedroom tax as a result of having the extra room. Accordingly, their homes became unaffordable. At an international level, the UN rapporteur excoriated the UK government's approach, arguing that it produced greater poverty: 'Those who are impacted by this policy were not necessarily the most vulnerable a few months ago, but they were on the margins, facing fragility and housing stress, with little extra income to respond to this situation and already barely coping with their expenses' (Rolnik, 2013).

It has been difficult to accept the assurance of then Prime Minister Theresa May in 2018 that 'austerity is over'. She announced that the 'end is in sight' for the period of prolonged suffering from massive cuts in public spending. Whether or not May was correct, austerity had produced a country with a state which had largely withdrawn from provision to a state which relied on ever-reducing income-based subsidies. Where the state remained involved in provision, such as the NHS, there was an estate, workforce and structure which was under-resourced; and, as became apparent as a result of COVID-19, a care home sector cut adrift from large-scale state support. There was a labour market which increasingly relied on zero-hours contracts, and an increasingly penal crime control complex.

Theresa May, of course, could not have predicted that, only two years after she announced the end of austerity, the financial crisis facing the UK, and the world, would be of even greater significance. There, thus, is a sense of fear among those working within and around the law – what could possibly be next? Of course, we welcomed, on 23 November 2020, ahead of a Spending Review, Chancellor of the Exchequer Rishi Sunak's announcement that "you will not see austerity next week, what you will see is an increase in government spending". Indeed, he promised an increase in funding for health, the police and education. He also presaged, however, a public sector pay freeze for all workers outside of the NHS, and a freeze on benefits. The UK's aid budget was cut from 0.7 per cent to 0.5 per cent of national income. Finally, he hinted that spending would not continue into the future at its current rate.

Our ideas

The message from these mixed signals is that a hierarchy of priorities is emerging. The prospect of public sector strikes, for example, lingers in the air, even as the NHS appears to be ringfenced from further cuts. This book aims to inform the public discussion of these hierarchies. Before areas are targeted for protection or defunding, it is important to ask: how has austerity impacted upon these areas of the law? What is more urgent, now that the pandemic has happened? Are existing legal structures sufficient? Above all, what is most important for us to consider, and possibly to change, right now?

It is our aim in this book to map out ways in which those already disadvantaged have been affected by COVID-19 across two broad areas: **justice**, and **the social**. These broad areas enable us to pinpoint issues which have been particularly affected by COVID-19 – such as, for example, the scandal over the procurement of Personal Protective Equipment (PPE) – through to issues where COVID-19 has highlighted pre-existing particular systemic inequities or by-products of global capital movement – such as around retail in the context of ESG (environmental, social and corporate governance) investing.

The chapters have been divided between those two broad areas, but, as always, the margins are fine and chapters could have been located in both areas. Partly for symmetry and partly because there is an inherent crossover between justice and the social – it would be difficult to have one without the other – the chapters and parts tend to blend into each other. It is not our concern, particularly, to interrogate the meaning of these labels, or key words, which is the stuff of other scholarship; but, if they mean anything, it is a concern with working towards equality, working towards understandings of solidarity and networks through which we can do better. Our animating concerns generally are the kinds of anxieties we have raised, and, to be sure, we are angry, but we also seek to offer positive messages.

What, after all, does something like corporate social responsibility have to say about the pandemic? What can tax or labour law offer the ways in which we see the pandemic? How can we link the issues around Black Lives Matter to the pandemic? However, our authors demonstrate that these kinds of questions are the wrong questions to be asking. The COVID-19 pandemic has impacted on all areas of law, and that impact has been experienced disproportionately along lines of race and poverty. This is our (and we are speaking collectively for us and the authors) key objective, whether that be through corporate social responsibility, health, housing and social care, or tax and labour law, or indeed the range of subjects dealt with here. Our authors carefully trace the responses to the pandemic back through different temporal periods and periodizations in their subjects, demonstrating the ways that the responses to the pandemic have often exaggerated and made apparent the issues which were already in place, often submerged or obscured. They see that the impact of the pandemic must be considered from the perspectives of both institutions and individuals. We have come together here to seek to influence the discussion of how to move forward and recognize the fragility in the present and the contingencies of the past.

The editors set the authors a distinctive and difficult task. The authors are some of the leading legal academic experts. Their outstanding work appears, often but with some notable exceptions, behind paywalls. We are fed up of writing for each other. This book offers a space in which all of us have tried to write for a different audience of everybody. We required our authors to write with no more than five references where possible. Gone are much of the references to our theory heroes. As editors, our role has been also to enforce a strict word limit of 4,500 words per chapter. The pleasure for us has been to sit down and read the chapters in which our wonderful authors have produced outstanding think pieces in as accessible a way as they can. Most of all, we want you as the reader to engage with our anxieties and hopes; we are not asking you to agree with us, which would be dull; but, in the pages which follow you may feel our anger and concern, and may share our hopes for a better world to come.

Structure and outline

Our first theme, justice, begins with a chapter in which the idea of Parliamentary democracy is unpicked through thinking about the ways in which Parliament has been side lined and marginalized during the responses to the pandemic, and new ways of government by guidance, Direction or letter or request have been forged (Cowan). What we have witnessed during the pandemic has been an enhancement of non–Parliamentary practices by the executive which have overridden some of our fundamental rights and values. Using a case study of the governance of residential security during the pandemic, this chapter demonstrates how questionable processes and practices of government have extended the terrain of government towards new administrative forms.

Building upon these themes, the next two chapters in this section consider the recent acceleration in the use of remote justice in the UK, prompted by COVID-19. They raise the question of how such changes affect litigants in person and other vulnerable litigants. Drawing on original research in the Asylum Tribunal, Gill highlights the challenges appellants encounter in their face-to-face hearings, including confusion, anxiety, mistrust, disrespect, communication difficulties and distraction to provide a framework for thinking about the consequences of the shift to remote hearings in this charged context. Mulcahy considers, on the other hand, the extent to which totally online trials have the potential to create a more level playing field in the criminal justice system. In doing so, the chapter argues that there is a danger that critics of the use of technology romanticize physical courthouses as places which are better at dignifying lay users of the justice system or encouraging their participation.

Then, focusing these risks on particularly vulnerable participants, children in the criminal justice system, Hollingsworth invites us to consider the experience of children and their families in courthouses. She demonstrates that the youth justice crisis in 2020 is no longer one dominated by volume; it is one that now, more than ever, exposes discrimination, disadvantage and disability. There are risks from both the economy and growing indications of a return to penal populism. These threats demand a more concrete base for children's rights.

This section then shifts focus on to the occupation of the contributors to this book – legal education – but through an analysis of a justice system that is racialized. Adebisi and Jivraj start from ideas about race, racism and the 'racial state', and the disproportionate effects of the pandemic on racialized populations, arguing for an understanding of the pandemic as a syndemic moment. The argument is that racism is the real pandemic, which is also a legal pandemic. The chapter considers how legal pedagogy can, and should, respond to these issues. This chapter offers resources to legal educators, who may be searching for resources as part of an effort to reconsider the boundaries of the subjects they teach. Thus, the authors offer a wider range of references to the reader with the frank intention of offering pragmatic recommendations for course development.

Justice has had a mixed reception among our authors – to put it at its highest – but the next chapter reports some of the findings of an ongoing research project about public compliance with the UK's COVID-19 lockdown. Halliday, Meers and Tomlinson discuss the results of their study suggesting that, despite notable and powerful public statements about the extent to which lockdown represented an unacceptable violation of basic rights and liberties, this claim failed to capture the public imagination. Instead, most people either regarded the violation of basic rights as acceptable, given the context of the pandemic, or simply failed to think of the lockdown in terms of basic rights at all. This provides a corrective to the negative perceptions, and demonstrates a kind of obligation consciousness that finds force in social solidarity.

The section ends with Sanchez-Graells' powerful discussion of the PPE procurement fiasco in the context of the English NHS, drawing attention to the problems which were in place at the start of the pandemic and which produced the fiasco. The chapter advocates that the procurement capability of the public sector needs to be re-established, which will require insourcing currently outsourced functions and providing substantially more resources. Reliance on 'strategic providers' and management consultants needs to be severely cut back and the development of more varied and resilient supply chains needs to be actively promoted. Finally, there is a clear need for more (and much better) contingency planning, which also needs to be properly resourced.

The second section on the social begins with that totem of the social, the NHS. Hervey, Antova, Flear and Wood present the results of a project in which they interviewed people in 'left behind' communities in the North of England and Northern Ireland. They argue that the gap between ordinary people's perception of the power of law to hold a government to account, and ordinary people's desire for law to be used in that way, and the reality, is too wide, and should be narrowed. Many of the people who participated in this study argued that the law should secure protection for 'ordinary people' against cronyism and corruption – at the very least through securing transparency. Those in power should not be above the law. Put simply, political constitutionalism, along with its economic analogue, austerity economics, have failed the 'left behind'.

A complementary study of care homes by Harding follows, explaining that there are multiple and overlapping reasons for the very high rates of COVID-19 infection and death in residential adult social care settings. Some are immediate policy decisions relating to the management of the pandemic including to discharge older people from NHS hospitals into residential and nursing homes without a negative COVID-19 test result, and to prioritize the supply of (scarce) PPE to NHS providers. Others are endemic to the regulation of residential and nursing care. Low pay and low status for care workers in this impossible financial context then translates into high staff turnover and a reliance on agency care staff (who work for multiple providers). A new model for adult social care, which focuses on fairness rather than profit, is the only way to create a stable, safe and sustainable care home sector for the future.

Alcock, Carr and Kirton-Darling reflect upon the potential for a long-term shift towards a socially oriented housing system in England and Wales as a result of COVID-19. For too long, the housing system has been limited by its own pre-conceptions of what is possible. This has been accentuated by the withdrawal of the state from housing provision, the shift towards regarding housing as an individual's asset rather than as a home, which has led to an inability to respond properly to the challenges and led to a failure to see housing as a public health response. Instead, rather than addressing the totemic problems of the private rented sector such as mandatory possession claims (which must be dealt with), they argue for a social politics of housing in which the state takes responsibility for safe, secure and sustainable homes, putting society first, above the profit-motive.

In a similar vein, Struthers discusses the stratified effects of COVID-19, and the responses to it, within the formal education sector in England based principally on socio-economic factors, with other social categorizations, including ethnic origin and disability. The chapter challenges the reader to consider whether there is a way to ensure that the UK's economic recovery from the pandemic is handled in a sustainable and equitable way, with the burden of debt repayment falling not just on the poorest and most vulnerable sectors of society. Wheeler then explores the potential of this challenge, but in the context of corporate social responsibility. The focus, here, is on Boohoo, a publicly listed company on the Alternative Investment Market, and demonstrates how the problems behind the rise of fast fashion, together with the credibility of ESG investing. The chapter reveals the fault line that separates workplace conditions and environmental degradation from monetary return on investment. It ends by offering some thoughts on the behaviour of those who enable industries such as fast fashion to take hold and thrive – consumers and investors.

Then, Meers looks back at the UK social security system's response to the pandemic and its impact on groups already subject to the disproportionate effects of the 'welfare reform' agenda. Using the concept of 'frontier problems', it looks at what social welfare challenges have been caused and exposed by COVID-19, and the role for the social security system going forward. It also looks forward to future responses by the government, setting out the lessons from the last decade of austerity scholarship and from the legal challenges in the UK – grouped under 'austerity law' – that followed the 2008 recession. What shape the future government response will take is currently unclear, but those who have engaged with the social security system or those that work in it will be all too conscious of the failure to heed these lessons. Building upon this, Bales reminds us that a labour market divided along classed, gendered and racialized lines is nothing new and is unsurprising in a capitalist system which was built upon the domination of the working classes and the historical erasure of colonial and women's labour from its establishment. Finally, Mumford and Lahey consider the path ahead for taxation measures in the aftermath of the massive borrowing that the government will be required to undertake to pay for supportive measures, like the furlough scheme, put in place during the crisis. Spending cuts and tax breaks are often different sides of the same coin. The spending cuts of austerity appear poised to be replaced by taxation increases after the pandemic, which is to be welcomed. This presents the opportunity, the authors argue, for a fundamental reconsideration of the principles of a key tax that has been recommended for reform, the capital gains tax.

These chapters combine to offer challenges for action, and cause for optimism. The road ahead is likely to be exceptionally difficult. This is also an exceptionally fast-moving subject. The brave assertions by a journalist, in the opening paragraph of this introductory chapter, that the impact of COVID-19 is not experienced equally may well be replaced by another moment that both distracts and focuses attention. As a number of potential vaccines appear to be on the verge of global approval, the actions of the Trump administration with Remdesivir now seem to offer a prescient warning. What follows next, after COVID-19, need not be as costly as what preceded it, and there are clear steps that may be taken in order to ensure that the legal system offers justice; that corporations and tax structures are based on values of true social responsibility; and, that the systems of health, care, housing, justice and education are able to serve all who need it.

References

Blyth, M. (2015) *Austerity: The History of a Dangerous Idea*, Oxford, New York: Oxford University Press.

Boseley, S. (2020) 'US Secures World Stock of Key Covid-19 Drug Remdesivir', *The Guardian*, 30 June, www.theguardian.com/us-news/2020/jun/30/us-buys-up-world-stock-of-key-covid-19-drug (accessed 20 April 2021).

Cook, D.M. (1988) 'Rich Law, Poor Law: Differential Response to Tax and Supplementary Benefit Fraud', Keele University, https://library.lincoln.ac.uk/items/11848 (accessed 20 April 2021).

Rolnik, R. (2013) 'Report of the Special Rapporteur on adequate housing as a component of the right to an adequate standard of living, and on the right to non-discrimination in this context', *United Nations General Assembly*, https://www.ohchr.org/EN/HRBodies/HRC/RegularSessions/Session25/Documents/A_HRC_25_54_Add.2_ENG.DOC (accessed 20 April 2021).

PART I

Justice

1

Ruling the Pandemic

Dave Cowan

Introduction

I have spent more time wondering about how to start this chapter on 'governing' during the pandemic than actually writing it. Perhaps it could start with the almost daily shock felt in reading headlines and tweets linking Personal Protective Equipment (PPE) contracts and key personnel with the ruling party. Or we might start with the shift in the way of legislating which, on analyses from both the left and the right, has undermined the rule of law and the accountability of the Executive. What was said – rhetorically – about the 'elected dictatorship' or the 'new despotism' has given way to fresh realizations about its existence; perhaps the question is not, 'who governs Britain?', but how is Britain governed? Legislation, and secondary legislation, have combined with other forms of what Robert Megarry termed (in 1944) 'administrative quasi-legislation'[1]; or, government by media briefing; or, in 240 characters, by tweet, exemplified by a tweet by Robert Jenrick, Secretary of State for Housing, Communities and Local Government telling us that he was stopping evictions.

Another way to start this chapter might have been with a recognition of how things have changed over time. Since the invention of the Code of Guidance by the promulgation of the Highway Code, and successive forms of government by guidance, practice, circular, or letter (all of which seem rather quaint now), governments have used these forms as obtaining self-government by consent. As Ganz suggested (1987: 98), it is an empirical question whether government by consent in this way is effective. However, the point made in this chapter is that the *how* of governance has moved on

---

[1] Megarry, R. (1944) 'Administrative quasi-legislation', *Law Quarterly Review*, 60(1): 125.

in non-uniform ways, generally outside the Parliamentary gaze, and outside circuits of accountability.

To be sure, the impenetrable system of social security rules in this country have been toughened in the pages of statutory and secondary legislation, which has, at least, been subject to limited Parliamentary oversight. However, it is when we drill down into our specialist fields that the method of governing becomes more opaque. I will use the specific example of the methods and mechanisms of governing residential security during the pandemic. By residential security, I am referring to something as basic as being able to stay in our homes; and, of course, during the pandemic that basic human need has become even more significant. Alcock et al, in this volume, discuss the specific issues around housing security, with a focus on security in the privately rented sector. This chapter is complimentary to that, as it focuses on the *techne* of government, as opposed to substantive rights.

What the case study exposes is how apparently binary lines between lawfulness and unlawfulness, and between formal and informal models of government have blurred. One might say, ''twas ever thus' – in the period until the late 1970s, when relations between central and local government were characterized as autonomous and laissez-faire, there are plenty of examples of government by circular which lacked any form of legislative backing, but which were simply accepted as providing the basis for an obligation. In my field, that process provided the foundation for the modern homelessness legislation. However, in providing a chronology of the technologies of government of residential security during the pandemic, I am demonstrating something rather different – the expectation of government and the Ministry of Housing, Communities, and Local Government that everybody will dance to their tune; a tune which was usually composed (or publicized) late on a Friday afternoon, for implementation at that time.

Legal form and legal force

At an early stage in their education, law students learn the difference between what is termed primary, secondary and tertiary legislation. Primary legislation refers to Acts of Parliament, such as the Coronavirus Act 2020, and students learn about the different stages such an Act is required to go through before it passes into law. Although those stages sound onerous, and can be, in the case of the 2020 Act, those Parliamentary stages were passed in just one day (certainly not unheard of at crisis moments), despite the significant centralization of control, and significant extension of powers given to certain officers, restrictions on human rights, and, as other chapters in this book explore, complicated sets of 'easements' and requirements, such as in relation to virtual hearings.

The Office of the Parliamentary Counsel's drafting guidance for legislation recommends in its opening paragraphs that the draftsperson tells the story (OPC, 2020: para 1.1.1), but, as Kirton-Darling and colleagues (2020: 6) argue, there is no single story in the Act. Rather, policy makers' choices '... were not a simple power grab but were circumscribed by the traditions of thought of groups of policy makers and the range of what was imaginable and manageable, as extended by circumstances of extreme urgency'. The Act is a mishmash of lots of different ideas, some of which are expressed in the vaguest possible terms, giving great powers to the government. Ewing (2020: 10), for example, draws attention to s 76 of the Act which says: 'Her Majesty's Revenue and Customs are to have such functions as the Treasury may direct in relation to coronavirus or coronavirus disease'.

It is this power which underlines the job retention scheme which Bales discusses in Chapter 14. Ewing also takes us into rather sticky legislative territory, because he notes that the scheme actually was brought into effect by Treasury Direction: 'This is a form of delegated power with which we are generally unfamiliar, and although the Direction uses the language of "entitlement", it is uncertain what legally enforceable rights it creates' (Ewing, 2020: 10). As Ewing suggests, and Bales' analysis of the scheme makes crystal clear, the issue with the Direction is not just about Parliamentary authorization but also scrutiny of the detail. The point Ewing makes about the form of delegated power is significant for this chapter because the Direction blurs the distinction between secondary legislation, tertiary legislation and other forms of quasi-legislation.

In the standard framing, secondary legislation (or Statutory Instruments) is subject to some form of Parliamentary oversight, which depends on the process selected by the relevant government. Over the last century, these have proliferated to the extent that they are now the principal tools of government. There are often over 3,000 of these instruments per annum, and they have come to provide the legislative form for implementing much contentious policy. Given the number of such instruments, and the limited form of Parliamentary scrutiny applicable to them (whichever process is adopted), meaning that they are almost never rejected, it is not surprising perhaps that mistakes are made. Noting in relation to Brexit that, by exit day (31 January 2020), there had been 622 related statutory instruments, Sinclair and Tomlinson (2020: 23) argue that there were consistent problems with their drafting. Many were replaced or withdrawn.

Some of these instruments address important errors that managed to slip through the scrutiny process. For instance, The Environment (Miscellaneous Amendments and Revocations) (EU Exit) Regulations 2019 corrected a host of errors, including a 'tick box' that was 'omitted in error' but was crucial to enable endangered species to be moved within the UK and an amendment which 'inadvertently altered the operation of an Article' relating to pesticide products (Sinclair and Tomlinson, 2020: 24).

The Hansard Society maintains a Coronavirus Statutory Instruments Dashboard, demonstrating that the same issues have arisen with secondary legislation. We can, perhaps, all recognize the sinking feeling that the civil servant must have had when laying the Charitable Incorporated Organisations (Insolvency and Dissolution) (Amendment) (No. 2) Regulations 2020, because 'Due to an administrative error, the version of the first regulations made on 6 July was not the final draft of the instrument and contained drafting errors and omissions'.[2]

There has also been much discussion about the impenetrability of the public health regulations, with government ministers and the Prime Minister regularly getting interpretation wrong in live interviews, subsequently having to issue retractions and clarifications. Remembering that criminal offences are created in these regulations, clarity of expression is key. So is some forewarning, but a number of the most significant regulations were laid before Parliament very shortly – minutes – before they came into force, which was exceptional. So, for example, even the title of The Health Protection (Coronavirus, Restrictions) (No 2)(England)(Amendment)(No 4) Regulations provides a clue as to the drafting issues (brilliantly discussed by Adam Wagner in the Better Human Podcast).[3]

These regulations were laid on 13 September 2020, at 11.30 pm, around half an hour before they came into force, and increased complexity in restrictions on public gatherings (the so-called 'rule of six'). It contained the (legally) perplexing provision that, where a group of no more than six people participates in an excepted (that is, lawful) public gathering, they cannot become a member of another group participating in the gathering or 'otherwise mingle with any person who is participating in the gathering but is not a member of the same … group as them'. The word 'mingle' became, for a limited time, a metaphorical figure of fun as politicians doing the rounds of radio and television studios struggled to define it.

However, the job retention scheme Treasury Direction was not a statutory instrument. That takes us to tertiary legislation, which are the ranges of materials which are mandated by legislation and which commonly create obligations on, give advice or explanations to, public authorities without

---

[2] See Hansard Coronavirus Statutory Instruments Dashboard, at www.hansardsociety.org. uk/publications/data/coronavirus-statutory-instruments-dashboard#scrutiny-procedures

[3] The podcast is available at www.youtube.com/watch?v=5JcIgjMQ_9o&feature=youtu. be

Parliamentary scrutiny. These are the kinds of directions, enforceable circulars, or statutory codes commonly used by government. Whether or not the Treasury Direction was one of these depends on whether it was properly made under s 76, 2020 Act. That provision, beguiling in its simplicity and brevity, may provide the relevant powers – certainly, the Treasury believes it does, as that is said to be the statutory authority in the Direction – but that demonstrates how such a general power in main legislation, subjected to the briefest scrutiny, has been used to disburse such eye-watering sums of public money, without any Parliamentary scrutiny. Truly, this is government by direction.

Otherwise, we are in the murky territory of 'administrative quasi-legislation', the emphasis here being on the administrative, as opposed to the legislation. It is legislation only in the sense that it can have governing effects without authority. The best example of this type of material are circulars and letters issued without any statutory authority.

The government has used these techniques of government liberally during the pandemic. Guidance issued around what people can and cannot do during the lockdown periods falls into this category. Routinely during the pandemic, this guidance has exaggerated the strength of the lockdown, made errors both in translating the regulations as well as of form (at the time of writing, the guidance on the move from the national second lockdown to the revamped Tier scheme appears to make a timing error, suggesting the second lockdown ends a day early), and has been used to justify 260-mile round trips. The second lockdown guidance document was updated eight times (and counting) (one of these, adding translated versions of the guidance in minority languages, was added nine days after the second lockdown began).

The guidance begins with the striking requirement that: 'You must not leave or be outside of your home unless where permitted by law'[4] – previous versions had included the proviso 'except for specific purposes' (there is a helpful Twitter thread on this, including links to a document demonstrating the ways in which the guidance was updated).[5] The regulations in fact require that: 'No person may leave or be outside of the place where they are living without reasonable excuse' (The Health Protection (Coronavirus, Restrictions) (England) (No. 4) Regulations 2020, reg 5(1)). A reasonable excuse is defined by way of exceptional categories. Driving lessons were included in the most recent guidance as an activity which was not permitted

---

[4]   Taken from a gov.uk webpage which is no longer available due to the changing nature of COVID-19 restrictions.

[5]   https://twitter.com/charlescholland/status/1327549545610358785

by the exceptions; the previous version was somewhat unclear because of an errant comma. For educators, the guidance distinguishes between formal and informal education and training, but that distinction does not appear in the regulations.[6]

It is not surprising, then, that enforcement agencies and others are unclear about what can and cannot be done under the regulations. Their wording is obscure, their translation into guidance inaccurate at best, and ministers as well as the Prime Minister made embarrassing errors about what is permissible. Parliamentary scrutiny has been absent, so that journalists and others (academics and lawyers) have been interrogating the regulations, which, as Ewing (2020: 24) notes, as a '… spectacle reinforces the marginalisation of Parliament'. As I go on to discuss in the next section, in the matter of residential security in the home, these blurry mechanisms of government and scrutiny have been taken to greater heights.

Residential security during the pandemic[7]

'Look, I have to be honest, this is getting silly now.'[8]

It is appropriate to begin this section with the caveat that housing law as it applies in possession cases is notoriously complex and even the simplest questions lack clarity. That caveat is to excuse the government ministers who have over-promised, demonstrated a lack of appreciation of how the possession process works, and have regarded governance as their own domain. It perhaps did not help the Secretary of State's focus that he was caught in the eye of a ministerial responsibility storm during the first lockdown.

The pandemic raised particular problems for those living in rented or mortgaged homes because of the potential for income loss during the period. As Alcock et al highlight in Chapter 10, those in privately rented accommodation were particularly threatened because of the lack of residential security, and comparatively high rent to income ratios.

The government's response to the potential for mass evictions and to the prospect of homeless people being particularly affected has been characterized by panicked techniques of governing beyond the rulebook, together with lashings of self-praise for their actions. For example, on 18 March 2020, MHCLG issued a press release: 'Complete ban on evictions and additional

---

[6]   https://twitter.com/charlescholland/status/1329863034895028224

[7]   I have found the work of Giles Peaker and the Nearly Legal Blog – www.nearlylegal. co.uk – invaluable in constructing this section and its chronology.

[8]   Giles, P. (2020) 'Lockdown 2 evictions', *Nearly Legal: Housing Law News and Comment,* https://nearlylegal.co.uk/2020/11/lockdown-2-evictions/ (accessed 26 April 2021).

protection for renters'.[9] The problem with this document was that the provisions in sch 29 of the 2020 Act did not create a complete ban. The schedule extended the periods of notice for those tenancies or licences which required formal notices (other than agricultural and family intervention tenancies) to three months from, in the case of private renters, two months (a whole extra month!). However, many of the most vulnerable people were not included in the legislation – for example, lodgers and those living in temporary accommodation as homeless households. Nor did the legislation prevent the possession process being commenced – indeed, throughout, landlords have been able to start proceedings.

The MHCLG sought to rebut what it called 'misleading information' in a series of inaccurate tweets: 'We want to be clear that the emergency legislation means there can be no evictions as a result of #coronavirus for 3 months – and we've taken the power to extend if necessary #covid19' with a picture caption saying: 'No renter who has lost income due to coronavirus will be forced out of their home'.[10] The Act had not stopped the possession process for previously issued notices, and renters who lost income during COVID-19 could still be served with a valid notice. Further, the Twitter thread suggested that the government had given 'very clear guidance' to judges and bailiffs so that it was extremely unlikely that any possession proceedings would continue during the period. However, any such administrative 'guidance', which would have been constitutionally tricky given the rule of law, did not appear to have been given.

What did occur in practice was an unruly mess, with some courts adjourning possession claims, others going ahead, with local practices predominating. On 19 March 2020, court guidance was provided which suggested that 'judges dealing with any possession claim during the crisis must have in mind the public health guidance and should not make an order that risks impacting on public health' – very far from the MHCLG's 'very clear guidance'. In any event, despite the social distancing requirement, courts remained open, and applications to suspend warrants of possession (the final throw of the dice of a renter facing eviction, often on the same day) were to be prioritized (a duty solicitor's perspective on this).[11]

---

[9] Ministry of Housing, Communities & Local Government (2020), 'Complete ban on evictions and additional protection for renters', *GOV.UK*, 18 March, www.gov. uk/government/news/complete-ban-on-evictions-and-additional-protection-for-renters (accessed 26 April 2021).

[10] https://twitter.com/mhclg/status/1240660753482485760

[11] Giles, P. (2020), 'Law in the time of Covid – Court duty work', *Nearly Legal: Housing Law News and Comment*, https://nearlylegal.co.uk/2020/03/law-in-the-time-of-covid-court-duty-work/ (accessed 26 April 2021).

Even on 15 April 2020, the court service was listing priority areas as including applications to stay enforcement of existing possession orders. By then, though, the civil procedure rules committee had stepped in, on 27 March 2020 issuing an emergency practice direction, which effectively stayed all proceedings including (as was subsequently held) appeals. That emergency practice direction was subsequently extended to 23 August 2020, heralded by Jenrick posting, on 5 June, the tweet which began this chapter. The idea that this was the government's doing stretched reality – this was the rules committee; and, again, the notion that somehow nobody would be evicted due to COVID-19 was incorrect (as not all occupation agreements require a court order to end them). Subsequently, a statutory instrument brought the practice direction into the main body of the rules (thus protecting it from challenge).

That extension to 23 August should have been designed to enable the government to prepare for cases to re-start after the end of the lockdown. Indeed, the Master of the Rolls had set up a working group that was developing the court's approach. There had been a suggestion that Jenrick had been working with the Lord Chief Justice to develop a pre-action protocol that would give tenants 'an added degree of protection'.[12] A pre-action protocol, however, has no practical effect on the substance of the law – and cannot defeat the mandatory nature of many possession claims in the private rented sector, so this comment demonstrated technical amateurism, at best. What then occurred is the stuff of a pantomime. On 20 August, the Lord Chancellor wrote to the Master of the Rolls directing that the civil procedure rules committee extended the stay on possession claims for a further four weeks. The committee agreed to do so, but only by a majority. Those two sentences in and of themselves are remarkable, in a constitutional sense, because of the separation of powers, and the simple idea that the Lord Chancellor can direct the rules committee to do something which has such an impact on the rule of law and due process. That is, perhaps, what persuaded the minority to refuse to follow the direction.

The pantomime continued on the following day, with an MHCLG press release promising that new six-month notice periods would be in place '... in all bar those cases raising other serious issues such as those involving anti-social behaviour and domestic abuse perpetrators, until at least the end of

---

[12] Giles, P. (2020), 'Optimism of the will, pessimism of the intellect', *Nearly Legal: Housing Law News and Comment*, https://nearlylegal.co.uk/2020/05/optimism-of-the-will-pessimism-of-the-intellect/(accessed 26 April 2021).

March'.[13] (It was said that the courts would prioritize priority cases.) Much of the procedural heavy lifting was done by the Master of the Rolls Working Group on possession proceedings, which worked out a process to prioritize those priority cases, and to create procedural opportunities for tenants to obtain advice and assistance while recognizing the limits of what could be done in this way. Mandatory claims – where the judge must make an order for possession and can do so on the basis of the claim form alone – were effectively slowed down by this procedure as 'each court centre will refer [such claims] to a judge at manageable frequency'.[14]

As it turned out, however, a rather more complicated picture emerged. Housing law, as suggested earlier, is noted for its opacity, which has only been increased by the new law (by which a statutory instrument amended the 2020 Act, sch 29) and procedure. This is most clear as concerns the notice periods. The exceptions include antisocial behaviour and domestic violence, but also riot and making a false statement to obtain a tenancy as well as death of the tenant and 'right to rent' (when no other grounds of possession are mentioned). When it comes to rent arrears, the rules provide that, if there are rent arrears of more than six months, and no other grounds for possession are relied on, then just four weeks' notice is required; in other cases, six months' notice is required. The courts do indeed prioritize emergency cases, which include extreme rent arrears, defined, in a private renting case as '9 months rent where that amounts to more than 25% of a private landlord's total annual income from any source'. There is space on the new court form for the private landlord to indicate that this rule applies, but it is unclear what documents a landlord must include to prove that statement.

Then, issues emerged over the enforcement of possession orders. That is done by court bailiffs in the main. On 21 October 2020, the Lord Chancellor wrote a letter to enforcement officers' associations confirming that enforcement agents are 'not to enter residential properties in areas that are classed as Local Alert Level 2 (high) or 3 (very high), for the purposes of enforcement including taking control of goods and carrying out evictions'. That was a quite extraordinary intervention because enforcement officers were under no obligation to accept any such direction in an unenforceable letter; but, rather more importantly and paradoxically, the highest judicial

---

[13] Ministry of Housing, Communities & Local Government (2020) 'Jenrick extends ban on evictions and notice periods', *GOV.UK,* www.gov.uk/government/news/jenrick-extends-ban-on-evictions-and-notice-periods (accessed 26 April 2021).

[14] The Master of the Rolls (as Head of Civil Justice) Working Group on Possession Proceedings, 'Overall arrangements for possession proceedings in England and Wales', September 2020, para 61(c).

officer was requesting enforcement officers not to enforce the law. The MHCLG also announced that there would be a 'Winter Truce' of evictions – a discursive statement which seemed, at best, inappropriate – by which Guidance would be issued to bailiffs instructing that they should not enforce possession orders in England and Wales between Friday 11 December 2020 and Monday 11 January 2021. There would be further guidance for cases that 'could cause undue damage and distress for landlords, other tenants and the wider community'.

Subsequently, on 5 November, the Lord Chancellor again wrote to the enforcement officers' associations with further 'guidance' requesting that they do not enforce possession orders during the second lockdown, 'except in the following limited circumstances: illegal trespass or squatting by persons unknown, nuisance of antisocial behaviour, domestic abuse, fraud or deception and properties unoccupied following the death of the defendant'. Additionally, he was intending to introduce an exception for cases with extreme pre-COVID-19 rent arrears about which further detail would be provided 'shortly'. It was this letter which led to Giles Peaker's outburst; as he put it: 'Evictions, or the lack of them, who gets evicted and who doesn't, are not at the whim and fiat of the Lord Chancellor. This needs to be put on a statutory footing immediately. I don't know a single housing lawyer, no matter who they act for, who thinks this is lawful'.[15]

Finally, the government moved to make regulations bringing these unenforceable letters into lawful effect (following pre-action correspondence from the National Residential Landlords Association). They contain an exclusion for substantial rent arrears which are defined as at least nine months' rent in arrears, but disregarding any arrears which accrue after 23 March 2020.

If we zoom out and ask why these possession orders can be enforced, we find a degree of – putting it non-technically – irrationality. First of all, the explanatory memorandum to these regulations made the point which appeared in much of the explanatory memoranda to statutory instruments during the pandemic periods:

> The purpose of this measure is to protect public health by preventing people being evicted at a time when the risk of virus transmission is very high and it may be more difficult for them to access services, and to avoid placing additional burdens on

---

[15] Giles, P. (2020) 'Lockdown 2 evictions', *Nearly Legal: Housing Law News and Comment,* https://nearlylegal.co.uk/2020/11/lockdown-2-evictions/ (accessed 26 April 2021).

the NHS and hindering local authorities in their public health response at a time when pressure on relevant public services is likely to be most acute.[16]

And

> At a time when risk of transmitting the virus is high and a number of significant restrictions are in force, the government also believes that it is necessary to prevent people being evicted.[17]

In which case, how can the exemptions to the non-enforcement rule be justified?

> To ensure the measure remains proportionate to the public health risk identified, in light of the competing public interest in ensuring access to justice, preventing harm to third parties and upholding the integrity of the rental market, the measure contains some limited exemptions from the ban on enforcing evictions. These exemptions are limited to circumstances where the government feels that the competing interests of preventing harm to third parties or taking action against egregious behaviour, are sufficient to outweigh the public health risks. These are: cases where the public health risks are judged as likely to be lower; where harm to third parties may occur if the order is delayed; or where there is a need to uphold the integrity of the residential housing market by addressing the most egregious cases involving unlawful entry, misleading statements or substantial rent arrears which cannot be attributed to the extraordinary circumstances faced by tenants since the pandemic was declared. ... Allowing evictions to be enforced in these circumstances while the ban is in force is also intended to ensure that the policy does not disproportionately negatively impact on landlords and enable them to re-let their properties to tenants in need.[18]

Of course proportionality is a relevant consideration, but eviction as a result of rent arrears (however extreme) or any of the other more egregious acts does not provide some sort of vaccine against COVID-19, placing additional

---

[16] www.legislation.gov.uk/uksi/2020/1290/pdfs/uksiem_20201290_en.pdf, para 7.1.
[17] www.legislation.gov.uk/uksi/2020/1290/pdfs/uksiem_20201290_en.pdf, para 7.7.
[18] www.legislation.gov.uk/uksi/2020/1290/pdfs/uksiem_20201290_en.pdf, para 7.9.

burdens on the NHS; and quite how the public health risks in such cases can be judged to be lower is unclear.

Conclusion

There have been 17 housing ministers since 1997, and housing is a subject in which expertise at cabinet and ministerial level has generally been lacking. The response of Jenrick to the pandemic richly demonstrated his level of appreciation of the complexity of the legislative terrain of which he is master. Yet, it also demonstrates something much deeper. While the Prime Minister was, at least, scrutinized by the media on policy and detail, the case study of residential security demonstrates that, in specific areas, government policy escaped even that level of scrutiny. To be sure, social media and other much-derided experts might have noticed, but the over-promising amateurism of government in this critical area has generally lacked scrutiny.

What the case study exposes is the way in which policy making has blurred the lines between different types of legislation, and producing entirely new ways of governing by letter, usually heralded by self-congratulatory and inaccurate tweets. Of course, it may well be said that this is the price we have to pay for governing in an emergency; and, no doubt, there is something in that. It might also be said that, certainly as far as secondary legislation is concerned, these processes have been in place for some time. The real test, however, will be how these new techniques of government are used and developed as we move out of lockdown and back to some sort of normality in everyday life. Only then will we be able to gauge, as Ganz (1987: 108) wondered, the extent to which our unwritten constitution is under threat.

References

Ewing, K. (2020) 'Government by decree', *King's Law Journal*, 31(1): 1–24.

Ganz, G. (1987) *Quasi-Legislation: Recent Developments in Secondary Legislation*, London: Sweet & Maxwell.

Kirton-Darling, E., Carr, H. and Varnava, T. (2020) 'Legislating for a pandemic: Exposing the stateless state', *Journal of Law and Society*, Special Supplement, Issue S2: S302–20.

Office of the Parliamentary Counsel (2020) *Drafting Guidance*, https:// assets.publishing.service.gov.uk/government/uploads/system/uploads/ attachment_data/file/892409/OPC_drafting_guidance_June_2020-1.pdf (accessed 26 April 2021).

Sinclair, A. and Tomlinson, J. (2020) *Plus ca Change?* Brexit and the Flaws of the Delegated Legislation System, London: Public Law Project, https:// publiclawproject.org.uk/resources/plus-ca-change-brexit-and-the-flaws-of-the-delegated-legislation-system/ (accessed 26 April 2021).

2

Remote Justice and Vulnerable Litigants: The Case of Asylum

Nick Gill

The recent acceleration in the use of remote justice in the UK, prompted by COVID-19, raises the question of how such changes affect litigants in person and vulnerable litigants. The latter include children and young adults, immigration detainees, those using English as an additional language, those facing mental health difficulties or who are neuro–diverse, those with alcohol or drug dependencies, and those who are excessively fearful and anxious.

Some of these characteristics can be especially acute among people claiming asylum. Like other jurisdictions, the UK's First-tier Tribunal (Immigration and Asylum Chamber) has expedited its roll-out of online procedures which were already underway before the pandemic. Substantive hearing lists were vacated from March to June 2020 and only Case Management Review hearings and immigration bail hearings were heard. These were conducted almost exclusively via telephone, with some hearings heard via video conference (see also Mulcahy, Chapter 3). At the time of writing (October 2020), the prospect of the pandemic continuing to prompt the use of these and similar measures, including for substantive asylum appeals, seems likely as COVID-19 cases are climbing.

I have led a team of researchers over the last several years in an attempt to understand appellants' experiences of asylum appeal hearings, conducting interviews with asylum appellants as well as legal professionals, and observing appeal processes from the public galleries of hearing rooms in the UK and various other European countries. Figures 2.1 and 2.2 depict a typical hearing room in the UK, with the public seating at the back.

Figure 2.1: Sketch of appellant's and interpreter's chairs in a hearing room

Source: Rebecca Rotter

Recently my collaborators and I have written a report entitled *Experiencing Asylum Appeals: 34 Ways to Improve Access to Justice at the First-tier Tribunal* which examines the experiences of people seeking asylum in the tribunal and suggests reforms (Gill et al, 2020). While not all appellants characterize appeals negatively, the report identifies a series of challenges appellants often encounter in their face-to-face hearings, including confusion, anxiety, mistrust, disrespect, communication difficulties and distraction. Although our research preceded COVID-19, these categories provide a ready framework for analyzing the impact of the recent move towards remote justice.

Confusion

Remote justice could mitigate some sources of confusion described in the *Experiencing Asylum Appeals* report. One example concerns legal etiquette during hearings. Most of the actors involved in asylum hearings are usually repeat players including the judge, both representatives and the interpreter. This makes asylum appellants' lack of knowledge about when to sit and stand, when to stay silent and speak, as well as how to address the judge, quite obvious and a frequent source of self-consciousness. The fact that all the parties might be unused to the remote technology could act as a leveller. Judges and the other repeat players may only recently have mastered the

Figure 2.2: Sketch of a hearing room as viewed from the public gallery

Source: Rebecca Rotter

technology themselves which could be helpful in reminding them how it feels to be disorientated and struggle communicating, stimulating empathy with appellants experiencing similar difficulties. Remote hearings might also lend themselves to longer introductions because judges must explain how the remote system works and what to do if technology fails, which could help to reassure litigants generally.

Other forms of confusion may be more acute though. Some asylum appellants are unsure about the purpose of the appeal even when face to face (Gill et al, 2020). When the whole hearing is confined to the screen, or even a telephone call, clarity may be further reduced.

Asylum appellants are also frequently ill-informed about the roles of the actors involved in hearings. We found evidence, for example, that appellants are often surprised that the solicitor, to whom they have disclosed their narrative in advance of the hearing, will not be speaking for them on the day. Rather, they sometimes meet their barrister only a few minutes before the hearing, and are expected to trust them immediately. One barrister gave this example:

> 'I said to the client this morning, "Hi, I'm Susan".[1] I introduced myself, then after a pause the client said, "Who are you?"

---

[1]   Pseudonym

> And I said, "I'm your barrister". I mean I had said that I was a barrister, but they just didn't get it'. (Female barrister, 25 years' experience, in Gill et al, 2020)

Rapidly forming relationships of trust is difficult enough face to face, but the ability of barristers and others to put appellants at ease remotely may be severely limited. Ways to break the ice like discussing common experiences of weather and traffic or sharing a coffee before the hearing are often impossible.

One way to think about legal hearings is in terms of genre (Mullings, 2020). Popular culture is rich in references to courts, and television has disseminated a crude popular understanding of what courts look like and what happens there. Litigants will consequently have a rough idea of the roles, setting and costume associated with them. When attending a hearing in person their knowledge of the genre prompts them to expect certain things, like unusual forms of turn-taking in speech or legal forms of address they would not hear elsewhere. The markers that help to establish genre in litigants' minds are largely absent online though. There is ceremony associated with legal hearings: not everyone likes the formality but the visible structure can help to define roles. In contrast, as Mullings (2020) explains, in remote hearings litigants may feel untethered from the cultural cognitive anchor of the court space.

There is also likely to be a certain amount of confusion arising from the use of the technology itself. Technical issues frequently frustrate the flow of proceedings (Byrom et al, 2020). Although some litigants are likely to be very familiar with telephone conferencing or screen-based forms of communication others may not be. The look and feel of specialist online systems in particular are likely to be unfamiliar to appellants even if they have used popular video conferencing platforms in the past. The disorientation involved in using a new platform can multiply quickly under conditions of stress.

The *Experiencing Asylum Appeals* report discusses not only the confusion that appellants experience but also some of the mitigating factors that can lessen it. Primary mitigating factors are (good) legal advice and representation. Under lockdown conditions though, or social distancing arrangements, many advice providers reduced their face-to-face provision, meaning that the quality of legal advice may well be stymied in the run-up to an appellant's hearing. Law centres, for example, have experienced a decline in their contact with many clients who cannot access their digital services due to poverty or inexperience.

Anxiety

Some appellants find their hearings stressful. This can manifest in various ways including becoming intimidated by the judge or the general situation and not being able to give their full evidence. One appellant told us that they lost their memory because of nerves.

> 'Before I go to that court I had so [many] things to say but when I was there it was all completely ... out of my brain, I didn't remember anything to say ... because the situation ... was really stressful and nervous and for me it was really big issue. I forgot everything'. (Afghan unrepresented appellant, in Gill et al, 2020)

Waiting for a long time for one's hearing date can exacerbate anxiety. Without being allowed to work or move on with their lives, some appellants obsess about the hearing, and when it finally arrives it can be overwhelming or surreal.

Freedom from Torture and the Helen Bamber Foundation (2020: 2) report that lockdown and social distancing can exacerbate asylum seekers' anxieties:

> many survivors of torture ... are experiencing a deterioration in their mental and physical health due to issues including isolation, uncertainty, disruptions in treatment, delays, concerns about their and their family members' health, fear for the future, lack of childcare, difficulties with accommodation and destitution issues. Survivors may also find the experience of 'lock-down' triggers traumatic memories of captivity or self-confinement, which were a characteristic of past persecution, leading to an increase in trauma symptoms and a decrease in coping mechanisms.

Being at home may reduce feelings of being overwhelmed, but it can also worsen things. Appellants may feel less well supported, for example, because they do not have friends with them who might have attended a physical hearing.

From the appellants' perspective, they may be very keen to get the hearing over with if they are extremely anxious about it. Although appellants who do not want to use online procedures can opt out of them, an appellant may not be able to predict the effect that anxiety is going to have on their ability to participate in advance. They may also be reluctant to ask for allowances on the basis of their anxiety. The Judicial College Equal Treatment Bench Book Committee (2020: 4) write that 'people in difficulty may say they are willing to continue, out of a sense of deference, unassertiveness or anxiety to get the hearing over with'.

This puts the onus on the judge to detect signs of debilitating anxiety during the hearing itself. Using remote hearings may make this harder, however. In a face-to-face hearing it might be possible to see the appellant shaking, or discern that they are giving whispered replies, but online only the face of the appellant might be visible, and the low volume of replies could be attributed to connection issues or compensated for by turning up the volume. Evidence suggests that appellants find it harder to challenge what is happening remotely too (Byrom et al, 2020).

A further difficulty when the appellant appears on screen is the possibility that they will react negatively to seeing themselves. It is quite common for anyone to feel embarrassed when seeing themselves. Some appellants are extremely self-conscious though, and sometimes hold highly negative self-images related to anxiety and experiences of trauma. Seeing themselves on screen could stimulate feelings of self-deprecation and unworthiness which may lessen their abilities to give evidence.

Mistrust

The *Experiencing Asylum Appeals* report discusses two types of mistrust: the feeling appellants have of being mistrusted by judges and others involved in the hearing, and the mistrust they have of the system.

In the first instance, appearing via videolink or conducting the appeal via telephone may make the assessment of credibility harder. Judges are deprived of the opportunity to see the entire body language of appellants, and eye contact in particular could be interfered with. Via videolink for example, appellants may naturally talk to their screens, which is where they can see the other participants, but their cameras could be located just above or to the side of their screen, resulting in a lack of direct view of their eyes when they are speaking which could give the impression of furtiveness. Poor lighting, small screen sizes, and constricted broadband width, resulting in a blocky picture, could all exacerbate the issues. While judges may have been briefed on the risks these issues present, appellants are still deprived of the full repertoire of body language they may have used to communicate.

In terms of appellants' mistrust of the system, some asylum seekers struggle to trust interpreters who are co-nationals or co-ethnics, owing to the bad experiences that prompted their flight. Furthermore, many have deep reservations about state authorities owing to the experiences that led to their flight or their experiences of border control en route. A common perception for example, is that the judge or their lawyer is not independent, but in fact is in league with the Home Office in some way.

> 'When I claimed asylum, and they said they will give me legal aid, I was afraid. Because legal aid is paid by the government.

So in my head I thought, if a lawyer is paid by the government, then it means that the government can influence the process. ... I felt like "Hmm, OK", I was suspicious'. (Male appellant, Cameroon, quoted in Gill et al, 2020)

Appellants' mistrust of the process can be affected by the publicness of the hearing. Traditionally journalists, interested parties and the public have had the right to attend hearings unless there are reporting restrictions or they are conducted in camera. On the one hand, making sure that justice is open to the public is important for building trust in the system. It is constructive to show the appellant that there is nothing to hide. Indeed, there has been much debate about the importance of maintaining open justice where appropriate during the pandemic, including making provision for journalists to see hearings where appropriate. Consideration has also been given to members of the public. Freedom from Torture and the Helen Bamber Foundation (2020), for example, recommend that a published protocol is made available for third parties to observe hearings or watch recordings taken by the tribunal after the event.

On the other hand, appellants who are concerned about malevolent forces in their home countries might understandably also be keen to know what will happen to any recording made of their hearing. There is a risk that public observers of asylum appeals will record or livestream the hearing on the internet, against the instructions of the tribunal and judge, which would have been harder in a face-to-face hearing. The worst-case scenario would be that either a videostream or a recording would be somehow accessible to a third party outside of the UK; and every measure must be taken, and seen to be taken, to ensure against this possibility because appellants may not disclose their full case if they are not convinced about this. How the official recording of the hearing is stored and how it is distributed is therefore of utmost importance. Remote hearings present a good opportunity for the tribunal service to improve its data collection and transparency, bearing in mind that no transcript or recording of asylum appeals is usually produced in face-to-face hearings. They might also be used to make it easier for vulnerable witnesses to safely take part in proceedings. However, this cannot come at the price of appellants' trust in the system. One solution may be to only allow the recording to be viewed or listened to in a court or tribunal building, but the appellant may still be reticent about this because they will not be able to see who watches it.

Face-to-face hearings are public and the security arrangements they entail are not perfect, but there are checks at the entrance to hearing centres, and judges and appellants can see the other parties in the room. The unease that could be generated when it is impossible for the appellant to see who is viewing (or will view) the hearing needs to be taken extremely seriously.

Disrespect

Some appellants report experiencing disrespect because they feel as though the process of appealing treats them as though they are criminals, or because they feel that judges are not taking a keen interest in their case. They feel devalued when judges or other actors in the hearing do not pronounce their names correctly. They sometimes find the questioning of the Home Office Presenting Officer to be patronizing and confrontational. They sometimes object to situations in which the repeat players in the room share a joke or informal conversation before the hearing, making them feel excluded. They are also aware of the marked difference in respect shown to them and to the judge, whose status is indicated by the physical architecture of the room such as their raised dais and ritualized behaviours, for example when the parties stand as the judge enters and leaves.

Remote hearings have the potential to improve appellants' perceptions of respect and disrespect in various ways. There may be fewer opportunities for the repeat players to hold informal conversations that exclude the appellant for example, and many of the ritualized aspects of the hearing will also be tempered (although forms of address like using 'sir' and 'ma'am' to address the judge may continue). Appellants may also be unable to detect when judges are bored and disengaged in the hearing.

On the other hand, it may be harder for the judge to demonstrate to the appellant that they are alert and paying attention to their case via remote means. Making eye contact, looking engaged and interacting frequently are all more difficult in remote environments. Difficulties of pronunciation of names may also be harder to clear up if audibility is imperfect or there is a poor connection.

Communication difficulties

Effective communication during the legal hearing demands that litigants understand the relevance of points raised, are able to follow proceedings, are able to make themselves understood, are able to introduce and respond to relevant issues, and that they understand the consequences of decisions or court or tribunal directions.

Face-to-face asylum appeals are often characterized by communication difficulties because the appellant is frequently operating in a second or third language. Over 13 per cent of cases involving an interpreter that we observed for the *Experiencing Asylum Appeals* report suffered significant problems

Figure 2.3: Where an interpreter is present, are there significant problems with the flow of interpretation or frequent confusion over certain words?

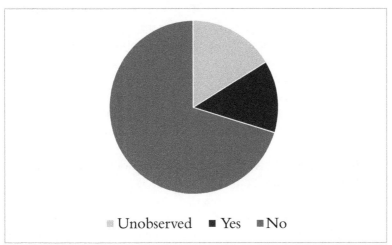

Unobserved ■ Yes ■ No

Note: Data refer to face-to-face hearings observed between 2013 and 2016. A version of the data is available here: https://reshare.ukdataservice.ac.uk/852032/. The total number of cases depicted by the chart is 173 which is the number of cases we observed where an interpreter was present. Unobserved means that the researcher either could not observe or was uncertain.

with the flow of interpretation or frequent confusion over certain words for example – see Figure 2.3.

Under remote conditions, the lack of visual cues is likely to hamper effective information exchange between the interpreter and the appellant even more. Their interaction is vulnerable even to minor distortions such as buffering delays. Interpreters have a difficult job that requires a good deal of skill and concentration and the additional cognitive demands of screen-based or telephone hearings may provoke fatigue and lead to mistakes.

The Judicial College Equal Treatment Bench Book Committee (2020) notes that there are particular difficulties with telephone hearings because of the reliance on the tenor of voice to convey meaning. Judges themselves should seek to avoid any tension in their own voices as a result, and also need to take 'particularly active steps' (Judicial College Equal Treatment Bench Book Committee 2020: 4) to ensure all the participants remain fully engaged. Judges and legal representatives managing and participating in hearings on screen or via telephone connections may be tempted to use relatively closed questions which do not afford the same opportunities for explication. They might also find it harder to interpret silences (possibly attributing them to the technology) that would have spoken for themselves face to face.

Another issue facing remote appellants is the challenge of finding a space that is private from which to participate. Parents may face challenges of disclosing sensitive aspects of their case if their children are within earshot. Children themselves may be exposed to hearing things that could traumatize them, so safeguarding is an important consideration in remote hearings:

> a child may be highly traumatised if they witness a parent's distress or hear their parent's past experiences. For example, hearing how a parent was arrested from home could cause a child significant fear and anxiety and they may believe this could happen again at any moment. Even a child who is not yet talking should not be considered safe from this kind of distress. (Freedom from Torture and the Helen Bamber Foundation, 2020: 5)

This issue is not confined to the hearings themselves: appellants need to be able to communicate freely with their legal representatives and any supporters they have in advance of hearings too.

There are also inequalities in practical access to technology. Wi-Fi, phone credit, broadband width and access to devices all cost money. Much of the guidance available for operating in a remote hearing is written too, which may render it useless for illiterate appellants. It may also not be available in a language they can understand.

Some of these issues may be addressed by providing access to an appropriate venue from which appellants can access the hearing rather than their home, although this in itself would need to be thought through carefully.

Distraction

Face-to-face hearings are *immersive* because a journey is required. But to what extent is this valuable? On the one hand, certain litigants could appreciate not having to travel. Litigants with certain injuries, sicknesses or disabilities, for instance, might appreciate the convenience of a remote hearing, sparing them a difficult journey to a hearing. Busy litigants – not to mention busy barristers, interpreters and judges – may also appreciate the reduced travel time, since face-to-face hearings can involve long travel times and a lot of waiting around. Expert witnesses may be more likely to attend remotely too.

On the other hand, a journey can focus appellants' and others' attention. The journey is a reminder that this is something of sufficient gravity to be set aside – literally and physically – from everyday life. Upon arrival the hearing participant is bodily surrounded by the hearing in the venue at which it takes place, even if their attention starts to wander, or they start to dissociate. In their home there may be multitudinous distractions ranging from serious obstacles such as the presence of abusive partners and the threat of off-screen coercive control, to overcrowding, to more minor forms of distraction such as television, internet surfing, and simply looking around the room. A screen (most likely a small one) is no match for the immersive experience of the face-to-face event for commanding the attention of all involved.

Furthermore, recalling traumatic experiences can often be difficult at the best of times, and if the appellant has done it various times before then a degree of jadedness can enter into recollections. Screen-based communications can be more tiring because of the intensity of focusing on a small screen and missing out on visual cues provided by body language in face-to-face interactions. This could lead to lethargic or curtailed responses to questions.

The technology itself may also become distracting. Fiddling with the screen brightness and contrast, worrying about the connectivity and availability of credit, battery life, reception, and broadband speed could all tax litigants' attention (again, a venue from which to participate remotely might help here). What is more, the features of homes that can impact on appellants' abilities to concentrate are not confined to technical ones. The Judicial College Equal Treatment Bench Book Committee (2020) raises the possibility that there may be unsuitable seating arrangements available at home, for example, which could quickly lead to posture-related discomfort.

Appellants are not the only ones affected by these considerations. Barristers, interpreters and judges may be more susceptible to challenges of distraction in remote settings because they are repeat players. They may be tempted to multitask while the hearing is on in the background. Mutually enforced, largely unspoken, standards of professionalism that were helpful in focusing attention in face-to-face settings may be lacking in remote situations.

Conclusion

It is fair to say that the moral coordinates of the debate about remote justice changed with the onset of the pandemic. For a time, at least during the full lockdown in 2020, no longer was the issue about whether online and remote forms of justice are preferable or comparable to face-to-face forms. Suddenly the issue was whether online and remote forms of justice were preferable to no justice at all, or at least much slower and more impoverished forms. In this context it is worth noting the efforts of court and tribunal staff and judges to keep justice moving during the pandemic. One of the most difficult aspects of seeking asylum is the interminable waiting, and so maintaining a sense of the possibility of progress is, all other things equal, a welcome achievement.

There are also some potential advantages of remote hearings such as reducing confusion over court and tribunal etiquette, reducing the association some appellants have with face-to-face hearings and disrespect, and improving the convenience of the proceedings. Taking these factors on board, there may be certain types of hearings that are suitable to be heard remotely. Much depends on the particular participants involved, but hearings dealing with routine questions or questions of law rather than contestations of fact may be examples. The latter tend to be at higher courts which are better resourced, with a greater proportion of professionals involved.

It is nevertheless necessary to raise concerns about the turn to remote justice. In asylum appeals, if the publicness of hearings is ambiguous then serious trust issues could arise. It may become more difficult to communicate effectively with judges, interpreters and lawyers. Inequalities could be introduced through uneven technical capacities. And the participants may be exposed to more distractions and obstacles such as off-screen coercion or inhibition by abusive partners or the presence of children.

For these reasons, in cases where oral evidence is likely to be needed, there should be a presumption against remote hearings if the appellant is unrepresented, requires a witness, needs an interpreter, is vulnerable, or if the case concerns traumatic material.

This should not be taken to indicate that paper-based hearings should become the norm though. Asylum appellants generally appreciate the opportunity to be heard by a judge. Wherever possible, every effort should be made to hold in-person hearings, with appropriate social distancing measures. To do this, court and tribunal estate capacity may need to be increased to meet the need for space. Nor should court and tribunal authorities take 'nonattendance' at a remote hearing as carte blanche to go ahead with a paper-based hearing when social distancing measures are in force, given the difficulties many people have in accessing and engaging with remote hearings.

Finally, if remote hearings are to become more common there should be guidance for asylum appellants in a medium they can easily understand. Judges, lawyers and various court and tribunal users have been issued with guidance and there is discussion of a new guidance note for judges. Asylum appellants themselves need more guidance in their own languages though, that does not rely on textual forms of communication (which assumes literacy). For asylum hearings in particular, information films in the main languages of asylum appellants should be produced.[2]

Acknowledgements

I gratefully acknowledge my co-authors on the Experiencing Asylum Appeals report (Gill et al, 2020), including Jennifer Allsopp, Andrew Burridge, Daniel Fisher, Melanie Griffiths, Jessica Hambly, Jo Hynes, Natalia Paszkiewicz, Rebecca Rotter and Amanda Schmid-Scott, for their contribution to the programme of work that made this chapter possible. I also acknowledge the financial support of the European Research Council, StG-2015_677917.

References

Byrom, N., Beardon, S. and Kendrick, A. (2020) *The impact of COVID-19 measures on the civil justice system: Report and Recommendations*, London: Civil Justice Council and Legal Education Foundation, www.judiciary.uk/wp-content/uploads/2020/06/CJC-Rapid-Review-Final-Report-f-1.pdf (accessed 26 October 2020).

Freedom from Torture and the Helen Bamber Foundation (2020) *The Courts, Tribunals and the Covid-19 Public Health Crisis*, London: Freedom from Torture and the Helen Bamber Foundation, www.helenbamber.org/wp-content/uploads/2020/05/Tribunals-courts-and-COVID-recommendations-Final.pdf (accessed 26 October 2020).

Gill, N., Allsopp, J., Burridge, A., Fisher, D., Griffiths, M., Hambly, J., Hynes, J., Paszkiewicz, N., Rotter, R. and Schmid-Scott, A. (2020) *Experiencing Asylum Appeal Hearings: 34 Ways to Improve Access to Justice at the First Tier Tribunal*, London and Exeter: University of Exeter and the Public Law Project, https://publiclawproject.org.uk/resources/experiencing-asylum-appeals/ (accessed 22 February 2021)

Judicial College Equal Treatment Bench Book Committee (2020) *Good Practice for Remote Hearings*, London: Judicial College, www.judiciary.uk/wp-content/uploads/2020/03/Good-Practice-for-Remote-Hearings-May-2020-1.pdf (accessed 26 October 2020).

Mullings, S. (2020) 'Fairness in new-tech court proceedings in the era of Covid-19', *The Justice Gap*, 23 March, www.thejusticegap.com/court-drama-genre-familiarity-and-fairness-in-new-tech-court-proceedings-in-the-covid-19-crisis/ (accessed 26 October 2020).

---

[2]   As a template see these videos for face-to-face appeals: https://geography.exeter.ac.uk/research/appeal/

3

Virtual Poverty? What Happens When Criminal Trials Go Online?

Linda Mulcahy

Introduction

The COVID-19 pandemic has created extensive problems for the criminal justice system and those who become embroiled with it. The lockdown in 2020 resulted in numerous courts having to shut down (see also Gill, Chapter 2). Trials in those that remained open needed more space to comply with social distancing measures with the result that the number of trials that courthouses were capable of accommodating reduced significantly. By June 2020, the backlog of Crown Court trials stood at 41,000, and it was recently announced that some criminal trials are now being postponed until 2023. Additional backlogs and delays are continuing to build up by the hour and will undoubtedly rise to an intolerable level if too much court business is adjourned.

Problems with organizing hearings is only the tip of an iceberg. Ten thousand people, or 11 per cent of the prison population are remanded in custody awaiting trial (65 per cent) or waiting to be sentenced (35 per cent). This means that the majority of those waiting for justice have not even been convicted of the crime with which they are charged. The situation will undoubtedly lead to an increased sense of uncertainty and intense stress for accused persons and their families at a time when public health officials are already concerned about the nation's mental health. The fact that prisons and remand centres are often located at a distance from prisoners' homes and that many of them are not accepting visitors during the pandemic will leave those on remand feeling even more isolated than usual. There has rarely been such strong evidence that justice delayed is justice denied.

This emergency is much more likely to impact negatively on the poor. Poverty has long been a reliable predictor of citizens' involvement with the criminal justice system, though the relationship between poverty, disadvantage and crime is a convoluted one. It relies on a complex causal dynamic involving income poverty, increased stress, strained family relationships, unstable childhood development and perceptions of relative poverty in engendering discord. Many people from disadvantaged backgrounds never have reason to be involved with the criminal justice system, but those from poor and disadvantaged families are much more likely to be charged, tried and go to prison than those from the middle classes. A staggering two fifths of children in secure training centres and young offender institutions have been looked after by the state compared with less than one per cent in the general population. It is also widely speculated that the disadvantaged are more at risk from COVID-19 because of poorer health, crowded living conditions and complex lives. These problems are further heightened for those on remand with public health officials warning that prisons are a 'hotspot' for the virus because of crowding and shared facilities.

In addition to making it more likely that someone will enter into the criminal justice system, poverty is also an outcome of engagement with it. Being subjected to fines by courts exacerbates financial hardship, and people with a criminal record are much less likely to be able to find employment in order to clear the fines. Moreover, the stigma of imprisonment has also been linked to a long-term wage gap between those who have been in prison and other workers. Punishment extends beyond those convicted of crimes to their families who commonly remain vulnerable to financial instability, debt and housing disruption. Fathers who have been in prison are much more likely to become estranged from their children so that social and emotional problems also flow in the wake of incarceration. The connection between race and poverty also rears its ugly head in the context of research on the criminal justice system. Black men are 26 per cent, and mixed ethnicity men 22 per cent, more likely to be remanded in custody at the Crown Court than White men. Indeed, over a quarter of the prison population (27 per cent) are from a Black or minority ethnic group (Prison Reform Trust, 2019).

The challenge posed by the editors of this volume is for authors to reflect on what good can come out of the pandemic. This is far from easy to address in the context of ever more evidence of a divided polity, but this chapter will look at the rapid rise in the use of video hearings caused by the pandemic and their potential to improve the lot of the poor. Academics, including myself, have been sceptical about the extent to which the needs of lay users and open justice are served when technology is used to circumvent the need for everyone to come to a physical court. What is different about developments during the pandemic is that they have prompted experiments in which everyone including elite legal actors have been forced online and made to reflect on the experience. In the sections which follow I outline developments to date before going on to consider the extent to which totally online trials have the potential to create a more level playing field in the criminal justice system. In doing so I argue that there is a danger that critics of the use of technology are in danger of romanticizing physical courthouses as places which are better at dignifying lay users of the justice system or encouraging their participation.

All change! Responding to the pandemic

The use of video technology in the court service has been a feature of the criminal justice system for some time. Vulnerable adults and children have long had the opportunity to give evidence and to be cross-examined on video, both pre-recorded and live. This has enabled trials to take place that might otherwise not have been possible because of the stress caused by vulnerable witnesses having to be in the same room as the accused. The Ministry of Justice launched a 'virtual court' pilot scheme a decade ago and claimed to have demonstrated that a videolink between a police station and a courtroom could be successfully used to conduct a first hearing in the majority of cases, though not all commentators, including the author, agreed with their assessment. It is also the case that long before the pandemic arrived on our shores, videolinks were also being routinely used for bail and some sentencing hearings.

This position changed rapidly in the UK with the onset of the pandemic. Since March 2019 we have seen a dramatic upturn in the use of videolink proceedings. The need for social distancing and isolation has had a significant impact on the use of the court estate. Only one hundred and fifty-seven courts, which form 42 per cent of the court estate, remain open to deal with priority cases on the basis that not everything can be done remotely. A further 124 courts and tribunals are open to HMCTS (Her Majesty's Courts and Tribunals Service) staff and the judiciary but not the public. These 'staffed courts' are being kept open to support video and telephone hearings and progress cases without hearings. This facilitates mixed mode hearings in which professionals remain in the court and the laity use videolink. Certain types of cases are seen as being more amenable to virtual trials than others. HMCTS has indicated that it is working to make it possible for the majority of remand cases to be heard by videolink during the COVID-19 crisis and anticipates defendants appearing from police custody suites, prisons and youth custody facilities.

The last few weeks have seen the production of new COVID-19-related law, guidance and Practice Directions on remote proceedings. The

Coronavirus Act 2020 c. 7 expands the availability of video and audio link in criminal proceedings, and permits the public to participate in court and tribunal proceedings through audio and video links if the judge is satisfied that it is in the interests of justice for everyone involved. In making their decision, judges and magistrates are expected to consider the details of the case, the type of hearing, how complex it might be and the participant's ability to use videolinks. Despite these many recent developments it is significant that very few criminal jury trials are currently being held, though the Lord Chief Justice has announced that he is committed to keeping the situation under regular review. With that in mind a judicial working group has been established to consider ways to re-start some jury trials once it is safe to do so. It is unclear at present how organizations representing the interests of lay and disadvantaged voices are feeding into the deliberations of the working party.

What's wrong with the use of videolinks?

Academics, including myself, have made a number of criticisms of the use of video technology in the courts, the most important of which for present purposes is the impact that it has on the poor to participate effectively in the criminal justice system. This is especially the case where defendants and witnesses appear on videolink from undignified and often shabby places of incarceration such as prisons and police stations. Technological solutions to the current COVID-19 crisis also need to be set against rising concerns about the digitally excluded. Digital poverty is caused by a number of factors. These include not having access to a computer or smartphone, relying on pay as you go contracts, not having access to an internet service in the home, having an internet service with low bandwidth and the problems caused by low levels of digital literacy. Factors closely associated with poverty such as income, health, unemployment, location and educational attainment (see Struthers, Chapter 11) also feature prominently in discussions of digital poverty. By way of example, it has been estimated that 8.2 million adults or 16 per cent of the population in the UK have never used the internet, with the majority being older people, the widowed or those with a disability. Location also plays an important part in digital impoverishment with approximately 30 per cent of households in rural areas only have access to slow internet connections of less than 1Mbps. Of those who are not online, 77 per cent are not working. In households earning less than £11,500 per annum, 47 per cent did not use the internet compared to only 4 per cent of those with an annual income of over £30,000 (Low Incomes Tax Reform Group, 2012). Trials by videolink are also especially challenging for those who are vulnerable by reasons of leading complex or chaotic lives because of alcohol or drug use; learning disabilities; significant mental health issues; homelessness or the fact that they victims of violent crimes or abuse. Significantly, these are all conditions that the poor are more likely to experience.

Recent research on virtual jury trials conducted by JUSTICE and the technology company AVMI in which *all* the participants joined a trial online from their own home using their own equipment clearly demonstrated the sorts of challenges that people face with technology (Mulcahy et al, 2020). In common with other studies (see most recently Rossner and McCurdy, 2020) easily accessible information about online support for lay users was essential to their ability to participate effectively in proceedings. The number of support staff in the JUSTICE experiments was increased from three to five technicians in a trial involving 20 people as soon as this was realized by AVMI. These staff took part in trial runs with everyone involved the day before the trial and were on hand to support individuals with technical problems on the day of the trial.

Despite this high level of technical support, it soon became clear in the JUSTICE experiments that a virtual trial is only as good as the weakest internet connection. Some participants lost their internet connection completely during the virtual trial and a small number in the first three trials were unable to re-join proceedings. Intermittent connectivity resulted in people entering and exiting the virtual courtroom unexpectedly with the result that it was not always clear who was 'in' or 'out' of the trial. Others had problems with their camera or audio connection meaning that they were able to be heard but not seen, or seen but not heard. These issues are likely to be exacerbated during the COVID-19 crisis when there is higher demand for internet services. While only a minority of participants had trouble with their connection on the day, those that did experienced considerable frustration and anxiety.

These connectivity problems matter because they can be a hindrance to perceptions of fairness and delivery of a fair trial. Seemingly small things, such as screen freezes, sound and audio being out of sync or sound cutting in and out, are not easily discounted in this context because vital evidence, visual cues or nuance in the presentation of evidence could easily be missed. These issues may be difficult to track if jurors do not fully appreciate the importance of them adequately hearing all of the evidence and alerting someone if they experience a problem.

Research tells us that appearing via videolink from their own homes can have the knock-on effect of rendering disadvantage even more visible than it usually is in the courtroom. When participants appear from their homes the rooms they are in become part of the virtual courtroom. The government has recently produced useful advice on video or phone hearing which makes a number of helpful suggestions as to how participants can prepare themselves and their surroundings. It advises participants to locate themselves in a quiet private space where they will not be interrupted, to sit with the light in front of them so that their face is not in a shadow and to make sure that the view behind them is neutral or blank, to drink only water, not to eat or smoke, and to ask permission if they want to move away from the screen during the hearing. The guidance is less helpful when addressing the issue of how participants living in crowded and shared homes can arrange their lives so that they can appear from a quiet location or how they can manage to sit close to an internet router when they do not have one. When someone's home becomes part of a virtual or mixed mode courtroom there is a problem of cluttered and chaotic living conditions being exposed to the court and impacting negatively on those appearing. Backdrops and lighting also have a particular impact on how well people with dark skin colours present. In the JUSTICE experiments these various issues eventually led to a decision to gather the jury together in one physical socially distanced hall, using equipment supplied by AVMI and supported by a team of technicians who were physically present. Satisfaction levels for those sitting on the mock jury increased significantly as a result.

A number of other reservations have been raised in the context of debate about mixed mode hearings or virtual trials. These commonly relate to problems that appearing remotely lacks the dignity or sense of civic ceremony which the architecture of law courts commonly engenders. It could be argued that journeys to court, which often allow participants to prepare themselves mentally for their appearance and performance, are disrupted as people move from home to the courtroom in a matter of seconds or are abruptly expelled from it just as quickly when no longer needed. Unassisted by a sympathetic court clerk or usher, and unaided by discreet visual cues from others present, there is a danger that participants fail to develop a good enough understand of what is happening. Appearing in court through a screen runs the risk of participants feeling remote or isolated from the justice system. Virtual trials can all too easily fall into the trap of being just another form of virtual reality.

I would not deny that some of these arguments are justified, but what if virtual courtrooms have the potential to increase the immediacy of proceedings and enhance participation? Is it possible that machine mediated interactions have the potential to create a more level playing field for all those involved than was the norm in 2019? Reactions to increased use of videolinks in courts have generally been opposed by members of the criminal bar, but what happens if we look at virtual trials through the eyes of those who have most to lose or gain in the criminal justice system – the victims and defendants who appear before courts?

Retaining an open mind in times of crisis

In this final section I consider two arguments about experiences of virtual trials which have been less regularly made in debate. Each requires the reader to retain an open mind about the benefits of technology that have only come to light with the increased incidence of completely virtual trials. In each instance I draw attention to the possibility that virtual trials may actually achieve things that physical gatherings in courthouses cannot. My first argument relates to an enhanced sense of engagement with proceedings. The second relates to the creation of a more dignified experience for defendants that aids their participation in their own trial.

An enhanced sense of engagement with the trial

There is a danger that criticisms of virtual trials and the enhanced use of technology provide us with a romanticized vision of trials that take place in physical courtrooms with everyone gathered together. Socio-legal scholars and criminologists have repeatedly drawn attention to the ways in which trials can serve as degradation rituals for the poor and disadvantaged. While some might argue that courthouses dignify proceedings, many of the buildings that house courts have the effect of belittling them or making ordinary people feel unimportant before they even enter them. The mock gothic exterior of Birmingham's Victoria law courts, the brutalist exterior of Bolton Crown Court and the imposing facade of the Crown courts in Newcastle and Sheffield send very obvious messages to the people that pass them about the nature of state power. More recently constructed courts may at first suggest a change in thinking in rendering justice more transparent, but the penchant for glass atriums can also be viewed as introducing a synopticon in which defendants and their family have to engage in walks of shame across public reception areas visible to all who stand outside and watch. Within courthouses, segregated circulation routes, airport security at the entrance and unwelcoming and uncomfortable scruffy waiting areas do little to dignify citizens. Within the courtroom, the laity are placed at the margins of the trial away from the centre where barristers perform or the heightened dais from which the judge stares. Distancing of the public in the courtroom has been motivated by convenience, the need to signify hierarchy and fears that some participants may intimidate others or effect an escape from custody. The laity have rarely been consulted about what they want from a court but I suspect it is not what they have got.

When policy makers talk about efficient use of court time they frequently mean efficient use of professional time. But those juggling jobs and caring responsibilities who have to use public transport to reach courts are also time poor. Appearing by videolink reduces the need of lay people to make lengthy journeys and to have to wait in alien surroundings and uncomfortable waiting rooms with poor refreshment facilities for long periods until they are called.

The JUSTICE experiments discussed earlier found that although virtual trials were at times a much more intense experience there was a much stronger sense of being closely involved in a group event when all the participants could be seen up close and clearly on screen. The design of the JUSTICE experiment had a positive impact on the 'sightlines' between people in the courtroom. These are often interrupted in physical courts because of the flattening of courtrooms since the 1970s. This means that when barristers stand up to speak, they often break the sightline between defendant and judge. In other cases, sightlines are deliberately interrupted because of fears of intimidation or jury 'nobbling'. One extreme example of this can be seen in the image of a courtroom in Bradford Combined Courts shown as Figure 3.1. In this example the public gallery is situated in the foreground with members of the public looking forward being forced to stare at a blank wall to the side of the judicial dais. In order to look into the well of the court members of the public have to swivel to their right and look through a smoked glass screen.

By way of comparison in the JUSTICE experiment (see Figure 3.2) all the parties could see each other's faces very clearly and were accorded equal visual status. When surveyed, participants argued that the presence of all key participants in the trial on a screen just a few centimetres away engendered a sense of intimacy which promoted engagement with the process. Intimidation of other people was also made more difficult by the

Figure 3.1: Courtroom in Bradford Combined Courts

Source: Simon Hicks, in Mulcahy and Rowden, 2020

Figure 3.2: Screenshot of the virtual courtroom on screen in fourth trial from the public gallery

Source: Mulcahy et al, 2020

fact that everyone is in full view of others. It was also more difficult to look someone directly in the eye with a view to intimidating them.

It could be argued that seen in this way completely virtual trials represent a more democratic way of managing a trial in which the laity and the legal professions all suffer the same advantages and disadvantages.

Dignification of the defendant

Of all the lay participants in the criminal trial it is somewhat ironic that the defendant is the most isolated and marginalized. This manifests itself in three ways. Firstly, while defendants once stood shoulder to shoulder with their lawyers at the bar of the court, it has since become the norm for them to sit three rows behind their lawyer. Whole trials can be conducted with defendants staring at the back of the person representing them, making it extremely difficult to catch their lawyer's attention or make comments on the direction of the defence or evidence. Secondly, from the 1970s, it has become the norm for the defendant's place in the courtroom to move from the middle of Crown courts to the very back of the court against the wall furthest from the judge. Thirdly, there has been a gradual and significant move towards the incarceration of those standing trial *in the courtroom*. Up until the

1980s a number of criminal courtrooms did not have an enclosed area for defendants, and when they did it often took the form of a simple rail. With centralized guidance for court design, there has been a trend towards more fortified enclosures for the defendant to be built. The 'standard dock', now a waist-height wooden barrier topped by glass screens, and the 'secure dock', which emerged at the turn of the 21st century (see Figure 3.3), has a wooden and glass wall that reaches to the ceiling and transforms the dock into a separate room within the courtroom. It is also the case that defendants appearing in physical courts have nowhere to place papers or make notes to assist them in following their own trial. Both article six of the European Convention on Human Rights and common law precedent stress the importance of the ability of defendants to participate in their trial and their right to counsel, but in the modern justice system contemporary design makes enjoyment of this right extremely difficult (Mulcahy and Rowden, 2020).

Completely virtual courts designed to date are far from perfect and there is still much work to be done to improve them, but they do at least remove these particular instruments of incarceration and marginalization. They dispense with the need for an enclosure for the defendant that is physically distinctive from those used by other participants. As can be seen from Figure 3.2, everybody sits in a similar frame and the defendant can be placed both literally and metaphorically at the centre of proceedings. The defendant is also able to sit at a desk where their monitor sits and can place papers or look at documentary evidence made available by the court clerk on a shared screen. In short, experiments forced on us by the COVID-19 pandemic have shown that virtual trials can enhance the ability of the defendant to participate in their defence and follow proceedings more carefully.

Figure 3.3: Front view of a secure dock

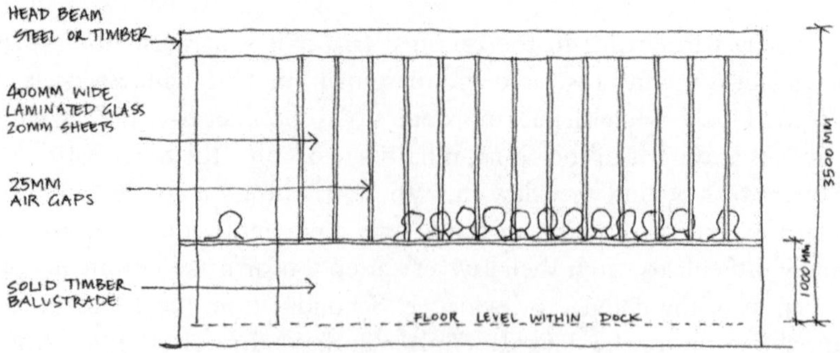

Source: Emma Rowden, in Mulcahy and Rowden, 2020

Virtual courts also have the potential to enhance the defendant's right to counsel. Studies of mixed mode proceedings in which the defendants appeared via videolink but others gathered in a traditional courtroom, have raised a number of concerns about the physical separation of defendants and their lawyers. Lawyers have argued that they remain torn as to whether to appear from the same room as the defendant so that they can provide face-to-face support, or attend the physical court where they think they can have more impact on the outcome of the trial. This can make it even more difficult for the defendant and their counsel to have discreet discussions than when they attend physical courts. In direct contrast, the visibility of the defendant in a virtual trial makes it much easier for them to signal that they would like to consult with their lawyer. The provision of a virtual and private breakout space also means that the defendant and their counsel can easily leave court for a private consultation without the trouble of having to find a vacant and private space in the vicinity of the courtroom. It also obviates the need for jurors to be escorted back to the jury assembly room and the judge does not have to make the journey to his chambers. Viewed from this perspective it can be seen that the right to counsel can actually be enhanced during a virtual trial.

Conclusion

Lawyers are often criticized for being hesitant about change in the administration of justice, but the pandemic has provided us with the chance to revisit the extent to which the current administration of justice serves the needs of the disadvantaged. There is much riding on current debate about the increased use of technology in the months, even years, ahead. Unless people stop committing crimes or the police stop arresting people the backlog of criminal trials can only get larger week by week. The English justice system has responded much more quickly than others to the need to behave differently while the pandemic alters our ability to interact in public buildings. For many of us online has become a lifeline by maintaining our ability to stay in touch, access support networks and get on with our lives. But the same opportunities are not available to everyone and the impact of the digital divide has never been more obvious or acute. As policy makers, HMCTS staff, the judiciary and the legal profession discuss how we can proceed in a legitimate and credible way it is critical that the poor remain at the top of our priorities and romanticized visions of what happens in physical courthouses is not allowed to cloud evaluations.

References

Low Incomes Tax Reform Group of The Chartered Institute of Taxation (2012) *Digital Exclusion: A research report*, www.litrg.org.uk/sites/default/files/digital_exclusion_-_litrg_report.pdf (accessed 1 September 2020).

Mulcahy, L. and Rowden, E. (2020) *The Democratic Courthouse: A Modern History of Design and Due Process*, London: Routledge.

Mulcahy, L., Rowden, E. and Teeder, W. (2020) *Exploring the case for Virtual Jury Trials during the COVID-19 crisis* (Three reports), London: JUSTICE, https://justice.org.uk/our-work/justice-covid-19-response/(accessed 1 September 2020).

Prison Reform Trust (2019) *Prison: The Facts*, London: Prison Reform Trust, www.prisonreformtrust.org.uk/Portals/0/Documents/Bromley%20Briefings/Prison%20the%20facts%20Summer%202019.pdf (accessed 1 September 2020).

Rossner, M. and McCurdy, M. (2020) *Video Hearings Process Evaluation (Phase 2) Final Report*, London: London School of Economics, https://assets.publishing.service.gov.uk/government/uploads/system/uploads/attachment_data/file/905603/HMCTS391_Video_hearings_process_evaluation__phase_2__v2.pdf (accessed 1 September 2020).

4

Genera-Relational Justice in the COVID-19 Recovery Period: Children in the Criminal Justice System

Kathryn Hollingsworth

When the UK government plans its COVID-19 economic recovery, children and their rights must be at the heart of decision-making. All children have been deeply affected by the pandemic. The closure of schools and leisure facilities, the contraction of essential children's and youth services, and increased exposure to stress, poverty, hunger, abuse and domestic violence during lockdown will have significant and enduring consequences and entrench existing disadvantage and discrimination along socio-economic, racial and ethnic lines (see Struthers, Chapter 11). This is especially true for children in conflict with the law. The response to the pandemic has heightened the conditions that draw children into contact with the criminal justice system (CJS) and had a detrimental impact on those currently within it, again perpetuating existing disparities especially for care-experienced and BAME heritage children. These are not, however, new problems brought about by the pandemic or the impending economic crisis. Rather, they are the very predictable consequences of a long-standing failure to address both the causes and responses to childhood offending in a way that is holistic, caring and rights-respecting, and in ways that are good for children, society and the economy.

Drawing on lessons from the decade of austerity, this chapter argues that the COVID-19 recovery period should be founded on principles of genera-relational justice.[1] A genera-relational approach to childhood offending recognizes both the pandemic's disproportionate impact on children and our unique obligations to them. The chapter concludes, optimistically, that recent policy shifts in youth justice – including the intersecting 'child-first', trauma-informed and public health approaches – offer more fertile ground for a just response to the impending economic crisis than existed in the post-2008 period. However, to ensure these are embedded and able to survive the vicissitudes of the economy or political mood, they must be accompanied by more robust accountability. There is a great deal happening in this area, so there is a lot of information to share.

Youth justice in the shadow of austerity

In the wake of the 2008 economic crisis, reforms by the in-coming coalition government brought positive results for children in or at risk of entering the CJS, including the conferral of 'looked after' status on all remanded children. But it was reform to the system of diversion, alongside changes to police crime recording practices, that was transformative, reversing years of penal expansion under New Labour. The result was a huge decline in the number of first-time entrants and children in custody, from 79,260 to 11,900, and 2,881 to 860 respectively, between 2008–9 and 2018–19.

The significance of these quantitative changes should not be under-estimated. But it is clear that they were driven by cost-savings rather than a principled commitment to children's rights, welfare, or to achieving qualitative improvements in their experience or treatment. This is evident from the sweeping cuts to policing, courts, local authorities and legal aid that resulted in increased delays and poorer outcomes. Good legal representation and intermediaries to aid effective participation have become more limited; the closure of courts and custodial institutions mean children remanded to custody have to travel further for trial and sentencing; and those sentenced to custody are often placed far from home, making family visits and reintegration more difficult. The Youth Justice Board de-commissioned beds in secure children's homes (the most appropriate – but most expensive – type of secure accommodation) but retained cheaper-to-run young offender institutions (prison-type accommodation, in which children experience high levels of bullying and self-harm, and which the Prisons Inspector has found to be unsafe). Children – sometimes as

---

[1]   See the section entitled 'Genera-relational justice in the COVID-19 recovery period' for a more detailed explanation of this term.

young as ten – are kept overnight in police cells because local authorities have insufficient places in secure children's home to meet their statutory duties to accommodate detained children. And the use of (some) private custodial providers working for profit contributes to poor treatment, as viscerally portrayed in the 2016 BBC *Panorama* exposé of Medway Secure Training Centre.

Austerity measures also left children more exposed to environments that increase the likelihood of childhood offending. One in three children now live in poverty, social networks have been disrupted by forcing movement to more affordable areas, and demand on local authority children's services has increased at a time when funding from central government was cut and council tax frozen; resulting in 23 per cent cuts to children's services over the past ten years. Youth justice grants – which make up a third of the budgets for local authority youth offending teams – were halved and local authorities had to divert some of the remaining youth justice budgets to children's services for child protection work. Spending by children's services on early intervention programmes was also diverted to late intervention, primarily to fulfil statutory duties including those owed to the increasing number of children in care. According to research by the YMCA England and Wales, youth services have experienced £1billion of cuts over the past decade. And although youth crime is down (partly due to population change and, as noted, a decrease in children entering the system), serious violent crime among young people has grown (offences involving knives or offensive weapons increased 11 per cent from March 2012), which in some authorities has coincided with an increased use of tasers and spit hoods, the use of gang injunctions, and more stop and search . This type of policing – as with other aspects of criminal justice – is now more than ever disproportionately used against Black communities resulting in diminished trust and – because reduced trust means people are less likely to plead guilty – higher sentences. The profile of children coming into the system is therefore one of increasing disproportionality (in 2008, 25 per cent of children in custody were from a BAME background; by June 2020, this had risen to 52 per cent), an over-representation of care-experienced children (about a third of boys and two thirds of 15–18-year-old girls in custody report having been in care), and an over-representation of children with communication difficulties, mental health problems and a range of adverse childhood experiences including bereavement, poverty, poor housing, domestic violence and neglect. In 2016, the UN Committee on the Rights of the Child expressed its 'serious concern' about the 'effects [that] recent fiscal policies and allocation of resources have had in contributing to inequality in children's enjoyment of their rights, disproportionately affecting children in disadvantaged situations'[2]; something clearly evident in youth justice.

However, it would be wrong to paint an entirely negative picture of youth justice over the past decade. As well as important wins for children's rights following successful legal challenges (including to childhood criminal records and the extension of child-specific rights to 17-year-olds in police detention), there have been important shifts in nomenclature and practice towards a 'child-first' approach based on better understanding of teenage brain development, as well as the impact of childhood trauma. However, without a solid and principled legal foundation it is hard for such shifts to become embedded and for real change to occur; a precarity that has been exposed by the COVID-19 pandemic, as crises tend to do.

COVID-19 and children in the criminal justice system

As with austerity, the response to COVID-19 negatively affects children in the CJS and at risk of offending. For children within the CJS, limits on face-to-face contact, introduced to reduce transmission, have had multiple consequences. Police investigations, charging decisions and trials have been postponed, compounding the already worsening delays caused by austerity measures. Even before the pandemic, some children were 'released under investigation' for 18 months or more, resulting in extreme stress, disruption to education and employment, and the charging of older children as adults if they turned 18 in the intervening period (thus losing access to child-specific protections, courts, and sentences). COVID-19-related delays heighten these problems and also mean that some children spend longer on remand as custody time limits are routinely extended (Fair Trial, 2020), contrary to international children's rights standards that demand expediency.

Where justice has continued for priority matters, much of it has been virtual via telephone or video link, including court hearings and in police stations (to allow lawyer-client conferences and, in some circumstances, police interviews to take place). Remote communication can be beneficial where it reduces the time children spend in police cells waiting for lawyers or appropriate adults, or in the back of a van travelling long distances to court for short bail or sentencing hearings. But these advantages are often outweighed by the heightened threat to other rights, particularly

---

[2]   United Nations Committee on the Rights of the Child (2016) *Concluding observations on the fifth periodic report of the United Kingdom of Great Britain and Northern Ireland* (CRC/C/GBR/CO/5), para 12.

the right to effective participation. Research consistently shows that children's understanding and participation in criminal processes is highly constrained because of their developmental stage, their inexperience and the prevalence of communication and learning difficulties (estimated to be at least 60 per cent for children in the CJS). These factors are compounded by remote communication which affects audibility, visual cues, the ability of lawyers to discretely check the child's understanding, and the child's willingness to speak and ask questions. It also affects the quality of legal representation: lawyers conducting conferences with a child in a police station by phone or video cannot be sure the child is alone and cannot be overheard; rapport-building and body language is hindered; and there may be inadequate time during and after proceedings to speak privately with the child, including to explain the outcome (Fair Trial, 2020). As we know, entering court rooms can be a horrible experience (Mulcahy, Chapter 3), but so can having a video link exposing your living conditions, or lack of access to Wi-Fi. The revelation of such social inequalities erects additional barriers between the child defendant and legal professionals, and assessing a child – for example for communication support or sentence – is also made more difficult (Standing Committee for Youth Justice, 2018; Fair Trial, 2020).

One positive trend to emerge during the pandemic is the reduced number of children in custody from 755 in March 2020 to 598 in June 2020. This is not, however, due to the End of Custody Temporary Release scheme, brought in as a response to COVID-19, from which no children benefitted. Instead, it is primarily a consequence of the delays and the reduced flow of children through the CJS.[3] The numbers, therefore, are likely to increase again as criminal justice returns to normal.

For children in custody during the spring 2020 lockdown, life was incredibly bleak. While most understood that staff shortages and transmission prevention necessitated regime restrictions, the severity of the lockdown was profoundly detrimental. Many children had only one or two hours out of their cell/room each day and little time in the fresh air; no face-to-face family visits or education took place and instead meaningful activity was reduced to packs pushed under doors (comparing poorly to the continuing educational provision for other vulnerable, but non-incarcerated, children). Fewer mental health assessments took place; time for association was severely limited; and support from charitable organizations (including advocacy

---

[3] It may also partly reflect sentencing courts taking account of the heavier impact of custodial sentences during the pandemic (the increased risk of transmission and harsh custodial lockdown regimes).

and resettlement support) reduced. Although extra phone credits were given and monthly video link family visits eventually instigated (for those families not excluded by the digital divide), the regime changes – given legal effect by Statutory Instrument with no consultation or child-rights impact assessment – differentiated little from those imposed on adults, despite the lower health risk to children from COVID-19 and the higher (mental) health risks and educational impact of isolation. When the restrictions continued even after lockdown eased in the community, the Prisons Inspector described these as 'avoidable and disproportionate'.[4] The only benefit to children of the regime restrictions was a reduction in the number of assaults and restraint. As a result, some children reported feeling safer. However, this was at a cost to children's overall welfare and rather than speak to any success in the COVID-19 -response, the increased feeling of safety merely highlights how unsuitable and dangerous custodial institutions for children ordinarily are.

Indeed, the negative impacts of the lockdown were entirely due to the pre-existing structure and organization of the custodial estate. The design, size and staffing levels of Young Offender Institutions and Secure Training Centres created the conditions and culture that resulted in children effectively living in solitary confinement for months. In secure children's homes, normal regimes (in relation to education and time out of rooms) continued. The COVID-19 crisis has therefore reinforced what many have argued for a long time: that the rights of children in custody are better protected when placed in small, care-based homes where positive relationships between staff and children can develop.

Children's vulnerability to serious offending may also increase as a result of the pandemic. We know that children with four or more adverse childhood experiences are 15 times more likely to commit violence and 20 times more likely to be imprisoned. We also know that during the pandemic there was an increase in family violence, rising unemployment and poverty, educational exclusion, and COVID-related bereavement. Many of these factors will worsen as the economic crisis hits.

There is also anecdotal evidence that lockdown alters patterns of childhood criminal exploitation particularly in relation to county line drugs trafficking, making it easier for organized crime groups to exploit children. Local children have been used to sell drugs in provincial towns rather than trafficking children from larger cities, making their involvement less visible to carers and the authorities because they are not missing from home for

---

[4]   HM Chief Inspector of Prisons (2020) *Report on short scrutiny visits to young offender institutions holding children*, London: Her Majesty's Inspectorate of Prisons, p 7, www.justiceinspectorates.gov.uk/hmiprisons/wp-content/uploads/sites/4/2020/07/YOI-SSV-2.pdf (accessed 21 April 2021).

extended periods or using public transport. During the pandemic many of these services closed, reduced or were available only online, perpetuating the digital divide. Of particular concern was the removal, again by Statutory Instrument and without consultation, of long-standing local authority statutory duties under the Children Act 1989 (including the duty for in-person six-weekly visits to children in care and timely reviews of care plans). A legal challenge by the charity Article 39 is currently ongoing.

Finally, because the police were not empowered to impose fixed penalty notices on children for breaching lockdown laws, arrest using other powers (such as breach of the peace) become a more likely enforcement option. And although increased police presence meant some vulnerable children felt safer and enjoyed positive engagement with officers (where they showed care and understanding), others felt the young and those from poorer communities were targeted in policing, including stop and search (Leaders Unlocked, 2020). The pandemic may, therefore, have increased 'system contact' which, research shows, is associated with re-offending.

Genera-relational justice in the COVID-19 recovery period

When we move into a period of economic recovery, lessons can be learnt from the impact of austerity on children in, or at risk of entering, the CJS. By replacing pragmatism with principle, the lives of children – and the rest of society – can be improved and long-term savings made. Such a principled approach can be founded on the concept of genera-relational justice (Hollingsworth, 2019).

Genera-relational justice brings together generational justice and relational justice. *Generational justice* is underpinned by three inter-related aspects of children's status as rights-holders: (1) the unique *vulnerabilities* of all children, deriving from their economic, political, legal and – in some cases – physical dependencies on adults, as well as their developmental stage; (2) children's unique *capacities* and *potential* for growth and development; and, therefore, (3) our unique *obligation* to all children to provide support and services to minimize their vulnerabilities and to develop their potential which, if neglected during childhood, will have longer-term costs to the individual and to the state (Hollingsworth, 2013). Generational justice demands priority investment in children and their rights. As a form of justice premised upon children's life-stage, it is an obligation owed to *all* children and not only those perceived as *especially* vulnerable or needy (which can be exclusionary of older children or those who present physically, psychologically or situationally as mature). This ensures, for example, that our growing understanding of the relationship between trauma and offending (including those induced by the pandemic) does not dichotomize children into those with a history of trauma (upon whom rights and understanding are conferred) and those whose vulnerability stems 'only' from childhood. This is not to ignore individual experiences or backgrounds. Rather, it demands as a starting point a very specific *child* (age-based) justice system, *within which* particularities can be accommodated.

This can be achieved where that system is based on mutually enforcing values associated with *relational justice*: contextualization, reciprocity and care. Contextualization pays attention to the child's specific characteristics and experiences (for example care status, or the impact of lockdown) and their familial, community and social context, including vulnerabilities that arise from prejudice or oppression based within socio-economic disadvantage, gender and race (and especially the intersection of all three). The constraining effects of these on the child, and how these factors shape their experiences of the CJS, should inform our response to the child's offending. Reciprocity and care provide the normative goals for that response. Reciprocity should ensure children have access to 'goods' necessary to thrive and make good choices (education, adequate housing, caring relationships and so on); punishment takes account of and is proportionate to life circumstances; and that children (and their capacities for future autonomy) are not irreparably harmed by the CJS (placing limits on how children are treated and imposing strong obligations around reintegration) (Hollingsworth, 2013). Care recognizes the centrality of positive relationships to children's ability to thrive before, during and after they leave the CJS. This requires supporting the continuation of the child's existing (non-oppressive) relationships (for example ensuring family participation through the criminal justice processes or facilitating meaningful contact in custody) and a focus on the nature of the relationships with criminal justice professionals: including police, social workers, lawyers, judges, and staff in custodial institutions. These should be characterized by empathy, understanding, dignity, recognition and fairness; in short, a form of 'caring justice' (Held, 2006).

How do these principles translate into policy? The starting point is that the approach to children who offend, or are at risk of offending, must be holistic. Two over-arching commitments are needed. Firstly, there should be priority investment in children. Maximizing the potential of *all* children is crucial for economic growth and is also likely to reduce the economic and social costs of serious youth violence – estimated to be £1.3 billion in 2018–19 by the Youth Violence Commission. One aspect of this would be a more whole-hearted shift to funding the emerging public health approaches to youth offending (where attention and resources shift from seeing criminality as individual 'choice', towards understanding and addressing the conditions that foster offending). Another would be a legal commitment to child-rights impact assessments of all policies and budgetary decisions, giving children priority in the short term in order to bring long-term savings, and bringing *ex ante* accountability where *ex post* accountability (for example through the courts) is sometimes ineffective, especially for challenges to the spending of scarce resources (as demonstrated by unsuccessful judicial review challenges to the lack of secure children's homes).

Secondly, a much firmer rights-basis is needed in law both to compel those financial commitments and also, in the context of youth justice, to protect from populism the more progressive and inter-related trauma-informed and 'child-first' approaches now adopted across the UK. Underpinning these approaches are norms and values that align with children's rights, but they also need to be based *in* rights. Children's rights – if enforceable in law – provide the legal accountability that allows demands to be made and breaches to be remedied and would create the legal environment within which trauma-informed and public health approaches could become embedded in long-term commitments. It is an approach already underpinning the Welsh Government's *Blueprint for Youth Justice*. However, England currently lags behind the regions regarding the legal protection of the UN Convention on the Rights of the Child (the key children's rights treaty), and a legislative commitment to the Convention is an essential starting point. A reconsideration of local authority statutory duties might then follow, for example to include youth and/or preventative services for which central government funding would then need to be provided. Inspection frameworks (of custody placements and youth offender teams) should also map more closely onto children's rights (including children's own views of how those services are operating) providing further *ex ante*, rights-based accountability and reducing the need for children to rely on rights-based legal challenges, which often have insurmountably high thresholds. Finally, legislatively embedding the UN Convention would give a firmer basis for children's participation to inform experientially the structure and funding of the youth justice system.

Genera-relational principles can also inform more specific immediate and longer-term changes needed to address the consequences of COVID-19. The most pressing issue is to prioritize cases involving children in police investigation, prosecutorial decision-making, and court hearings. This is particularly important for 17-year-olds at risk of crossing the threshold into adulthood. Children should be diverted as early and as much as possible, to clear the backlog and decrease system contact. Video-enabled proceedings should be used if compatible with children's rights (for example bail hearings to avoid children spending extended periods being transported to court), but there is too little evidence yet to support more extended use given the likely impact on effective participation and welfare. The rights of children in custody must also be urgently addressed. As children in the community return to school, educational provision and time out of cells must be increased (preferably in small association groups), with prioritization of necessary Personal Protective Equipment (PPE) and testing, as recommended by the Children's Commissioner.

Longer-term, principle-based reform would help to protect the CJS – and the children in it – from the detrimental impact of future outbreaks and economic recession. Many of the necessary reforms have repeatedly been called for by civil society organizations, the UN Committee on the Rights of the Child, and the Taylor Review of Youth Justice. A small number of issues are highlighted here.

Firstly, the minimum age of criminal responsibility should be increased from ten to 14, in line with international standards, to protect younger children from the harms of the CJS and reduce system contact. Alternative responses through the care-system, if the behaviour or its consequences are sufficiently serious to warrant a state response, would require investment in children and health services, including for intensive fostering placements or secure children's homes. These responses would also provide an opportunity to increase public and political confidence in alternatives to youth justice for *all* children.

Secondly, we can learn from jurisdictions such as New Zealand and allow criminal cases to be transferred to family court, and/or introduce 'crossover' proceedings. 'Crossover' proceedings allow the same court to deal holistically with offending *and* care and protection issues (often inter-linked). This allows for a trauma-informed response, rather than one founded solely on principles of punishment. Other lessons might be drawn from New Zealand's Rangatahi courts, introduced to address the disproportionate representation of Maori children and responsible for monitoring the child's progress against their 'family conference plan' (required in criminal proceedings). The courts – held on the Marae (meeting place) with Maori judges and elders – provide a forum within which genuine participation can take place, where the child's cultural heritage and belonging to the community can be fostered (achieved by encouraging the child to recite their pepeha (their genealogy), by hongi (touching noses) and the sharing of food). The multiplicity of ethnicities in the UK makes a direct transplantation of such courts impossible, but they could provide a blueprint for a legal framework for follow-up courts, held in local community locations, employing people from the child's own community, with a strong re-integrative focus.

Thirdly, reducing the numbers of children on remand is a priority given they make up a third of the children in custody, of whom two thirds are subsequently acquitted or receive a community sentence. This could include higher age-limits for custodial remands, more investment in local authority care (to provide feasible alternatives), and increased training of youth justice social workers, lawyers, magistrates and judges. More meaningful community sentences are also needed that help children reintegrate (increasing skills and education), informed by their own views, and with strict limits on breach (reciprocity involves partnership with young people; breach is sometimes indicative of the state's failure to provide support or meaningful activity for the child).

Finally, the Children's Commissioner recommended (in light of the pandemic) that the Youth Custody Service be entirely separate from the Prison Service so that a child-specific approach imbues all its work. We are reminded during COVID-19 that children feel safer in smaller units, supporting the case for care-based homes to replace youth custodial institutions, even the new secure schools (which focus on education but are still large institutions with little explicit emphasis on 'care'). There should be a focus on positive, care-based relationships reflected in recruitment, training and staff rewards/promotions. Changes should be made to the Children Act 1989 so that *all* children in custodial institutions (and not only those on remand) are, in law, 'looked after children' (recognizing that their parents are unable to fulfil fully their own duties to their incarcerated child).

Conclusion

The youth justice crisis in 2020 is no longer one dominated by volume; it is one that now more than ever exposes discrimination, disadvantage and disability. Principle not pragmatism needs to underpin our response to the COVID-19 crisis. As well as providing a more just approach, society benefits if costs associated with crime – personal costs to victims, health costs, criminal justice costs – are reduced, and young people are supported and motivated to make positive contributions to society. Given the recent shifts in youth justice to a trauma-informed, child-first approach, the ground for building a new, more principled youth justice system underpinned by genera-relational justice is firmer now than in 2008. But there are risks from both the economy and growing indications of a return to penal populism (including the recent indications that the government will review the sentencing for murder of 15–17-year-olds, so-called 'Ellie's law'). These threats demand a more concrete base for children's rights. What is needed now is the political will, and the longer-term perspective, to ensure that the changing language and tentative moves towards a new approach to youth justice that have emerged in recent years form the cornerstone of youth justice in the COVID-recovery period.

References

Fair Trial (2020) *Justice under Lockdown.* A survey of the criminal justice system in England & Wales between March and May 2020, https://www. fairtrials.org/publication/justice-under-lockdown-england-wales (accessed 21 April 2021).

Held, V. (2006) *The Ethics of Care: Personal, Political and Global*, Oxford: Oxford University Press.

Hollingsworth, K. (2013) 'Theorising children's rights in youth justice: the significance of autonomy and foundational rights', *Modern Law Review*, 76(6): 1046–69.

Hollingsworth, K. (2019) 'Children and juvenile justice law: the possibilities of a relational-rights approach', in J. Dwyer (ed) *The Oxford Handbook on Children and the Law*, Oxford: Oxford University Press.

Leaders Unlocked (2020) *Policing the Pandemic*, http://leaders-unlocked.org/ publication/policing-the-pandemic/ (accessed 21 April 2021).

Standing Committee for Youth Justice (2018) 'They just don't understand what's happened or why': A report on child defendants and video link, https://www.ayj.org.uk/news-content/they-just-dont-understand-whats-happened-or-why-an-ayj-report-on-child-defendants-and-video-links (accessed 21 April 2021).

5

Racism as Legal Pandemic: Thoughts on Critical Legal Pedagogies

Foluke Adebisi and Suhraiya Jivraj

Introduction: race, racism and intersectionality

> George Floyd's last words were 'I cannot breathe'. But, the truth is that it is we who cannot breathe amid all the ongoing hatred and racism. It is devastating to see that many people survive the global pandemic (COVID-19) only for their lives to end by another human. Hence, it is important to end this evil cycle before it puts an end to us.[1]

Quite soon after the COVID-19 pandemic reached the UK, its disproportionate impact on Black and other people of colour in our communities and among NHS staff became apparent. We watched the viscerally arresting pictures of the first NHS deaths displaying Black and Brown faces on our news screens. We waited desperately for answers and solutions in the subsequent official reports (PHE, 2020) with the banal ministerial claims that the 'virus does not discriminate' ringing in our ears. However, we knew, as Omar Khan, the former Director of the UK's leading race think tank, the Runnymede Trust, was quick to remind those of us that

---

[1] Faris, A. (2020) 'Racism, the real global pandemic', *Voices of Youth*, https://www.voicesofyouth.org/blog/racism-real-global-pandemic (accessed 6 November 2020).

Figure 5.1: Black Lives Matter Protest, London, 6 June 2020

Source: James Eades, from Unsplash

needed reminding: 'racism is a matter of life and death'[2] which the pandemic has merely served cruelly to expose and exacerbate. 'Racism is the real pandemic' – as the banners of Black Lives Matters (BLM) protesters (shown in Figure 5.1) proclaimed – because COVID-19 does discriminate through inequalities in health, education, housing and employment, impacting and determining 'the lives of BAME groups from cradle to grave'. In November 2020, the American Medical Association, recognized racism – systemic, cultural and interpersonal – as a 'public health threat'[3].

That the severity of the suffering from the pandemic was experienced most acutely by Black and other lives prompted all of us to reconsider injustice. In this chapter, we extend this reflection to the profession of the authors of this book: legal education. As a starting point, it is clear that justice is not available for everyone: from police brutality and deaths in custody against Black lives and those of indigenous and other people of colour across the globe including in (former) colonial centres like the UK; to the sheer

[2]   Khan, O. (2020) 'Coronavirus exposes how riddled Britain is with racial inequality', *The Guardian*, 20 April, https://www.theguardian.com/commentisfree/2020/apr/20/coronavirus-racial-inequality-uk-housing-employment-health-bame-covid-19 (accessed 6 November 2020).

[3]   American Medical Association (2020) Press Release, November 16, https://www.ama-assn.org/press-center/press-releases/new-ama-policy-recognizes-racism-public-health-threat (accessed 6 November 2020).

negligent disregard which led to the burning of Grenfell Tower; to standing by as people fleeing persecution drown in the waters that surround us. This horrific everyday racism is known to most of us because we see it, even if we do not pay attention or heed the calls for change in education, health, policing and elsewhere. Moreover, the specific recent pre-COVID-19 socio-economic impact of racism on women of colour, compounded by the UK government's austerity measures has been practically invisible to the public and policy makers. Again, despite decades of research and activism that foregrounds 'intersectionality' – so easily and often slipped into tokenistic equalities discourse these days – is signalling co-constitutive factors of marginalization as expounded and theorized by the women of colour from Anzaldua to Lorde to Crenshaw. As these scholars, poets, activists and lawyers remind us, along with so many others, the notion of 'We the People' in the American Declaration of Independence, the fundamental notion of equality afforded to all citizens of modern liberal democracies, rarely materially and meaningfully includes and speaks to the lived realities of women of colour. The law (from supreme constitution law to ordinary legislation) is therefore heavily implicated as embedder and perpetuator of racism.

This 'premature death' or the necropolitical (Mbembe, 2019) is part of what critical race scholars refer to as the 'racial state', in which the concept of race is about the different political and legal methods that regulate certain populations within society, rather than it being about the colour of people's skin and having some kind of biological essence. We can therefore understand 'race' as actually a process produced by social forces of state power that leads to racialization and racism, which are experienced as persistent structures and formations, not fleeting events. As science journalist and broadcaster, Angela Saini in her recent book entitled *Superior* (2020) has highlighted how racist ideas supporting the biological, intellectual and cultural superiority of the 'white race', and the resultant dehumanization of Black and other lives through the legal justification of slavery which has fed into mass incarceration and police brutality (including in the UK), are making a comeback in frightening and covert ways.[4]

This is all the more reason for legal academics – as well as others – lawyers, policy makers and students to engage in the decolonizing process within education (as we discuss in the final section) to understand the ways in which law is integral to and a purveyor of the racial capitalist state. This is a violent state which accumulates wealth on the backs of bodies of colour, women of colour within the NHS and elsewhere or through other forms of reproductive labour. Intersectionality and other manifestations of racialization are therefore not to be taken lightly or in tokenistic ways but rather studied for

---

[4] Saini, A. (2020) *Superior: The Return of Race Science*, London: Fourth Estate.

the complex and deep-seated co-constitutive factors of marginalization that make up the racial capitalist state; of which austerity and now COVID-19 serve to continue, not just despite the force of law, but because of it.

In making the argument that racism must be understood as a legal pandemic, this chapter explores the continued deployment of race within law and beyond as a biological and therefore racialized concept. It highlights how this 'race thinking' in the time of COVID-19 compounds intersecting socio-economic and other inequalities that racialized populations already experience, as we demonstrate by focusing on the specific case study of garment workers in Leicester. At the beginning of the first lockdown, the image of sweatshops located in our midst caught media attention and fuelled racialized logics locating super-spreading and fear of contagion centrally within migrant populations rather than focusing on the issues of continued premature death – a form of blatant legally sanctioned racism in full view. However, in the final section of this chapter 'What now? Developing anti-racist legal education', we draw on our experience as teachers to argue that through pedagogy another world is possible. By engaging other teachers and students we can collectively expose the racist violence and force of law as well as chart paths and potential for social justice.

COVID-19: racialization and premature death

Thus, it can be argued that we are in the eye of a continuing cyclic syndemic moment. Such a moment is where the respiratory virus of COVID-19 interacts with other factors, such as socio-economic inequality and other co-morbities, that affect the transmission, mortality rates, and containment of the virus itself. According to the Office for National Statistics (ONS, 2020) for all ages the rate of deaths involving COVID-19 for Black males was 3.3 times greater than that for White men of the same age, while the rate for Black females was 2.4 times greater than for White women. Such a moment is itself an epistemic creation, in a world that is also epistemically created and legally ordered. What we mean by this, is that the vulnerability to death continually produced by 'racism as structure' (a pre-existing and concurrent pandemic) has created a convergence point with COVID-19, in a world in which what we experience as reality is often socially produced by knowledge systems that have themselves been organized into hierarchies that map onto racial hierarchies emanating from scientific racism. Consequently, we sit at a historical and contemporary convergence point where racism, sexism, classism, ableism, environmental injustice, and heteronormativity meet and materialize in human bodies. The mortality and materiality lines that COVID-19 draws fall closely on the lines of the pre-existing 'syndemic'; namely the exacerbating the disparities already woven into state structures that disproportionately harm their population through differing systemic process such as welfare, policing, immigration, education and health.

One key question for legal academics in this moment, is how to focus on engaging with the ways the law gives meanings to our social realities is complicit in the making of vulnerable bodies – bodies made vulnerable for the purposes of extracting capital and labour as well as hoarding power. Markers of difference, such as gendered and racialized markers, that are structurally imposed around the body, yield greater vulnerability to conditions of mortality. The more violent the state in these terms, the more violent the state of marked bodies, as state and individual violence converges on their bodies. Racialization – the marking of bodies as inferior or superior – also has, and is always intended to have a particular kind of impact or what we call 'material effect'. Without the functionality of material effect, such racialization serves no purpose. In other words, we often gather data along racial lines to measure differences in circumstances produced by systemic structures, hence material effect. This material effect produced by the state's systemic structures is mainly the extraction of capitalist labour and the hoarding of power. Therefore, while intentionality to these purposes in racialization may not be proven or disproven, intentionality becomes superfluous when effect is always discernible. We conventionally think of racism being a product of individual malice, therefore it is expected that this malice and its effect should be intentional. However, when racism operates in a systemic way (as it mostly does through racializing processes), the people who put the processes of the state into operation may have the purest of intentions, and yet the state structures will still yield disparate outcomes along racial hierarchies. Consequently, to end racism, we must rethink our conventional definitions and understandings of racism.

Thus, it is not just the meanings that we attach to racial differences that have ontological significance, it is also the destiny that those meanings bring about. Racialization euphemistically operating as 'race' or the more nebulous 'ethnicity', erases the processes of structural programming and re-presents such programming as naturally occurring. It erases the fact that racialization – the making significant of 'race' and the racism (individual and structural) that follows – makes bodies sick. Bodies are made vulnerable to mortality by casting certain bodies into the 'zone of non-being'.

In Gordon's (2015) reading of Fanon's conceptualization of the zone of non-being, Gordon explains how the Man of Europe is made universal – the template for all humanity. Consequently, we have a system of laws, policies, regulations and conventions that arise from a position that arose from a condition that normativized the White, European, heteronormative, able-bodied, property-owning man. Bodies that fall outside of this normativity are pathologized – that is, placed at varying degrees of vulnerability to death, depending on how far from this artificed norm they fall. Therefore, in the micro and the macro, racialized bodies were always going to be more vulnerable to the syndemically occurring pandemic called COVID-19.

A salient illustration of this phenomenon is the situation of garment workers in Leicester (as Wheeler discusses in Chapter 12). Under lockdown regulations for England, garment factories in Leicester should have remained closed during lockdown. However, these factories allegedly locked in their workers, while continuing production, placing their workers under difficult conditions of labour – not only exposing them to transmission of COVID-19 in unsafe conditions, but also making them work for longer hours than for which they were paid. Most of these workers were women who only spoke Gujarati – women in bodies epistemically marked by gender, race and history. When the news broke that Leicester's spike in COVID-19 infection and subsequent second lockdown may be linked to the fact that these factories continued working, the workers were blamed for living in overcrowded housing conditions. Their living conditions were non-normative, and thus these were pathologized. But the making of profit – which is normative – was not pathologized. This is reminiscent of the pathologizing of the origins of the disease in Wuhan's wet markets in China. At the time, calls were made for the banning of (non-normative) wet markets, and people presenting with supposedly 'Chinese' features were subject to physical and verbal assault across the normativized world.

Consequently, these different effects of racialization include not only vulnerability to direct effects of racism, but also more exposure to morbid material conditions such as poor mental health, poor housing, more dangerous working conditions (note the racial and gendered make-up of key and front-line workers), propensity to use crowded transport, (non)ability to work from home and so on. Racialization also manifests in the type of business and livelihoods that are made more vulnerable by the government policies in reaction to the pandemic – taxi drivers, small ethnic businesses and cottage industries face immediate disproportionate financial threat.

This leads us to the conclusion that this syndemic and the studies of it, cannot be solely focused on the numbers of the dead. We must look at the structures and processes that occasion increased vulnerability to death. But we must also look at the law which enables and maintains this epistemic hell for some, especially with reference to the universalizing of the Man of Europe. An example of this is the privileging of certain identities in migration, citizenship and belonging, how analogies of hard borders result in more dead bodies in the water, and more lives destroyed within those borders, for example the Windrush scandal. Note also who these borders are hard for, and who these borders are not hard for. Thus, citizens from non-EU countries (often former colonies), the majority of whom are racialized

Black or Brown, are faced with an uphill process to regularize their status as citizens, they pay higher fees for this process than citizens from the EU. Citizens from non-EU countries, through the hostile environment, are also more likely to be subject to intrusive checks on their belonging-status in housing, employment, education, health and so on. Thus, for fear of severe government sanction, service providers and agents in these areas feel less inclined to enter into transactions with non-EU people or even British citizens who may appear racially not to belong, thus further making non-White belonging to this space more precarious.

Thus, these racialized disparities continue to be reproduced in education, housing, as well as the criminal justice system, to name but a few. It is important that we think of these structures and processes beyond the artificial binaries of living and dead. As reports into economic disparities resulting from COVID-19 show, the living who already live subject to a wide range of socio-economic inequalities and health disparities have had those disparities exacerbated by COVID-19 and government policies in response to COVID-19. When we focus on the false inevitability of pathology of certain racial groups, we ignore the wider societal structures that create normativized bodies and the privileges that accrue to those bodies – privileges that seem to be naturally occurring. We ignore the complicity of the law in maintaining the illusion of inevitability and inescapability. This type of thinking leads to consternation when similar mortal proportionality is not found in Asian and African countries that can map in a comparable fashion to the mortality rates of people with African and Asian backgrounds in the UK. The marking of bodies seems to rob us of the ability to reason and engage in critical thinking which we envisage to be a significant outcome of legal education. This suggests a need to revisit the direction, content and purpose of legal education.

What now? Developing anti-racist legal education

If, as we suggest through our analysis, echoing the voices of recent anti-racism protests, racism is the real pandemic and indeed a *legal pandemic*, what should we as lawyers do now? Individually and collectively, we (the co-authors) have both employed our roles as teachers, colleagues and mentors to educate ourselves and those around us. First, it is crucial to understand how normativity (as we referred to it earlier) has been established through the force of law in embedding, perpetuating and implementing racism that has been around for centuries and pre-dates the killing of George Floyd and others. Yet barely any legal pedagogy of this kind exists in the UK beyond a handful of optional modules often taught by the relatively small number of legal scholars of colour who survive against the odds within the academy of the global north.

There is therefore an overwhelming need to redesign pedagogy and curriculum, not to erase what is already there which seems to be a key concern of those who have critiqued 'decolonizing the curriculum' or other similar decolonizing movements. Rather our aim is to make visible and foreground the facts, histories and perspectives of those that have been kept outside of the European canon as eminent anthropologist David Scott has shown us in his crucial work *Conscripts of Modernity: The Tragedy of Colonial Enlightenment*.[5] The process of socio-legal erasure is not accidental; we only hear the story of slavery and its abolition from the perspectives of the British colonial state and its apparatus including the academy, not from those that were enslaved, their families or indeed those left behind in the territories of West Africa and beyond. But their realities do exist as do their future imaginaries, whether of pan-Africanism and/or based on radical Black thought like that of Steve Biko. These perspectives, facts and realities, whether from Africa and/or other settler colonies including indigenous law should not remain invisibilized within the so-called canon and universalizing rhetoric of law and lawyers. One hopes that a redesign may allow future 'worlds otherwise' including these perspectives to emerge. It is not only 'bad scholarship' to continue without redesigning and rethinking, but it also does not quench the thirst of our increasingly diverse student body to 'decolonize the curriculum' and improve access to knowledge that reflects their intersectional lived realities. This movement, reinvigorated in the UK and globally by the Rhodes Must Fall movement in South Africa from 2015, has become so powerful that its graduates in the UK have gone on to set up their own campaigns and social enterprises such as the *Black Curriculum* and *Kids of Colour*. They are leading the way for curriculum and pedagogic changes within British primary and secondary education.

These demands for change in education have been made and set in motion, and we have no option now but to act as students increasingly utilize what power they do have to shape their education and futures as racial capitalism cracks under the weight of the global pandemic. Whether drawing from our own work – Foluke Adebisi's anti-racism reading list (2020) on her blog African Skies,[6] Suhraiya Jivraj's anti-racist legal pedagogy

---

[5]   Scott, D. (2004) *Conscripts of Modernity: The Tragedy of Colonial Enlightenment*, Durham: Duke University Press.

[6]   Adebisi, F. (2020) 'An Anti-Racism Reading List', *African Skies Blog*, https://folukeafrica. com/an-anti-racism-reading-list/

resource[7] – or the increasing amount of other similar information, there are now more ways in which to propel legal education towards its force for social justice, rather than epistemic and other forms of violence. Both our resources highlight the expanse of literature and knowledge that already exists in relation to law; but, equally importantly, other areas where more knowledge production is required and needs to be supported as well as funded. Suhraiya's resource in particular builds upon a teaching and innovation project with her law students to co-produce research and recommendations specifically for higher education settings, including ways in which to prepare oneself on the journey to developing anti-racist curricula and also classrooms. Students consistently inform us of micro-aggressions experienced in class including seeing themselves routinely presented back to themselves through negative stereotypes as either perpetrators or victims.

However, as we have both argued extensively elsewhere, even when choosing to be institutionally involved in 'decolonizing', 'inclusive' or 'liberated' curriculum frameworks we must also be vigilant about the fact that all these terms are fraught with difficulties in the current neoliberal university context. 'Decolonizing' in particular has become increasingly institutionally co-opted rather than understood 'as an ongoing process of conceptual thinking and consequent material actions ... which should not be appropriated or politically abstracted from the indigenous and other communities from which they have arisen' (Jivraj, 2020: 15; see also Foluke's African Skies blog mentioned earlier). In fact, most 'decolonization' efforts in UK higher education fall short of actual decolonization and are driven by colonial logics that privilege the commodification of labour and space. Decolonization seeks to disrupt these colonial logics. Yet the neoliberal university, subject as it is to auditing and inspecting against colonial criteria that reduces space and labour to financial value, can only survive through the colonial logics of commodification of space, nature, humanity and variably valued labour. Moreover, decolonizing movements within British universities have predominantly been student-led and therefore come from very particular anti-racist pedagogic trajectories, with very few like the University of Kent (DecoloniseUoK Collective, 2020) developing into short-term staff-student collaboration rather than institutional policy.

Starting from the point of pedagogy has been critical to addressing several key law and policy or ethical drivers for change. Educators after all are subject to the Equality Act 2010[8] and the public sector equality duty to

---

[7]   Jivraj, S. (2020) *Towards Anti-Racist Legal Pedagogy: A Resource*, https:// research.kent. ac.uk/ decolonising- law- schools/ (accessed 6 November 2020).

[8]   https://www.legislation.gov.uk/ukpga/2010/15/contents (accessed 6 November 2020).

have due regard to eliminating discrimination, and advancing equality of opportunity across the nine protected characteristics (age, disability, gender reassignment, marriage and civil partnership, pregnancy and maternity, race, religion or belief, sex, and sexual orientation). In reality this means that universities and teachers are required to go beyond paying lip service to the provision and delivery of teaching that is non-discriminatory in terms of overt racism but also tackling subtle and everyday forms of racism, sometimes referred to as micro-aggressions or (un)conscious bias. We know that these quotidian forms of racism so embedded within society alongside gender, sexuality and disability biases feed into the headlines around 'attainment gaps' or rather awarding disparities. While arguably the Equality Act has insufficient teeth for rigorous implementation the Higher Education and Research Act 2017 (HERA)[9] which established the Office for Students, a regulatory body now requires universities to have a 'work plan' with targets to tackle the significant gaps in the attainment between White and 'BME' students although we view this trend as awarding gaps placing emphasis on the role of universities and what they are failing to provide for students of colour rather than categorizing the students as the source of the 'problem'. We also know that 'attainment' and other career disparities exist not only in legal education – despite students of colour entering higher education institutions with similar if not higher grades – but also the professions. According to the Solicitors Regulation Authority (SRA) this includes 'BAME solicitors' being paid less including during training contracts and being less likely to become partners in larger firms than their White colleagues.

We must therefore put in the work to tackle the existing inequalities legally and ethically, particularly, as we know that the 'attainment gap' is a product of what we teach, and therefore can be more accurately described as an awarding gap or disparity. By calling this disparity an 'attainment' gap, we focus attention on our students' supposed deficiencies and deflect responsibility from institutional structures. This is an approach which feeds into pre-existing racialized tropes about lack of aspiration, while simultaneously avoiding any need for institutional change. As the Equality and Human Rights Commission report (2019) and other research has highlighted, students of colour face a complex myriad of racism on campuses and in the classroom as well as in the curriculum.[10] This has only been exacerbated by health

---

[9]   https://www.legislation.gov.uk/ukpga/2017/29/contents (accessed 6 November 2020).

[10] Equality and Human Rights Commission (2019) *Tackling racial harassment: Universities challenged*, www.equalityhumanrights.com/sites/default/files/tackling-racial-harassment-universities-challenged.pdf (accessed 6 November 2020).

and social mobility inequalities during the pandemic. As we have discussed earlier, COVID-19 does discriminate.

Many scholars and health professionals have echoed this, challenging the UK government's rhetoric that COVID-19 does not discriminate between people. Gurnam Singh, for example, explicitly states that we need to be aware of how further to tackle the impact of these intersecting inequalities on BAME students in particular:

> There is a large body of evidence confirming that BAME students face a variety of conscious and unconscious discriminatory practices in traditional classrooms. For instance, BAME students' behaviour is more likely to be rated harshly compared to similar behaviour of white students, staff tend to express more positive and neutral speech towards white students than toward BAME students. And in terms of assessment, BAME students are consistently given lower marks and less favourable feedback than their white counterparts. Though this is an under researched area, evidence suggests these biases are/can be replicated online.[11]

One step we can all take is to consider how some of the great work being done in optional modules can be centred within a law curriculum to ensure we are collectively acting and working towards an anti-racist pedagogy. As our resources highlight, what may seem a daunting journey – and it is a long-term, life-long one – we can take one step at a time. We can stop pretending that the murder of Stephen Lawrence and the Macpherson Inquiry should not feature within a criminal law module rather than be relegated to an option module on policing or criminology. All law students should know about the insurance law cases such as the Zong case (Gregson v Gilbert (1783) 3 Doug. KB 232) which sought enforcement of an insurance contract to compensate slave ship owners for 'loss of cargo' (slaves who were thrown overboard) and not the slaves or their families.[12] It is absurd and frankly offensive that students are not aware of this when previous and current government ministers attribute to Britain's role in the abolition of slavery rather than the compensation of slave owners for what is essentially the murder of the enslaved people deemed to be property and cargo thrown

---

[11] Singh, G. (2020) *Covid-19 does discriminate – so we should tackle its impact on BAME students*, https://wonkhe.com/blogs/covid-19-does-discriminate-so-we-should-tackle-its-impact-on-bame-students/ (accessed 7 November 2020).

[12] http://www.commonlii.org/int/cases/EngR/1783/85.pdf (accessed 6 November 2020).

overboard. Especially when these historical wrongs have continuities in the contemporary capitalist state that leads to migrant workers being locked in to continue their forced labour under the deathly conditions of COVID-19. Our teaching and research therefore need this context and can make overt reference to the origins of property law in enslavement and imperialism. Note how as Brenna Bhandar in her book *Colonial Lives of Property: Law, Land, and Racial Regimes of Ownership*[13] explains, there is a close relationship between how the person is understood in law and how we legally understand property. We could also point our students to Charles Mills' dismantling of the social contract which he argues is actually superseded by a racial contract – a global system of domination which produces and maintains the racial disparities we discussed earlier. A global system of domination in which the law cannot help but be complicit. Yet, this scholarship and research also simultaneously forms a counter-knowledge that defies the discourse of scarcity 'of other perspectives' or research and scholarship by people of colour. Again, these narratives and thinking they expose are more a marker of institutionalized whiteness and the upholding of White supremacy within law and legal knowledge than about the *lack* beyond the legal pandemic of racism.

Conclusion

The other chapters in this volume conclude with reflections on the government's response to the COVID-19 pandemic, and lessons that might be learned. This chapter, however, ends by speaking directly to legal academics. For those eager to reconsider basic assumptions in pedagogy, the references in this chapter provide a starting point. In teaching and researching law, generally, it is critical that we remain faithful to a truly meaningful engagement with an intersectional approach. Thus, we should refrain from fragmenting for example, the emergence of property, from the current climate emergency which arises from violent appropriation, unequal accumulation and overexploitation of real property. This is something that indigenous scholars in Abya Yala and Turtle Island (Indigenous Americas) remind us so well whether through co-creation of their national Constitutions with indigenous values or campaigning for gender and climate justice as a single issue. Most recently, in the 2020 United States elections, we see that the work of Black women in particular, like lawyer and politician Stacy Abrams of Georgia, have mobilized communities through various means, including education, to tackle voter suppression and policy brutality, to

---

[13] Bhandar, B. (2018) *Colonial Lives of Property: Law, Land, and Racial Regimes of Ownership*, Durham: Duke University Press.

initiate a paradigm shift away from a denial of White supremacy, at least at a symbolic level.

We must therefore take the lead of historic and contemporary fighters for justice to let our teaching and research demonstrate how this present necropolitical world and order, with its geopolitical disparities, emerges from making racialized populations increasingly vulnerable to death. We must resist, as Black studies scholar Kehinde Andrews and so many others remind us that the struggle to produce and protect our knowledges is real, visceral and every day and even espouses the language of 'BAME'. Despite the UK government's Equalities Minister claiming that we should not teach Critical Race Theories, which incidentally emerged in the US from Critical Legal Studies and is now being witch-hunted there, we do need to teach perspectives and theories that expose the realities that people of colour are subjected to through law. We can also teach the possibility of otherwise worlds because we should not just teach the world we have; we should also teach the world we want to see. A world woven in a new design.

References

Decolonise University of Kent Collective (2020) *Towards Decolonising the University: A Kaleidoscope for Empowered Action*, edited by D. Thomas and S. Jivraj, Oxford: Counterpress.

Gordon, L.R. (2015) *What Fanon said: A Philosophical Introduction to his Life and Thought*, New York: Fordham University Press.

Jivraj, S. (2020) 'Decolonizing the Academy – Between a Rock and a Hard Place', *Interventions*, 22(4): 552–73.

Mbembe, A. (2019) *Necropolitics*, Durham: Duke University Press.

Office for National Statistics (ONS) (2020) Coronavirus (COVID-19) related deaths by ethnic group, England and Wales: 2 March 2020 to 15 May 2020, https://www.ons.gov.uk/peoplepopulationandcommunity/birthsdeathsandmarriages/deaths/articles/coronaviruscovid19relateddeathsbyethnicgroupenglandandwales/latest (accessed 6 November 2020).

Public Health England (PHE) (2020) *Disparities in the risk and outcomes of COVID-19*, London: Public Health England, https://assets.publishing.service.gov.uk/government/uploads/system/uploads/attachment_data/file/908434/Disparities_in_the_risk_and_outcomes_of_COVID_August_2020_update.pdf (accessed 6 November 2020).

6

Rights and Solidarity during COVID-19

Simon Halliday, Jed Meers and Joe Tomlinson

'This is the worst interference with personal liberty in our history for what, by historical standards, is not a very serious pandemic ...'. (Sumption, 2020)

The development of social solidarity and of social cohesion is the real headline story of the pandemic. (Reicher, 2020)

Introduction

Public understanding of the risks posed by COVID-19 understandably has focused squarely on health and mortality. As government officials throughout the UK during the first few months of the crisis offered daily hospitalization and death counts, minds inevitably concentrated on the medical risks of COVID-19. Yet the subject of this book is the social costs that will also come in the wake of the pandemic: problems of social disadvantage and suffering that will be less visible – perhaps less compelling in the public imagination – than the primary health impacts. How might law matter to such social problems? What role can law play in the alleviation of this social suffering?

When answering such questions, it is tempting to frame the discussion purely in terms of what government, Parliament or the courts might do to alleviate suffering. The image of law here is one where it has a formal status: enacted through Parliament, interpreted and developed in the courts, and enforced by administration. Equally, the understanding of law's relationship to society is primarily a 'top-down' instrumental one: law as a tool of governance to bring about change in society. There is much to commend this way of thinking about law and society. It captures a great deal of what lawyers and social scientists study when exploring law's potential to improve society and the actual impact of law on society. However, to understand the role of law in the response to social suffering fully, we must make two basic adjustments to this familiar way of thinking about law in society.

First, we must recognize that law is not only an instrument of governance but is also a means of challenging the ways in which we are governed. The rule of law, though a much-contested term, speaks of the basic idea that government is constitutionally constrained in what it might do. The familiar contrast between the rule of law and arbitrary action highlights the role of law in holding government to account and reversing abuses of power. Equally and relatedly, the notion of fundamental rights – values for a godless age, as Francesca Klug put it (Klug, 2000) – articulates foundational legal limits. The dynamic between those with power in society and those subject to that power is structured in a way in which basic rights and liberties must always be respected – and law may be invoked to enforce such respect.

Second, we must recognize that we can speak of 'law' not only in formal terms, but also informally. Particularly if we concern ourselves with the ways in which 'law' is invoked in challenging the excesses, abuses or negative effects of public and private power, we should focus our enquiry on what those doing the challenging think of as 'law'. Attempts to alleviate social problems, even to change society, have frequently drawn on senses of 'law' that would not be recognized within formal conceptions. Most obviously perhaps, such informal senses of 'law' have a long and powerful pedigree in the history of revolutions, sometimes expressed as recovering a form of earlier legal truth that has been covered over by history, as in the English Civil War, at other times articulating new rights claims that run against the grain of history, as in the American and French revolutions. Thus 'law' in the thoughts and actions of ordinary people is as important to socio-legal study as formal conceptions of legality. It is this 'bottom up' and informal sense of legality that forms the focus of this chapter.

The lockdown imposed by the four governments of the UK in late March 2020 represented an extraordinary, rapid and radical restriction on normal life for the entire population. What did the UK public think about this unprecedented governmental intervention? Specifically, what was the popular rights consciousness with respect to the lockdown restrictions? Our thesis is that, despite notable and powerful public statements about the extent to which lockdown represented an unacceptable violation of basic rights and liberties, this claim failed to capture the public imagination. Instead, most people either regarded the violation of basic rights as acceptable, given the context of the pandemic, or simply failed to think of the lockdown in terms of basic rights at all. We suggest that such popular rights consciousness has been shaped by the strength of social solidarity during the crisis – what we might describe as a kind of popular 'obligation' consciousness.

This social solidarity has proven to be remarkably resilient, enduring over time. Indeed, even in the face of some very public breaches of lockdown by some very public figures – prompting allegations of hypocrisy that might be thought to threaten the sense of obligation to each other – solidarity seems to have remained intact. Social solidarity has thus operated as something of a double-edged sword: while much lauded as an extraordinary feature of UK society's response to the pandemic, it likely operated to suppress a sense of grievance over the government's pandemic response policy. The implications of this in terms of the relative acceptability of rights claiming during a time of atypical solidarity are considered in the concluding section.

Key social claims during the COVID-19 pandemic

The two quotations that preface this chapter (the first from a retired Supreme Court judge, the second from a member of the Scottish Government's COVID-19 advisory group and the UK-wide 'Independent SAGE' group of scientists) capture two of the major social claims – ones we might relate to the topic of law and rights – that have been made about changes to UK society during the COVID-19 pandemic.

The claim about the loss of liberty is readily appreciable. In March 2020, the country was, in effect, put under house arrest, as Lord Sumption put it. People could not leave home without a reasonable excuse, extended families could not see each other, funerals of loved ones could be attended by only a small number of family members, none of whom was permitted to visit the loved one before they died in hospital or care homes. This extraordinary and extreme change to the conditions of life and death did not, of course, go unprotested. In addition to the critique of the policy from prominent figures such as Lord Sumption, there was considerable sceptical commentary on social media and online platforms, as well as some public protests.

The claim about social solidarity is as readily appreciable as the loss of liberty. Everyone was encouraged to stand outside their homes on a weekly basis and applaud NHS and other keyworker 'heroes', child-drawn rainbows appeared on windows throughout the land, over a million people signed up to be NHS volunteers, and the Queen delivered an address to the nation that was understood to reference the solidarity of her subjects during the Second World War.

As part of a larger study that seeks to understand why people do and do not comply with behavioural restrictions during the pandemic, we explored public opinion about these issues of basic rights and social solidarity. These data allow us to reflect on the extent to which these claims have found traction within the public consciousness. The research, funded by the Nuffield Foundation, is ongoing at the time of writing. It comprises three elements: (1) the tracking of legislative developments in response to the pandemic; (2) a qualitative study of 100 participants' experiences of, and reactions to, the lockdown and subsequent behavioural restrictions; and (3) a national panel study of respondents' compliance behaviour during the pandemic, comprising three waves of surveys. In this chapter we focus on the third, quantitative element of the project and report findings from the first two surveys.

Given the pace of policy developments during March 2020, and in order to get an initial survey into the field quickly, we used the services of a national polling company to obtain survey data. Our data were collected from members of the YouGov panel of UK individuals who have agreed to take part in surveys. The total sample size for Survey 1 was 1,695 adults. Fieldwork for Survey 1 was conducted online and undertaken 27– 29 April 2020. The total sample size for Survey 2 was 1,158, all respondents having taken part in Survey 1. Fieldwork for Survey 2 was also conducted online and undertaken 8–12 June 2020. Nonetheless, although our panellists for Survey 1 were selected at random from the base YouGov sample of over 185,000 individuals, and although in relation to both surveys the figures were weighted to be nationally representative of all adults (aged 18 and over), it is still a non-probability sample. Caution should accordingly be exercised when making inferences about the wider UK population.

On rights consciousness

In our surveys we collected data from respondents about their attitudes to various recently introduced rules that imposed behavioural restrictions on the general public. For the purposes of this chapter, we can focus on seven of the rules explored in Survey 1 at a time when the lockdown restrictions were fairly uniform throughout the UK. For the ease of presentation, we might organize the rules into three groups as follows:

Shopping rules:

- You must not go to the shops solely to buy non-essential items.
- You must not go to the shops more than once a day.

Sociability rules:

- You must not arrange to meet up socially with someone outside who is not a member of your household.
- You must not make a social visit to the home of a family member (unless you are caring for them).

- You must not make a social visit to the home of a friend or neighbour (unless you are caring for them).

Recreation rules:

- You must not visit your second home or holiday accommodation.
- You must not go for a recreational drive.

In relation to each rule, we asked respondents to indicate by way of a Likert scale the extent to which they agreed or disagreed with the following statement: 'This rule violates my basic rights'. In the charts in Figure 6.1, the averaged-out findings for rule groups are presented (there being very little variation in the findings between rules within each group). As we can see, there is little difference in attitudes across the rule groups as to whether the lockdown rules violated a sense of basic rights. Roughly only a third of respondents agreed that they did. The general picture here is of reasonably weak support for the notion that the lockdown violated a sense of basic rights.

The general picture of weak popular support for the notion of basic rights violation is accentuated by the data from some further questions on rights consciousness. With these questions we aimed to gain a sense of the extent to which respondents felt that, should there be a sense of a rights violation, it was nonetheless acceptable in the context of the COVID-19 pandemic. In other words, we were keen to probe the extent to which the public's rights consciousness embraced a sense of what lawyers describe as 'proportionality' in rights thinking. The essence of the idea here, reflected in

Figure 6.1: Shopping, sociability, recreation

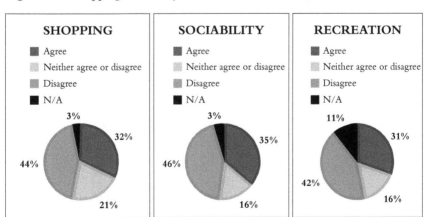

Note: In Shopping, Agree is 32%. In Sociability, Agree is 35%. In Recreation, Agree is 31%.

legal doctrine, is that an infringement of rights may be acceptable where the purpose of the infringement is sufficiently important to justify interference with the right.

To achieve this, we presented our survey respondents with a number of specific rights ideas, framed in everyday terms and not the language of legal rights instruments:

- my right to earn a living;
- my right to worship as I please;
- my right to enjoy the outdoors as I please;
- my right to spend time with family and friends;
- my right to fully support those who need me;
- my right to live life as I choose.

We then invited respondents to indicate whether the lockdown violated these rights; whether it violated these rights but, given the circumstances, the violation was acceptable; or whether lockdown did not violate these rights.

As Figure 6.2 demonstrates, the idea that gained most traction in the public consciousness with respect to an unacceptable rights violation concerned supporting others (12 per cent). This is interesting as it is more connected with social rather than individual benefits. Yet, overall, the findings from Survey 1 suggest that there is very little support for the claim that the lockdown was unacceptably violating a sense of basic rights. Indeed, in relation to each rights idea (with the exception of the right to worship), the majority of respondents indicated that the violation of rights was acceptable within the context of the COVID-19 pandemic.

Figure 6.2: Specific rights ideas

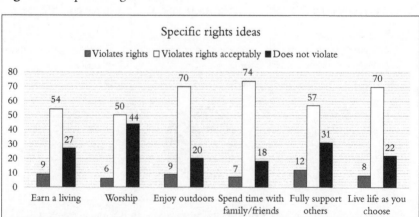

In Survey 2 we extended this list of rights ideas. In the period between Survey 1 and Survey 2 there had been significant public commentary about the re-opening of schools and the potential health risks this might pose, with strong views expressed on both sides of that debate. Equally, after the death of George Floyd in the US, there had been public demonstrations throughout the UK under the banner of the Black Lives Matter movement, though a number of politicians had warned against public protest in light of the infection risks this might pose. Indeed, as Hervey et al note in Chapter 8, in some instances the police issued fines for breaches of COVID-19 restrictions in relation to such protests. We were keen, therefore, to ask respondents about their perceptions of rights as they might relate to these issues. The following rights ideas were added to our list:

- my right as a parent or guardian to choose what is best for my child;
- my child's or grandchild's right to an education;
- my right to protest outside with others.

Although in relation to the first two of these three new rights ideas (about children and education) there was a high proportion of respondents indicating that the question was not applicable to them, we can still see that the rights consciousness of the public across these issues also seems to be weak (see Figure 6.3). And again, excluding the 'not applicable' responses, the majority of respondents in relation to each rights idea indicated that, although they felt there was a rights violation, they viewed it as acceptable in the circumstances.

These findings suggest that rights consciousness among the public may be more nuanced than we might have imagined. At the very least, we might suggest that, in the context of an extreme set of circumstances such as a

Figure 6.3: Further specific rights ideas

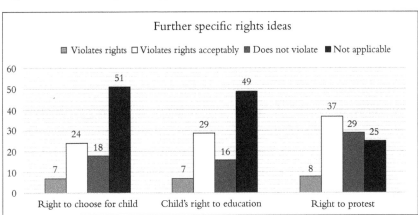

pandemic, a large proportion of people are willing to tolerate interference with their rights for what they see as a legitimate purpose. Our qualitative data offer some indication of what such a legitimate purpose might be: a sense of social solidarity and collective need. The quote by Lord Sumption at the start of this chapter forms part of a longer media interview where he criticizes the COVID-19 lockdown restrictions as an unjustified curtailment of the public's liberties. We played this interview to 100 focus group participants and invited them to respond. Many of them disagreed with Lord Sumption's sentiment. As one participant put it:

> I do not really share his sentiments and agree with what some of the other participants in this thread have said. I feel that this is a whole society issue and everyone has a role in defeating this virus .... In the grand scheme of things, I feel that having a lockdown is not really that inconvenient if it means saving and protecting lives .... Yes, it may not personally affect a lot of those whose liberty has been taken away, but this is not just a personal problem, it's a collective society issue.

This theme of social solidarity was explored further in the panel study. It is to these data that we now turn.

On solidarity (or obligation consciousness)

In both Survey 1 and 2 we probed the extent to which our respondents felt some kind of solidarity with others during the pandemic. To get at this, we asked a question about the extent to which respondents would be prepared actually to do something to improve the wellbeing of others (see Figure 6.4). We selected a range of groups, recognizing that people may feel stronger senses of solidarity in relation to some groups than others – for example family more than neighbours. Given the emphasis within government policy messaging at the time on the importance to the NHS of public compliance with the pandemic lockdown, we included NHS workers as one of the groups in the survey question.

The data, unsurprisingly, indicate that the strongest sense of solidarity was felt towards one's family. Yet, feelings of solidarity towards NHS workers were also very high, with 81 per cent of respondents indicating that they 'absolutely' or 'probably' would actually do something to improve their wellbeing. Feelings of solidarity towards NHS workers were higher, indeed, than those towards neighbours (70 per cent) or fellow countrymen and countrywomen (65 per cent).

Figure 6.4: Would you be prepared to actually do something to improve the wellbeing of the following? (Survey 1)

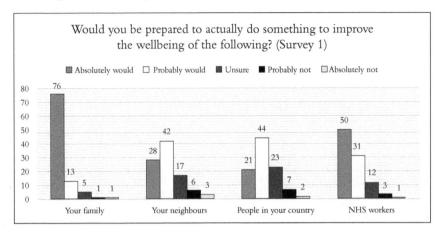

Figure 6.5: Would you be prepared to actually do something to improve the wellbeing of the following? (Survey 2)

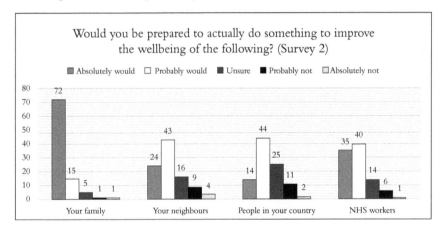

As the pandemic continued, there was media commentary about the potential 'fraying' of solidarity within the UK. Our findings from Survey 2 (see Figure 6.5) offer some support for this idea, though the key finding is that the majority of our respondents, at the time of our second survey, were still expressing a willingness to assist others towards their wellbeing.

The focus of our research, and the core of the government's messaging during the pandemic, was about compliance with lockdown rules. Accordingly, we also asked respondents about the extent to which they felt they owed it to others to comply with the rules. Our data about this specific sense of an obligation to others confirms the earlier findings about solidarity.

Figure 6.6: To what extent do you feel you owe it to the following people to comply with the lockdown rules? (Survey 1)

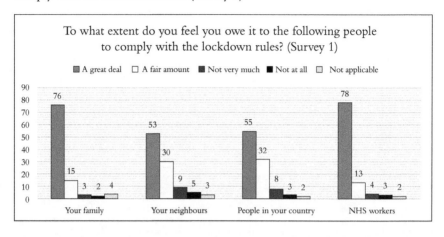

As the graph in Figure 6.6 shows, a sense of compliance obligation towards people's families was, unsurprisingly, very high (91 per cent). Remarkably, however, the extent of felt obligation towards NHS workers matched the feelings towards family (91 per cent). But more generally, across the board, our respondents overwhelmingly felt they owed it to a range of other people to comply with the lockdown restrictions.

Just as with our data on a willingness to do something for others' wellbeing, our data in Survey 2 on compliance obligation also suggest that there may have been some 'fraying' of solidarity within the UK, though the effects seem smaller. Again, overwhelmingly, the data suggest a continuing strong sense of solidarity amongst UK residents, with families and the NHS coming out as being particularly notable targets for solidarity feelings. The comparable data from Survey 2 are shown in Figure 6.7.

These data about a continuing strong sense of solidarity among our respondents are all the more remarkable in light of some high-profile political events that occurred around the time of our surveys. Shortly before Survey 1, the Chief Medical Officer for Scotland, the public official fronting the Scottish government's public campaign urging compliance with lockdown restrictions, was discovered breaking the rules herself by visiting her second home. She resigned in the wake of the scandal. Similarly, between Surveys 1 and 2, Neil Ferguson, a prominent member of the UK government's scientific advisory group (SAGE), resigned when a media story broke about him breaking the lockdown rules. Equally – and perhaps most spectacularly – not long before Survey 2, the UK Prime Minister's senior aide, Dominic Cummings, as Hervey et al describe in Chapter 8, was accused of breaching COVID-19 restrictions with his family. He, however,

Figure 6.7: To what extent do you feel you owe it to the following people to comply with the lockdown rules? (Survey 2)

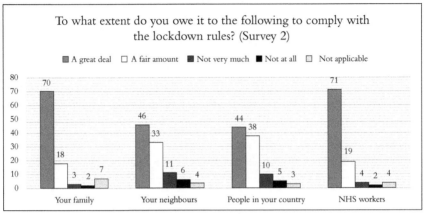

did not resign. Considerable media and political outrage was expressed in consequence, reflecting, it was thought, a real depth of public anger about governmental hypocrisy – as highlighted in a *Daily Mail* poll which suggested a level of public outrage, even of normally loyal Conservative supporters to the government, with regular expressions that there appeared to be 'one rule for them and one rule for us'. As Andrew Rawnsley noted in *The Guardian*, reflecting on the findings of a separate public opinion poll on the matter, 'The public ... thinks [Cummings] is a law-breaking liar who should be sacked if he doesn't resign' (Rawnsley, 2020).

In light of these events, we included a question in Survey 2 that elicited our respondents' perceptions about such matters (though we did not specifically reference any of these scandals): 'Thinking about how public officials and politicians themselves have acted during the crisis, in your opinion how hard are they trying, if at all, to act fairly?' The results, as shown in Figure 6.8, suggest that the public was quite divided about the fairness of personal action on the part of public officials and politicians.

Yet, despite 55 per cent of our respondents expressing a negative assessment about the efforts of politicians and public officials to act fairly themselves during the crisis, levels of felt obligation towards each other remained high. Legitimate and sizeable public anger about those who influenced the content of lockdown restrictions failing to abide by them did not, it seems (at least at the time of our second survey), significantly damage the sense of mutual obligation. As the quote from Reich at the beginning of this chapter suggests, social solidarity is actually the bigger and more enduring story here.

Figure 6.8: How hard are politicians and public officials trying to act fairly themselves?

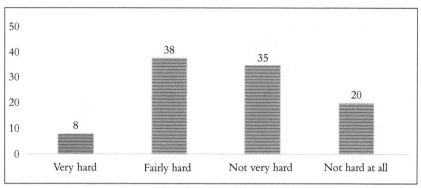

Rights in a period of heightened solidarity

The use of law to alleviate social problems – for example, by commissioning the services of a lawyer in a dispute or using legal ideas to bring about change – is not a straightforward matter. Indeed, such uses of law represent a kind of midpoint of a longer process. After the midpoint come various stages of litigation or campaigning that may eventuate in success, compromise or the abandonment of one's efforts. Before the midpoint come the crucial stages whereby a targeted sense of grievance comes into focus: first one must have a sense that something is wrong, or has gone wrong; second, one must have a sense of another party being to blame, or having responsibility for making things better; and it is only when one receives short shrift that we get to the midpoint where the use of law comes into focus as a potential tool to effect change. The study of rights consciousness is important because it relates to the first of these crucial pre-midpoint stages. To what extent do people 'name' their situation as a problem to be solved? In what ways, if at all, do they identify their circumstance as one of basic 'rights' being compromised or, more broadly, having a legal dimension?

Our data suggest that the restrictions imposed on the UK public are not, in the main, being identified as particularly problematic. Our suggested explanation for this is that it is because of the strength of social solidarity at this unusual moment in the country's history. Rights consciousness and solidarity are locked into a kind of seesaw dynamic: the stronger the solidarity, the weaker the rights consciousness. At the same time, the rights idea that seems to have the greatest traction in such an environment relates to the ability to perform an essentially social act: caring for another.

At a theoretical level, the logic of basic rights is that they provide a common foundation of political conditions that all in society may enjoy. Accordingly, rights consciousness in the minds of ordinary people becomes, to some extent at least, a matter of comparison – about identifying that, while others in society are being treated as they should, the same cannot be said for oneself (also see Hervey et al, Chapter 8). Thus the assertion of rights becomes one of attempting to remedy the unfairness of that deficit. The consequence of this is that when we are 'all in this together', and there is no one to compare oneself against, the purchase of rights consciousness dissipates. This is a particularly salient finding against which to interpret the actions of the powerful, whether that be the Cummings affair, the actions of Neil Ferguson, or the Scottish Chief Medical Officer.

Of course, from one perspective, the idea of solidarity is particularly positive. There is much to applaud about solidarity, particularly after the great rift of Brexit, and especially in a country that, since the late 1970s, has drifted increasingly westwards towards the strong individualism of the US. Yet, we must not forget that every perspective has its blind spots; and the blind spot of the solidarity perspective is that, in important senses, and as this book seeks to explore, we are not, in fact, 'all in this together'. Some are more privileged and less vulnerable than others, certainly in the economic aftermath of the pandemic. And so the study of solidarity is, perhaps, equally important to our understanding of the conditions under which people may use law to alleviate social suffering. An extraordinary period of crisis-driven solidarity may constitute rather hostile terrain for rights thinking and rights claiming.

It seems clear that, in the absence of an effective vaccine, the pandemic will continue for some time. It is equally likely that health and mortality concerns will continue to feature significantly in public thinking. The challenge for those who find themselves in positions of relative social disadvantage is, first, to name that situation as a problem to be solved and, second, to overcome the apparent difficulties of asserting one's rights at a time when the public may not be able see the logic of the claim, and the mood may be against it.

References

Klug, F. (2000) *Values for a Godless Age: The Story of the United Kingdom's New Bill of Rights*, London: Penguin.

Rawnsley, A. 'Dominic Cummings took the public for fools. Now they want his head', *The Guardian*, 31 May, https://www.theguardian.com/commentisfree/2020/may/31/dominic-cummings-took-the-public-for-fools-now-they-want-his-head (accessed 20 April 2020).

Reicher, S. (2020) 'Social Solidarity and social cohesion: The headline story of COVID-19', *Campaign for Social Science*, 2 June, https://campaignforsocialscience.org.uk/news/social-solidarity-and-social-cohesion-the-headline-story-of-covid-19/ (accessed 20 August 2020).

TheBridgeVids (2020) 'Lord Sumption discusses Coronavirus lockdown on BBCR4 PM with Evan Davis', www.youtube.com/watch?v=86P7EEJeNKM (accessed 20 August 2020).

7

COVID-19 PPE Extremely Urgent Procurement in England: A Cautionary Tale for an Overheating Public Governance

Albert Sanchez-Graells

Introduction

One of the notorious failings of the UK government in its reaction to the first wave of the COVID-19 pandemic was its inability to ensure that the health and social care frontline had proper and undisrupted access to essential personal protective equipment (PPE), such as masks, gowns and gloves. The story of the failings leading to the PPE fiasco runs largely in parallel to the also failed attempt at boosting the availability of ventilators through the 'Ventilator Challenge', and the not more successful subsequent 'Test and Trace' programme, including its doubling down in 'Operation Moonshot' – which, at the time of writing, has been assessed to be having a marginal impact on the prevention and management of the second wave.

These stories offer a cautionary tale for the future management of extremely urgent public procurement, which will become ever more important given the serious risks of social and ecological breakdown derived from climate change. These stories show the very significant problems that result from having a public sector with insufficient procurement capability, an inadequate procurement strategy and (perhaps more importantly) a very weak procurement governance system largely incapable of ensuring the accountability for outsourced tasks in the public interest (Boeger and Sanchez-Graells, 2019). Perhaps even worse, these stories are not news at all, and the underlying problems not only concern extremely urgent procurement, but also complex procurement projects, as the second phase of the Grenfell Tower Disaster Inquiry is further evidencing.

In this chapter, I will concentrate on the PPE fiasco in the context of the English NHS to explore these broader governance issues. By focusing on the case study of PPE procurement during the first wave of the COVID-19 pandemic, my main goal is to lay bare the more general problems in the UK government's approach to the governance of public procurement and its increasing insularity as a result of Brexit, with the hope that this will show a path for change that could avert even more significant fiascos in the face of the massive challenges that climate change is yet to bring.

Background

There is no need to rehearse here the reasons why the continued availability of adequate PPE is essential to the ability of the health and social care frontline to do their best to save lives. The PPE fiasco put lives at risk – those of the health and social care workers, as well as the patients and residents, and their broader communities – and most likely was a contributing factor to the disgraceful unnecessary loss of some of those lives (see also Harding, Chapter 9). National Audit Office (NAO) reports on the UK government's procurement during the COVID-19 pandemic,[1] and on the PPE fiasco[2] have laid bare the systemic failings, which have also been criticized by the Public Accounts Committee.[3] However, it may be naïve to hope that they will bring a sufficient degree of much-needed accountability for the many failings involved in the expenditure of over £5.5bn in PPE between March and July 2020. Litigation about the PPE expenditure promoted by The Good Law Project resulted in a judicial finding that the 'Secretary of State acted unlawfully' by breaching procurement transparency requirements,[4] but this has also failed to have any major political consequences or to bring additional information to light. There are issues still requiring further investigation, perhaps in a future public inquiry, such as which companies benefitted from

---

[1]   National Audit Office (2020) *Investigation into government procurement during the COVID-19 pandemic*, 26 November, HC 959 Session 2019–21.

[2]   National Audit Office (2020) *The supply of personal protective equipment (PPE) during the COVID-19 pandemic*, 25 November 2020, HC 961 Session 2019–21.

[3]   House of Commons Public Accounts Committee (2021) *COVID-19: Government procurement and supply of Personal Protective Equipment*, 10 February, HC 928 Session 2019–21.

[4]   *Good Law Project & Others v Secretary of State for Health and Social Care* (2021) EWHC 346 (Admin) at [135].

VIP treatment in the award of PPE contracts. In this chapter, I will rely on the patchy publicly available information. However, it suffices to support a couple of troubling observations, which will frame the analysis.

The first observation is that the problems underlying the PPE fiasco were manifold, including the incapability of the Department of Health and Social Care (DHSC)'s long-arm supply chain management entity (NHS Supply Chain) to nip the crisis in the bud and put in place workable arrangements (Hall et al, 2020). The NHS Supply Chain's centrality to the problem is perhaps best reflected in the (quiet) resignation of its top management between the first and second waves of the pandemic. However, this should not obscure the higher-level responsibilities of DHSC and NHS Improvement/NHS England in this context, which should also not be deflected to the army of management consultants engaged to sort out the PPE fiasco (as well as the rest of the aforementioned procurement problems).

Many governments around the globe also failed in the face of the significant, perhaps unprecedented challenge, of securing access to PPE under extreme urgency and massively disrupted marketplace conditions. However, my first claim in this chapter is that the UK government not only was particularly ill-positioned to deal with the pandemic as a result of years of austerity and the institutional unsettling resulting from the continuous reform of the NHS, its internal market and its supply chain – but also due to the imminence of Brexit and its political ramifications.

The second observation is that (for once), procurement law can hardly be blamed for the operational problems that manifested in the insufficiency and oftentimes unsuitability of PPE. Where unforeseeable and extremely urgent circumstances not attributable to the public buyer arise, public procurement rules get out of the way to free public buyers to do all they can to get the required supplies and equipment (Sanchez-Graells, 2020a). In the early stages of the pandemic, both the European Commission and the Crown Commercial Service confirmed in explicit guidance that pandemic-related procurement would be exempted from compliance with the EU and UK procurement rules, so long as that was proportionate and strictly necessary. Accordingly, the shortages of PPE cannot be attributed to procurement red tape or the need to follow anti-commercial practices – however much that would have chimed with the 'bonfire of procurement red tape' narrative spun by Johnson and Cummings in the post-Brexit context. The 'deactivation' of public procurement law thus created a regulatory gap through which to channel the expenditure of eye-watering amounts of public funds through 'unregulated procurement' and, unavoidably, exposed public governance to the ever-present risks of corruption and abuse (Sanchez-Graells, 2020b).

In that regard, my second claim in this chapter is that, in its desperate reaction to the PPE fiasco, the UK government misused and abused the disapplication of the standard procurement rules on the basis of the 'extremely urgent need' exemption. This resulted in the opaque award of large numbers of high value contracts to companies that would not survive basic screening under normal conditions. Granted, a relaxation of the procurement rules was needed. However, that is no justification for the dubious procurement practices that are starting to be uncovered, as evidenced in the NAO reports and judicial decisions published so far.

The weakened governance of centralized NHS procurement

Excessive centralization of NHS procurement

To understand some of the root causes for the PPE fiasco, it is necessary to take a step back and gain some perspective on the recent evolution of the governance of NHS procurement in England. As a starting point, it should be noted that, until relatively recently, each NHS organization (notably, NHS trusts) was carrying out its own procurement independently. In that context, the procurement function was very close to the frontline.

Progressively, however, where there were advantages to be had through collaborative procurement (such as reducing administrative burdens or securing better value for money), regional networks or 'hubs' emerged to procure goods and services for a number of NHS trusts. Also progressively, nationwide centralized procurement frameworks for common use goods (or consumables) were put in place to drive down costs, and these framework agreements were managed by a newly created entity: NHS Supply Chain. This organic phenomenon of consolidation or collaboration in the procurement of *some* supplies and services for the NHS led to a situation where, in 2017, NHS procurement expenditure was roughly split across three procurement routes: 20 per cent direct expenditure by NHS trusts, 40 per cent expenditure through collaborative procurement in NHS hubs and 40 per cent expenditure through centralized mechanisms managed as 'consolidated procurement' by NHS Supply Chain.

The UK government then decided to accelerate significantly and massively extend NHS procurement centralization through a so-called New Operating Model (NOM; see Sanchez-Graells, 2019). The NOM currently in place seeks to accumulate 80 per cent or more of total NHS procurement expenditure through NHS Supply Chain. In public management speak, this has been presented as synergies and economies of scale justifying the further centralization of NHS procurement. In practical terms, the system seeks to create cost cuts in NHS procurement to redirect those funds to the frontline. This is part of a broader strategy seeking to minimize the additional funding required by the NHS to prevent its collapse.

While NHS trusts are, in principle, free to use the services of NHS Supply Chain or to carry on with their independent procurement strategies, the introduction of centralized funding for the NOM in 2019 created a massive disincentive for NHS trusts to procure independently. DHSC withheld close to £250m from trust funding and directed it to NHS Supply Chain (under the so-called 'top slicing model'), which meant that trusts were locked in the system and had to use NHS Supply Chain to try to recover via lower prices the upfront contribution to its funding. Further, in the wake of the pandemic, the use of NHS Supply Chain was made mandatory.

From a governance perspective, the NOM and the strategic role NHS Supply Chain develops within it are troublesome, not least because NHS Supply Chain is, in reality, a corporate front used to hold a complex network of outsourced contracts that creates multiple layers of intermediation. (also see Wheeler, Chapter 12) Any given class of NHS supplies – for example PPE, or ventilators – has been placed under a 'Category Tower' that is managed by a 'Category Tower Service Provider' (CTSP). The CTSP designs a 'market strategy' for the procurement of the given supplies, which is likely to be contracted to a small number of providers (sometimes only one) under a framework agreement. Further, the logistics required to distribute the centrally procured supplies to the frontline are also outsourced to a private operator. In this setting, the procurement function is three or four times removed from the frontline; and, the NOM has created very problematic institutional barriers and dynamics that jeopardize the necessary alignment between the procurement function and operational needs. If a product ordered by an NHS trust through the NHS Supply Chain platform does not arrive to the frontline, it will be difficult to establish whether the problem (and responsibility) lies with the logistics operator, the manufacturer, the CTSP, NHS Supply Chain, or any combination of the these. This will also make fixing the problem rather difficult, not only because of the multiplicity of points of failure, but also because none of these organizations want to be left to bear the cost.

Inadequate, separate outsourcing of the influenza stockpile

The NOM has no influence over the management of the UK strategic influenza pandemic stockpile, which is under a separate outsourcing contract. The relevance of this stockpile for the COVID-19 pandemic is that, while the different diseases require different elements of PPE, the widely held view is that at least *some* of the products in the stockpile could have been used to plug some gaps in the shortages of PPE. In that regard, the strategic stockpile could have served as a bridge solution while the problems in the NOM were sorted (as will be discussed later). The difficulty here is that the management of the strategic stockpile has been riddled with problems over the last two years – including a controversial sale of the outsourced provider during the first wave of the pandemic – and the levels of the stockpile have also been significantly reduced in recent years (from £831m in 2013 to £506m in March 2020, in value terms), and known to have included PPE that had run out of date. This is part of the broader problems concerning the rejection of the recommendations of the New and Emerging Respiratory Virus Threats Advisory Group (NERVTAG) (for example, to include eye protection in the stockpile, or to purchase larger volumes of gown), as well as the shortcomings in the UK's readiness for a flu pandemic identified in 'Exercise Cygnus' – its report had been buried by the government for too long (but that is a story for another day). This mismanagement made resorting to the influenza stockpile particularly difficult and reduced its potential contribution to addressing the PPE shortage at the height of the first wave of the COVID-19 pandemic.

Brexit as further erosion of NHS procurement governance

There is a further major source of weakened health care procurement of relevance for the COVID-19 pandemic: Brexit and its political ramifications.

The deleterious impact of Brexit on health care procurement was perhaps more obvious regarding the strain that 'No Deal' Brexit preparations put on the system, which was not sufficiently close to having all preparations in place when No Deal Brexit was narrowly averted (for the first time). While some of the 'Brexit stockpile' seems to have helped the NHS cope with some COVID-19-related shortages (for example of medication), the fact that the NHS procurement function was significantly overloaded to prepare for Brexit could not have helped manage the early stages of the COVID-19 challenge; and, perhaps speculatively, it could be argued that this could have contributed to the late reaction (discussed later).

Less obviously, but perhaps with larger practical significance, Brexit and the UK government's policy of disengagement from collaborative EU projects meant that the UK did not participate in the early joint procurement of PPE coordinated by the European Commission in the framework of the Joint Procurement Agreement (JPA). The circumstances surrounding the UK's absence from the EU's bulk-purchase of PPE have been controversial but – on the face of significant revelations in mainstream media and an embarrassing U-turn by a top civil servant after having confirmed to the Commons Foreign Affairs Committee that the UK took a 'political decision' not to join the EU scheme to source medical equipment – it is hard to accept the government's position that there was no political decision not to participate and that this was rather the result of an unfortunate miscommunication.

Be that as it may, it seems obvious to me that the growing insularity of post-Brexit UK (particularly under the Johnson government) is a further contributing factor to the PPE failure and, more broadly, to the further weakening of the UK's public procurement governance system.

PPE procurement: NHS Supply Chain's failed stress test

> Behind the tweets [of procurement leaders in the UK's National Health Service] – coded, because the managers feared bosses' wrath for publicizing the shortages – lies the story of a government slow to recognize the scale of PPE that would be needed during the pandemic, of shifting guidelines that left staff feeling confused and vulnerable, and of a belated operation to source the vast number of items needed that left the UK playing catch-up with other nations to secure its share of scarce supplies.[5]

So far, I have identified the governance problems of the excessively centralized NHS Supply Chain under the NOM, the mismanagement of the outsourced strategic influenza pandemic stockpile and the additional burden and insularity resulting from Brexit as the most relevant ones. From those, the governance problems structurally unaddressed in the NOM, as well as important shortcomings in its operative structure, were the first ones to create significant difficulties.

By the time the urgent need to procure PPE became too obvious for anyone to ignore, the system was already showing signs of collapse. There was a competition between NHS Supply Chain and NHS trusts (and hubs) to secure the supply of PPE in what now was a sellers' market and where the UK buyers were competing globally for limited available supplies. In this context, price rises and supply chain disruptions could be expected. To try to mitigate this problem, DHSC attempted to make the use of NHS Supply Chain mandatory, to avoid competition between buyers from within the NHS system. However, this put extreme pressure on NHS Supply Chain to deliver and, as even the patchy record shows, it failed. There were in part coordination problems but, more importantly from a governance perspective, NHS Supply Chain started to engage in a strange strategy of 'demand management' that seemed oriented not to satisfying the most pressing needs of the frontline, but to safeguarding central stocks to back up

---

5   Foster, P. and Neville, S. (2020) 'How poor planning left the UK without enough PPE', *Financial Times*, 1 May, https://www.ft.com/content/9680c20f-7b71-4f65-9bec-0e9554a8e0a7 (accessed 21 Apr 2021).

the government's claim that there was no general problem of PPE availability, but just some difficulties in local distribution – which would deflect the blame from the centralized system to local NHS trusts. Coupled with the Secretary of State for Health and Social Care's accusation that doctors were overusing PPE,[6] the whole situation was flammable. Unsurprisingly, this resulted in local NHS trusts (and hubs) disregarding the policy of centralized procurement and continuing to (try to) procure PPE directly.

There is little clarity on the organizational changes introduced to try and overcome NHS Supply Chain's inability to source the required volumes of PPE, but there is evidence of the involvement of Deloitte in the creation of a parallel 'PPE procurement cell' to bypass (or complement?) NHS Supply Chain. This could only have further exacerbated governance problems, especially as Deloitte's position would not have (easily) fit within the NOM system. Moreover, the centralized efforts to source PPE were less than successful in themselves. From the evidence on the public record, the episode of the military airplane awaiting a delivery in Turkey that was only partly fulfilled by the supplier(s), and eventually turned out to be mostly unusable is perhaps the starkest example of the shortcomings of the strategy. And all of this occurred in the context of repeated and multiple claims from industry that offers to provide suitable PPE were largely ignored or turned down.

This demonstrates that not only that the NHS procurement function had been weakened by an inadequate governance structure, but also that DHSC had no contingency planning or strategy in place; and that, most likely, there was a general complacency or excessive expectations on the ability of the NOM, and NHS Supply Chain in particular, to scale up operations and ramp up the level of centralization. It also became obvious that the system did not have sufficient capacity to redeploy its existing resources (say, from different category towers) to the procurement of PPE. Further, the engagement of external management consultants to deal with the problem is telling of the limited capacity (or willingness?) of the civil service to step in when outsourced mechanisms fail. This is a much broader problem than just the procurement of PPE, or health care procurement, and seems to be the pervasive result of the austerity preceding the period.

PPE procurement: a chancers' paradise

From a different perspective, the extreme urgency of the procurement of PPE has evidenced the inadequacy of the governance mechanisms to cope

6   Stewart, H. and Campbell, D. 'NHS workers angered at Hancock's warning not to overuse PPE', *Guardian*, 10 April, https://www.theguardian.com/society/2020/apr/10/matt-hancock-urges-public-not-to-overuse-ppe (accessed 21 April 2021).

with systemic 'unregulated procurement'. As mentioned earlier, EU and UK procurement law contain an exemption for the procurement of extremely urgently needed supplies. Under that exemption, public buyers are free to pursue 'commercial approaches' that would not normally be available to them, such as not carrying out the required vetoing of potential suppliers, the conduct of direct negotiations with existing suppliers, proactive approaches to potential suppliers, or ancillary issues such as pre-payments. However, this exemption is not designed to be applicable at a systemic level, as evidenced by its malfunctioning in the COVID-19 context – in the UK, and elsewhere (Sanchez-Graells, 2020b).

More importantly, being exempted from the detailed requirements of public procurement rules does not mean (or *should not mean*) that the public buyer can award contracts as it sees fit without considering whether they represent value for money (making allowance for distorted market conditions and abnormal risk-taking), fail to discharge minimum levels of due and professional diligence, continue to prevent the exploitation of conflicts of interest and, ultimately, refrain from using the award of public contracts to pursue political goals and facilitate profiteering.

I am not saying that all of this definitely happened, but there are robust indications in the public record that those appear to have been the consequences. Perhaps this is most clear in the award of direct contracts for non-PPE supplies (such as the award of some of the ventilator contracts, or some of the management consultancy contracts), but there are a plethora of examples of failed PPE contract awards and awards to providers that were clearly speculating in the market – some of them on the strength of political connections. Future official reports or inquiries may provide further details, but the award of contracts for the supply of PPE to companies with no track record whatsoever, companies created a few months prior, or companies run by NHS procurers should have raised a few red flags at the time and should lead to further political scrutiny and accountability as the evidence crystallizes.

It would be all too easy to think that desperate times call for desperate measures and shrug our shoulders. It would also be too easy to think that the end justifies the means so that, if X or Y company delivered the goods, we should not worry about how they obtained them or what they kept in their pockets. All of this matters because the evidence that emerges from the extremely urgent procurement of PPE in the context of the first wave of the COVID-19 pandemic will be evidence of what is rotten or dysfunctional in a system that will only be facing increased challenges in years to come. My money is on a set of findings that will largely be coincidental with the learnings we should have extracted from recent Brexit-related procurement scandals (the reader will remember FerryGate),[7] so I do not expect a surprising diagnosis. What one can perhaps expect is that *at this point* the weight of the evidence will be enough to prompt meaningful system readjustments.

System fixes

In this chapter, I have tried to stress how the PPE procurement fiasco was not the unavoidable consequence of the pandemic and that the UK health care procurement system was in a particularly weak position to deal with it as a result of its previous excessive and inadequate centralization; the inadequate oversight, mismanagement and underfunding of the outsourced strategic stockpile; and the additional impacts of Brexit. This turned the implementation of 'unregulated procurement' for the extremely urgent purchase of PPE into a governance Hydra that ate up NHS Supply Chain and resulted in the implementation of expensive and largely inadequate stopgap management solutions, and the waste of significant resources in a desperate attempt to scramble PPE supplies. It also created a regulatory vacuum which facilitated the improper award of contracts in an opaque manner. Regardless of whether all details are accurate, I believe that the overall analysis is a fair reflection of the sorry state of affairs of procurement governance in the UK, as evidenced by the COVID-19 'stress test'. Perhaps the better question is what this means for the future.

To my mind, the existential challenge of climate change should be put at the forefront of policy and legal analysis – together with the also existential challenges of the development of digital technologies and social media, which are closely intertwined with the climate emergency. From those perspectives, before too long, the ecological and social breakdown resulting from climate change will pose urgent challenges to all governments. And public procurement will, once again, be an essential part of an adequate response. There are a few things that need to be done to prevent falling into the trap of 'unregulated procurement' on the basis that extreme urgent needs become the 'new normal'.

Without attempting to be exhaustive, I would advocate the following. First, the procurement capability of the public sector needs to be re-established, which will require insourcing currently outsourced functions and providing substantially more resources. Second, reliance on 'strategic

---

[7]   National Audit Office (2020) *The award of contracts for additional freight capacity on ferry services*, 11 February; National Audit Office (2019) *Out-of-court settlement with Eurotunnel*, 9 May.

providers' and management consultants needs to be severely cut back and the development of more varied and resilient supply chains needs to be actively promoted. Third, there is a clear need for more (and much better) contingency planning, which also needs to be properly resourced. Fourth, we need to reorient procurement to put sustainability at its core. Fifth, we need to harness the potential of digital technologies to achieve higher levels of sustainability and, more generally, to achieve the UN's sustainable development goals.[8] Sixth, we need to facilitate and support the emergence of transnational and global institutions and governance networks capable of coordinating domestic procurement efforts aimed at tackling cross-border and global challenges.

The practical obstacles are significant, and the obvious constraint is that all of this would require significant resources and sustained effort to implement and consolidate changes that are not easy fixes of what is, in effect, a rather dysfunctional complex system. However, I hope the COVID-19 story will serve as a cautionary tale. If we fail to fix the system, it will fail when put under significant stress. And the only thing that we should not doubt is that systemic stress is coming our way.

References

Boeger, N. and Sanchez-Graells, A. (2019) *Classic Debates in Public Service Outsourcing*, University of Bristol Law Research Paper Series, 8, 2019, https://ssrn.com/abstract=3564225 (accessed 16 October 2020).

Hall, D., Lister, J., Hobbs, C., Robinson, R., Jarvis, C. and Mercer, H. (2020) *Privatised and Unprepared: The NHS Supply Chain*, University of Greenwich and We Own It, https://weownit.org.uk/privatised-and-unprepared-nhs-supply-chain (accessed 16 October 2020).

Sanchez-Graells, A. (2019) 'Centralisation of procurement and supply chain management in the English NHS: some governance and compliance challenges', *Northern Ireland Legal Quarterly*, 70(1): 53–75.

Sanchez-Graells, A. (2020a) 'Procurement in the time of COVID-19', *Northern Ireland Legal Quarterly*, 71(1): 81–7.

Sanchez-Graells, A. (2020b) 'Procurement and Commissioning during COVID-19: reflections and (early) lessons', *Northern Ireland Legal Quarterly*, 71(3): 523–30.

---

[8] See United Nations, *17 Sustainable Development Goals*, https://sdgs.un.org/goals (accessed 16 March 2021).

PART II

The Social

8

Accountability for Health and the NHS under COVID-19: The 'Left behind' and the Rule of Law in Post-Brexit UK

Tamara Hervey, Ivanka Antova, Mark Flear and Matthew Wood

Introduction

In the documentary film *Brexit, Health and Me*,[1] the drill rapper Drillminister reflects on accountability for political decisions affecting the health of the UK population and the NHS in England, Scotland, Wales and Northern Ireland. The Drillminister interview is replete with references to legal forms of accountability: criminal processes, including imprisonment, for stealing, fraud and 'joint enterprise', as well as investigatory processes designed to promote transparency, such as Royal Commissions.

Interviewer: Your song 'NI Backstop' for me was a song about educating, but also that encapsulated the arguments so well. What made you want to do that?

Drillminister: Because my main ops is government, my main ops is the people that's putting us down. What I'm saying, in certain lines like, um, 'Before the referendum, did the average Joe know what Brexit was?' – before the

---

[1]   Available at: https://education.shoutoutuk.org/

referendum, not after, where everybody's saying, 'Brexit, Brexit, Brexit', saying the buzzword – did they know what Brexit was? No, they didn't. They had no clue, otherwise they wouldn't have been driving around with big buses saying, 'Yeah, 150 million … [corrects self] 350 million … is going back to the NHS', which is a lie. Which, right now, why is no one in jail for that? Because if I'm a fraud man, and if some Uncle is coming and saying, 'Yo, I'm putting blah, blah, blah into your account' … you'd be like, 'Yo, Uncle, you're putting that money in my account, yeah'. That man'd be in jail. …. But yet you were able to say 350 million, and got your vote through, and now we're all effed ….

Interviewer: What do you think should happen? Cos obviously the 350 million going back to the NHS, on the big red bus by Boris Johnson, it's been discredited, obviously, it's not true, what do you think should happen to MPs who abuse our trust, and the general public, like that?

Drillminister: Um, to be fair, when you're doing something so important, I know it sounds extreme, you have to do jail time. You have to. Guys are doing jail time for less, on the roads. Just, um, joint enterprise, if you know what that is – that's you was in the wrong place, at the wrong time, you never did anything, you never touched anything, you weren't a part of anything, you were there. So, if you were there, with Boris Johnson, when he's saying 350 million, knowing that there's an old pensioner, who is actually believing in that policy – she actually believes in the NHS, she might have been a retired nurse, and she believes in this country and believes in that – and you misled that woman with 350 million – to then rob from her pension now (because that's how she's going to have to pay that back) – what? You're telling me there's no jail time? There's no joint enterprise? There's nobody investigating that? There was nobody saying, 'How did that …?' … There was no commissions brought to say how did this even come about?

Using an evocative narrative and extended metaphor, Drillminister likens the claim that leaving the EU would mean significantly more money would be spent on the NHS to a fraud on a naïve retired nurse, who believes in the NHS and the trustworthiness of governmental promises. The negative consequences for her quality of life of the false promise of Brexit are such that those making that promise should, in Drillminister's view, be legally accountable, and indeed accountable through criminal processes. In Drillminister's logic, the £350 million promise is a fraud, and the consequences for that fraud should be no different from the consequences for someone who is able to steal money from a pensioner's bank account through a fraudulent hoax. Although he was not the author of the promise, (now) Prime Minister Johnson was present, and therefore Drillminister reasons that Johnson is as culpable as the perpetrator (Dominic Cummings), as an accomplice in the criminal sense of joint enterprise. According to Drillminister's logic, PM Johnson, and his aide Cummings, should be prosecuted for fraud, and, as they are guilty of such a significant crime, should be imprisoned.

This interview captures in a particularly eloquent form a theme which we found repeatedly in our conversations with people in the street in 'left behind' communities in the north of England and Northern Ireland. The concept of the 'left behind' holds great salience for health governance in the aftermath of Brexit and in the ongoing COVID-19 pandemic. Austerity economics and a widening of the gap between the richest and the poorest have contributed to the emergence of a group of people who are geographically removed from London and other large cities, for whom life has become significantly more precarious over the last decade. There are signs that the impact of the COVID-19 pandemic and the public health and economic responses taken to it are affecting the 'left behind' particularly badly. The links between poverty and ill-health are well-established. Underinvestment and constant reorganization without adequate resourcing in the NHS, especially in England, have contributed to worsening health indicators. Pockets of COVID-19, such as associated with crowded housing, have emerged, and people who live in those places continued to suffer further detriments, as local lockdowns, and the 'tier' system, became the norm into autumn and winter 2020–21.

The 'left behind' people we talked with in Derry, Newry, Rochdale and Rotherham do not trust politicians (of any political persuasion), but they trust and believe in the NHS. *They also believe that the law will (or at least should) hold politicians to account for the consequences of their actions* for the NHS and for health. To what extent is this the case in the UK's constitutional settlement for health and the NHS? This chapter looks at some high-profile examples to see the extent to which ordinary people's beliefs stack up against the legal and constitutional reality. One example is primarily about Brexit (the original subject of our research); the others are primarily about COVID-19.

Brexit and COVID-19 interact in their effects on the NHS and health, in multiple ways. The end of the transition period, 31 December 2020, after which the UK left the EU's single market, will result in a negative impact on the UK economy, which will combine with the COVID-19 recession. NHS staffing levels, and especially nursing and social care, are likely to be severely challenged, as the 'hostile environment' associated with a new immigration policy makes the UK a less appealing place to live and work. Supply of medicines and medical devices (including Personal Protective Equipment (PPE)) will be affected, particularly given the nature of the trade agreement between the UK and the EU. Opportunities to collaborate with European partners, in biomedical research, in public procurement of (eventual) vaccines or treatments, in sharing of epidemiological data, are diminished. Regulatory standards, including concerning safety of medicines or devices, clinical trials, could change significantly. The challenge of Brexit for COVID-19 is especially serious in Northern Ireland, because of its integrated health system with Ireland which remains an EU Member State, and because of their shared geographical space (the island of Ireland) within which communicable diseases circulate.

No legal protection for the 'devolveds': the *McCord* litigation

In 1997, Raymond McCord's 22-year-old son died as a victim of paramilitary action in Northern Ireland. Like many who live in Northern Ireland, McCord has experienced at first hand the pain of the particular history of the island of Ireland, and its difficult and at times tragic relationship with England and English rule. The Good Friday/Belfast Agreement 1998 offered hope for peace and reconciliation. One part of that Agreement was North-South cooperation: a suite of ways in which people and public services especially in the north of the island would collaborate and integrate for the benefit of all. The legal and economic structures for these efforts were made significantly easier by the fact that both Ireland and the UK were members of the European Union. Products, services and people could easily cross the land border, with minimal formality, because of the security provided by EU law underpinning economic and inter-personal interactions, and the residence rights of people who are not UK or Irish nationals. Public health standards are the same, because of EU regulation of food and other vectors of disease. Communicable disease control included cooperation and data sharing through the EU's Centre for Communicable Disease Control.

Health became a particularly successful part of North-South cooperation. A single children's heart surgery unit for the whole island was established in Dublin. Shared cancer services were set up for the north. Children and adult mental health services began to be provided by integrated teams. Ambulances no longer attended an emergency depending on the jurisdiction in which that emergency occurred. People working in health and social care cross the border every day, including many people from central and Eastern Europe, drawn to the opportunities offered by working and living conditions in the west of Europe. Membership of the EU, and shared health infrastructure and activities, became part of the landscape of peace on the island of Ireland.

The UK Brexit vote threatens that settlement. Although the vote across the whole UK was (narrowly) for Brexit, Northern Ireland voted against. The people we spoke with in Newry and Derry felt this strongly: they spoke of 'the English Brexit'. People also spoke passionately about how detrimental it would be to lose the integrated nature of health services on the island. Someone in Newry described 'a chain of negative effects' of Brexit on the NHS and on health in Northern Ireland, including staffing problems, longer waiting times, and medicines and vaccines shortages. Someone else worried about how children with disabilities would be affected. Many people confided their fears of re-bordering of Ireland, evoking stories of past violence, and an uncertain future where a hard-won freedom of movement would be once more taken away. The health corridors established under the North-South cooperation are a specific instance of a bigger narrative, in which people are afraid for their lives post-Brexit, especially in Derry, because of the physical geography of the island. Because of the significant disruptions implied, a 'No Deal' Brexit presented a particular threat to peace, security, prosperity and health in Northern Ireland.

Some people we spoke with in Northern Ireland suggested physical violence (killing, shooting, punching, slapping) as a way of holding English politicians, specifically Johnson, to account for the effects of Brexit. Some suggested political ("Don't vote them in") or moral accountability ("Shame on him"), and others said that politicians could not be held to account or that they did not know how. But a stronger theme in our conversations was *legal* accountability. There should be "a law to remove Johnson", we heard; or Johnson should "be arrested", be "taken to court", "prosecuted", "sent to jail", and we should "get a top lawyer on him". Some thought of criminal liability, such as for fraud; others of civil liability; and some resonated with the transparency associated with legal and quasilegal proceedings: Johnson should be "made to tell the truth and show his papers"; "present [his] figures and analysis".

McCord, along with two others, set out to use the law to hold Johnson to account for the potential consequences of a No Deal Brexit for Northern Ireland. McCord's representative in Northern Ireland's High Court explained during the proceedings that 'to leave without an agreement would create chaos, economic misery and a real threat to the peace process in Northern

Ireland'.[2] The High Court gave permission to apply for judicial review of the Johnson approach to Brexit (which meant No Deal Brexit was a real possible outcome) on only one of the grounds argued: a point involving the European Union (Withdrawal) Act 2018, section 10. That section requires 'a Minister of the Crown', in exercising powers under the Act, to act 'in a way that is compatible with the terms of the Northern Ireland Act 1998'. It prohibits regulations which 'diminish any form of North-South cooperation' or create or facilitate physical infrastructure on the border 'between Northern Ireland and the Republic of Ireland'. Section 10, McCord argued in effect, has a kind of constitutional status which precluded a negotiation approach that would lead to a No Deal Brexit. The Court of Appeal concluded that, in negotiating with the EU on the UK's Exit, Johnson's government was exercising prerogative powers which are not justiciable ([2019] NICA 49). Nothing about section 10 constrains that exercise of that prerogative power.

The implications of the *McCord* ruling embody a particular form of political constitutionalism, that does not allow for judicial oversight of the devolved settlement of the UK. This notion of the UK constitution centralizes what is *de facto* English (Westminster) power, and prevents Northern Ireland, Scotland and Wales from seeking a different path. The Johnson government's rules for a 'UK internal market' are a case in point: they will prevent any of the devolved nations from adopting a different approach to England in many aspects of public health. The lack of legal oversight of the relationship between Westminster and Belfast, Cardiff or Edinburgh is a weakness in the UK's constitution. It is a weakness which may yet undermine the hitherto different approaches to COVID-19 in the devolveds.

Furthermore, it is a weakness which does not match the expectations of those with whom we had conversations in Northern Ireland, to the effect that *legal* forms of accountability are necessary for legitimate decision-making across the UK. This notion, that the country's rulers are de facto 'above the law', became embodied in the question of whether public figures associated with the government were complying with COVID-19 guidelines and laws.

One rule for them, another for us

As the COVID-19 response took effect across the UK, curtailing freedom of movement and isolating households, many people were unable to see their families and closest friends, even those for whom they normally provide care and support. Stories circulated in mainstream and social media about elderly

2   *The Irish Times* (2019) 'No-deal Brexit would cause chaos in NI, legal challenge hears', 6 September, https://www.irishtimes.com/news/crime-and-law/no-deal-brexit-would-cause-chaos-in-ni-legal-challenge-hears-1.4010316. (accessed 6 May 2021).

people dying alone in care homes, their families unable to be with them for their last moments. In a few instances ([2020] EWCOP 23), families resorted to the courts in order to bring their parents and grandparents home for the last hours of their lives. Neil Ferguson resigned from his role on the SAGE (Scientific Advisory Group for Emergencies), describing as an 'error of judgment' meeting with his girlfriend in his home, though no police action was taken. Overall, however, reports of people flagrantly breaking the lockdown rules were rare: the vast majority of people across the UK accepted the need for isolation and remained at home, within the guidelines, only going out for their permitted exercise, for essential shopping, to seek medical care, and if they had to attend work as key workers.

According to the BBC Fact-check website, on 27 March 2020, Dominic Cummings, Johnson's senior aide, and architect of the Leave campaign, drove his wife, Mary Wakefield, and their four-year-old child to his parents' house in County Durham.[3] He did this, he claimed, because his wife had become ill, and he feared that he would do so too. The following day Cummings had COVID-19 symptoms and self-isolated in his parents' property until 12 April 2020. At that point, Cummings wanted to return to work in London. However, his wife was concerned that the illness had affected his eyesight, and so, in order to test whether he was safe to make the longer drive to London, the family drove to Barnard Castle, some 25 miles away. They stated that they left their car, and took a walk along the river, a local beauty spot.

The question arose as to whether Cummings' behaviour amounted to a breach of the law. It certainly seemed to be a breach of the guidelines at the time, which stated that if anyone experienced symptoms, the whole household should remain at home and self-isolate. However, Cummings cited another part of the guidelines which gave some leeway to parents of young children: 'We are aware that not all these measures will be possible if you are living with children, but keep following this guidance to the best of your ability'.

The relationship between the COVID-19 guidelines and the relevant legislation was, and remains, quite complex, not least because of the practice of the Johnson government of announcing new guidelines – in daily televised briefings or sometimes even by Twitter – in a very timely manner, to reflect the available public health data and governmental decisions based on that data. The ability of the civil service, many of whom were working from home with school-age children, to keep pace with legislative drafting was severely strained. Parliamentary or other scrutiny was non-existent.

---

[3] Reality Check team (2020) 'Dominic Cummings: Fact-checking the row', *BBC News*, 30 May, https://www.bbc.co.uk/news/52828076 (accessed 6 May 2021).

The relevant law at the time Cummings drove to Durham was regulation 6 of the Health Protection (Coronavirus, Restrictions) (England) Regulations 2020. This regulation provided that people should not leave their homes 'without reasonable excuse'. The regulations included a non-exhaustive list of reasonable excuses, such as seeking medical help, travelling to work where necessary, and obtaining essential supplies such as food or medicine. Whether taking one's child to their grandparents to be cared for constituted a 'reasonable excuse' was never tested in Cummings' case, because Durham Constabulary took the view that Cummings had not committed an offence.

Just a month later, in early June 2020, the Black Lives Matter movement led to protests across the UK. Some, such as on the remote Shetland Islands, were very carefully orchestrated to ensure compliance with applicable social distancing rules, and involved small numbers of people physically separated across large spaces. However, in cities such as London, Belfast and Bristol, despite the organizers of the protests seeking to secure compliance with the rules, police issued fines under the relevant COVID-19 regulations. Images and first-hand accounts of the Belfast protest, for instance, show that protesters were each standing within a carefully measured space in an open public square. Yet the police issued fines – in some cases fining organizers before a crowd of protesters had even gathered. The relevant regulations at the time permitted up to six people to gather outdoors, so logically a fine could only be issued to a group of seven or more. Yet this was not the case. Litigation challenging these fines is ongoing.

The discrepancy between the treatment, on the one hand, of those like Cummings and, on the other hand, of those like the organizers of the Black Lives Matter protests is striking. It resonates with a theme we heard often in our street conversations: those in power are not treated like 'ordinary people'. They do not experience interactions with public services, such as the police force, or indeed the NHS, in the same way. We heard people suggesting that the NHS is under-resourced and ill-equipped (including to respond to a pandemic) because people like the Prime Minister would not use the NHS themselves, because they can afford private health care. They would not experience long waiting times, inability to see a GP on the day you become ill, or poor service. There is one set of rules for ordinary people, and another for those in power.

Government outside the law

Many of our street conversations went further. Not only do the 'left behind' people with whom we talked feel that the law should hold people like Johnson to account for their actions; and that those in power should experience the same treatment when interacting with public entities like the police or seeking health care. Many of the people with whom we talked also feel that politicians are actively self-serving, taking advantage of their political power for personal gain. The vast majority of these people with whom we talked explicitly saw no distinction between different political parties in this regard: political parties are "all full of millionaires". All politicians, we heard, "work for themselves, not the poor people".

What the people we talked with want is a government that understands their position, and can therefore represent their needs. They feel that the country should be run by "ordinary working-class people … not all these people earning however many thousands of pounds". These conversations suggest a significant problem with the reality of representative democracy, the mainstay of the UK constitution and the source of legitimacy. One woman in Rotherham, who told us she was terminally ill with bowel cancer, put it particularly poignantly: these politicians who lie and "take naps in Westminster" (probably a reference to Jacob Rees-Mogg MP, whose photograph reclining on the green benches in the House of Commons was widely circulated) could never represent her as they could not possibly understand her life as a constant struggle to secure enough income to survive.

But, further, we heard that the 'left behind' feel that those in power are deeply untrustworthy and actively exploit situations of uncertainty, disorder or chaos for their own ends. When we discussed the NHS and the UK's health with people in Derry, Newry, Rochdale and Rotherham, we were mainly talking about Brexit, but what people told us could equally be said of COVID-19. A repeated theme in our street conversations is the idea of politicians as "gangsters": people who operate outside of the formal or official legal system. We heard that people believe that the "bigwigs upstairs" (a metaphor replete with resonances of pre-1940s social class relations) line their pockets with "backhanders".

As the Johnson government's arrangements for procurement of PPE – essential to secure the safety of front-line health and social care staff – became clearer, the Good Law Project became convinced that people with these kinds of opinions have a point. The Good Law Project,[4] founded by the tax QC Jolyon Maugham, challenges abuses of power, exploitation, inequality and injustice.

According to the Good Law Project:

> Whilst our EU partners were putting together emergency procurement arrangements in late January, it wasn't until March that Government put together an emergency scheme to protect our doctors and nurses and care workers.

[4]   See goodlawproject.org.

By then the global market for PPE had tightened considerably and Government was having to play catch up – ditching the normal rules that secure good value for public money and which guard against corruption in the process. On 27 March Government opened its portal inviting tenders for PPE on the gov.uk website and received 24,000 offers from 16,000 suppliers. It has spent – and this is the Treasury's own figure – a staggering £15 billion. And, surprisingly, three of the biggest beneficiaries were companies specializing in pest control, a confectionery wholesaler and an opaque private fund owned through a tax haven.

Why? We do not know. And Government is not helping – it has ignored the usual rule that contracts should be published within 20 days.[5]

The Good Law Project, along with EveryDoctor,[6] has commenced judicial review proceedings against Pestfix, Clandeboye and Ayanda.[7] The contract with Pestfix, for instance, was originally reported in error to be for £108m, which would have amounted to around one third of the government's total spending on PPE at the time. The contract with Ayanda, a 'family office' owned through a tax haven in Mauritius, was worth £252m. The firm is said to have connections to Liz Truss, the Secretary of State for International Trade. None of the companies hold significant assets in the UK. These factors prompted speculation on social media that there are links to government, and that the contracts are concealing corruption and cronyism. At the very least, say critics, the government must be incompetent for awarding contracts to these kinds of suppliers, as opposed to established domestic market actors, especially when it subsequently turned out that some of the products supplied cannot be used as they do not meet safety standards.

The Good Law Project is seeking a declaration that the contract award decisions, and contracts, were unlawful. Judicial review is a blunt instrument for the kind of legal accountability that would reassure people like those with whom we spoke that the government has their best interests, and those of the country as a whole, at heart. The principal purpose of the litigation, however, is to secure greater transparency over government decisions that resulted in public money being spent, by companies with no experience in the field, on sub-standard equipment, that was not delivered in a timely manner, and that was needed to secure safe working environments for NHS

---

[5] https://goodlawproject.org/update/the-ppe-fiasco
[6] https://www.everydoctor.org.uk/
[7] https://www.crowdjustice.com/case/108million/

staff in the context of the COVID-19 pandemic. In this regard, law can be used, at least to some extent, to make Johnson "tell the truth and show his papers" and "present [his] figures and analysis".

Conclusion

The people we spoke with in 'left behind' communities in the north of England and Northern Ireland felt strongly about the NHS and about health in general. They do not, in general, trust politicians, irrespective of party, but they do believe in the rule of law and the importance of legal accountability. The gap between their perception of the extent to which political actions with significance for health are subject to legal accountability processes, and the reality, is significant. Although we were talking with people about a different context – the effects of Brexit on the NHS and health – their views have significant relevance for COVID-19 governance. Political constitutionalism, along with its economic analogue, austerity economics, have failed the 'left behind'. Many of the people we spoke with do not recognize as legitimate a governance structure, or a government, without legal control. The law should secure protection for "ordinary people" against cronyism and corruption – at the very least through securing transparency. Those in power should not be above the law. That is a basic tenet of the rule of law. The gap between ordinary people's perception of the power of law to hold a government to account, and ordinary people's desire for law to be used in that way, and the reality, is too wide, and should be narrowed.

Health is a devolved power in the UK. The legitimacy of public health decisions, and questions of NHS resourcing, structure and how the NHS responds to a pandemic, all rely on a constitutional settlement that respects the power of the devolveds (Northern Ireland, Scotland and Wales) to depart from English decision-making and to withstand the hegemony of England in the UK. Other federal or quasi-federal democratic states embody within their constitutions the possibility – usually constrained by strong locus rules to prevent frivolous litigation – for judicial oversight of relations between the federal centre and the devolved entities. The UK's constitutional settlement suffers from a significant weakness in this regard. This deficiency should be revisited to secure legitimacy of health governance going forward.

As we move to a post-Brexit, post-COVID-19 future, we must urgently revisit the relations between law and politics in the UK constitution.

9

COVID-19 in Adult Social Care: Futures, Funding and Fairness

Rosie Harding

The impact of the COVID-19 pandemic on the UK residential social care sector has been immense and tragic. Elderly, vulnerable and frail individuals living in residential care settings who should have been 'shielded' from the virus have died in disproportionate numbers. There are multiple and overlapping reasons for the very high rates of COVID-19 infection and death in residential adult social care settings. Some are immediate policy decisions relating to the management of the pandemic including to discharge older people from NHS hospitals into residential and nursing homes without a negative COVID-19 test result, and to prioritize the supply of (scarce) Personal Protective Equipment (PPE) to NHS providers. Others are endemic to the regulation of residential and nursing care, including the financial models that allow private equity firms to make significant profits while local authority funded placements pay at below cost, family members are required to pay care 'top-up' fees, and self-funded residents are expected to cross-subsidize those funded by the state. Low pay and low status for care workers in this impossible financial context then translates into high staff turnover and a reliance on agency care staff (who work for multiple providers). Brexit has compounded this issue, with estimates suggesting there were over 120,000 vacancies in adult social care in late 2019. In this chapter, I will argue that a new model for adult social care, which focuses on fairness rather than profit is the only way to create a stable, safe and sustainable social care sector for the future.

Introduction: COVID-19 in care homes

Residential care settings in the UK were hit particularly hard by the initial outbreak of COVID-19. At the regular Downing Street daily briefing on 15 May 2020, Matt Hancock, Secretary of State for Health and Social Care, claimed that the government had thrown a "protective ring" around care homes "right from the start" of the pandemic. Statistical data collated on deaths involving COVID-19 during the first wave of the virus unfortunately tell a very different story. Far from protecting care homes from the outbreak, some 6,811 care homes in England (44 per cent) had reported suspected or confirmed outbreaks of COVID-19 by 23 July 2020.[1] Similar outbreaks were experienced elsewhere in the UK, with 66 per cent of care homes in Scotland reporting outbreaks, and several care homes reporting multiple COVID-19 deaths in quick succession.

Evaluating the quantitative scale of the outbreak in care homes is made more difficult by the publication of multiple sources of statistics, with different measurement periods, and definitions. In order to compare deaths across UK jurisdictions, the most reliable data are those which report the total number of deaths registered which mention COVID-19 on the death certificate. Table 9.1 shows total deaths from COVID-19 in the UK to 18 September 2020. The total numbers here are higher than those published by the UK Government Department for Health and Social Care (DHSC) in their daily dashboard.[2] The total population and the care home resident population in each of the four UK nations are included to demonstrate the scale of the impact of COVID-19 in care homes. As can be seen from these data, deaths of care home residents account for over 40 per cent of the total deaths in the UK from COVID-19, despite care home residents making up just 0.7 per cent of the UK population. Some of this tragic impact can, of course, be attributed to the particular vulnerabilities of care home residents, many of whom are older and living with a range of co-morbidities that place them at particular risk of severe disease if infected with COVID-19.

Social care workers were also badly affected by COVID-19, with 268 deaths of social care workers recorded in the period March–May 2020. Statistical analysis has shown higher rates of death for both male and female

---

[1] Public Health England (2020) 'COVID-19: number of outbreaks in care homes - management information', https://www.gov.uk/government/statistical-data-sets/covid-19-number-of-outbreaks-in-care-homes-management-information (accessed 31 August 2020).

[2] The https://coronavirus.data.gov.uk/ dashboard only includes deaths within 28 days of the first positive COVID-19 test, and therefore is an underestimate of the total number of deaths involving COVID-19.

Table 9.1: Registered deaths involving COVID-19: general and care home populations UK nations[3]

	Total deaths	Total population[4]	Care home resident deaths	Care home population
England	50,066[5]	56,287,000	20,581[6]	418,710[7]
Wales	2,577[8]	3,152,900	745[9]	24,178
Scotland	4,236[10]	5,463,300	1,966	35,989[11]
Northern Ireland	891[12]	1,893,700	436[13]	16,007[14]
UK	57,770	66,796,900	22,035	49,4884

3   Data drawn from multiple sources from the Office of National Statistics, National Register of Scotland, and the Northern Ireland Statistics and Research Agency for deaths registered up to 18 September 2020.
4   Office for National Statistics Population Estimates as at mid-2019: www.ons.gov.uk/peoplepopulationandcommunity/populationandmigration/populationestimates
5   Office for National Statistics: www.ons.gov.uk/peoplepopulationandcommunity/birthsdeathsandmarriages/deaths/bulletins/deathsregisteredweeklyinenglandandwalesprovisional/weekending18september2020#comparison-of-weekly-death-occurrences-in-england-and-wales
6   Composite figure from ONS analysis to 12 June 2020: (www.ons.gov.uk/peoplepopulationandcommunity/birthsdeathsandmarriages/deaths/articles/deathsinvolvingcovid19inthecaresectorenglandandwales/deathsoccurringupto12june2020andregisteredupto20june2020provisional#deaths-involving-covid-19-among-care-home-residents) and CQC Notification data 13 June 2020–18 September 2020 published by ONS at: www.ons.gov.uk/peoplepopulationandcommunity/birthsdeathsandmarriages/deaths/datasets/numberofdeathsincarehomesnotifiedtothecarequalitycommissionengland
7   Office for National Statistics: www.ons.gov.uk/peoplepopulationandcommunity/birthsdeathsandmarriages/deaths/adhocs/12215carehomeandnoncarehomepopulationsusedinthedeathsinvolvingcovid19inthecaresectorarticleenglandandwales
8   Office for National Statistics: www.ons.gov.uk/peoplepopulationandcommunity/birthsdeathsandmarriages/deaths/bulletins/deathsregisteredweeklyinenglandandwalesprovisional/weekending18september2020#comparison-of-weekly-death-occurrences-in-england-and-wales
9   Notifications to the Care Inspectorate Wales: https://gov.wales/notifications-deaths-residents-related-covid-19-adult-care-homes-1-march-25-september-2020-html
10 National Records of Scotland: www.nrscotland.gov.uk/statistics-and-data/statistics/statistics-by-theme/vital-events/general-publications/weekly-and-monthly-data-on-births-and-deaths/deaths-involving-coronavirus-covid-19-in-scotland
11 Public Health Scotland: www.isdscotland.org/Health-Topics/Health-and-Social-Community-Care/Publications/2018-09-11/2018-09-11-CHCensus-Report.pdf
12 Northern Ireland Statistics and Research Agency: www.nisra.gov.uk/publications/weekly-deaths
13 Northern Ireland Statistics and Research Agency: www.nisra.gov.uk/publications/weekly-deaths
14 The Regulation and Quality Improvement Authority: www.rqia.org.uk/RQIA/files/0f/0ff745be-514f-4013-8309-7d63de74bbc1.pdf

social care workers than others of the same age and sex in England and Wales.[15] As with other parts of society, the pandemic catalyzed a general increase in excess mortality, with people living with dementia (who make up some 70 per cent of care home residents) particularly badly affected. More than a quarter of deaths with COVID-19 in the 'first wave' of the pandemic in the UK were of people who also had a form of dementia. Social isolation during lockdown also had a disproportionate impact on people with dementia and their family carers, leading to loneliness, significant deterioration in dementia symptoms, and earlier than expected deaths.[16]

The effects of COVID-19 in the social care sector have been attributed to a wide range of causes. The discharge of 25,000 people from hospital into care homes in March/April 2020 without testing for COVID-19 was certainly one way that the virus entered the social care sector.[17] The general lack of availability of testing for care home staff and residents until July 2020 meant that the scale of the outbreak went unrecognized for too long. Shortages in testing thereafter have allowed new outbreaks to take hold in some care homes. There was poor access to affordable PPE for care homes, with reports of orders being cancelled to prioritize supply to the NHS and prices being pushed artificially high. Particular (and predictable) issues relating to the use of agency staff have emerged as potential mechanisms of cross-infection between care providers. The lack of sick pay for some care staff has also been identified as a problem, such that some care workers may have had to choose between paying their bills or going to work when ill or exposed to the virus. These specific failings undoubtedly all had an impact on the spread of COVID-19 in care homes during the first few months of the COVID-19 pandemic. The DHSC have since included care homes in the national PPE strategy, and made additional funding available to care homes to support infection control.

There is, however, a wider systemic problem at the heart of the COVID-19 catastrophe in adult social care, which helps to explain how these failings arose. In the next section, I explore the ongoing 'crisis' in adult social care, showing how the consequences of an unfair adult social care system created

[15] www.ons.gov.uk/peoplepopulationandcommunity/healthandsocialcare/causesofdeath/bulletins/coronaviruscovid19relateddeathsbyoccupationenglandandwales/deathsregisteredbetween9marchand25may2020

[16] Alzheimer's Society (2020) 'Worst Hit: Dementia During Coronavirus', https://www.alzheimers.org.uk/get-involved/our-campaigns/coronavirus (accessed 1 October 2020).

[17] Committee, House of Commons Public Accounts (2020) *Readying the NHS and Social Care for the COVID-19 Peak*, https://committees.parliament.uk/publications/2179/documents/20139/default/ (accessed 29 September 2020).

the conditions that allowed the COVID-19 pandemic to spread so quickly, and with such devastating effects within care homes.

The crisis in adult social care

Headlines proclaiming the existence of a crisis in adult social care have appeared with alarming regularity for more than a decade, in part as a consequence of the chronic underfunding of social care during the years of austerity following the 2008 financial crisis (Harding, 2017b). The crisis in adult social care is multifaceted, but includes significant unmet care needs, poor-quality care, neglect and abuse, a high reliance on precarious and low wage labour, a significant public funding gap, an unfair funding system, and high risks of provider failure.

While unmet care needs are a significant problem across all older adults in England, the prevalence of unmet care need is highest in those in lower socio-economic groups, and those with lower educational qualifications (Vlachantoni, 2019). The reasons for this gap are complex, but are linked to the criteria for public funding of care, which requires that anyone with capital (excluding the value of the home they live in) of over £23,500 must pay the full cost of their care, and only those with less than £14,250 in savings will be eligible for care funded by their local authority. Even those whose assets fall below the threshold and are therefore eligible for local authority support may have unmet care needs where the support they receive does not cover the full extent of their needs.

Quality of care has been a particular problem for many years, and is intimately bound up with the prevalence of precarious and low wage labour in adult social care, particularly domiciliary care (Hayes, 2017), and difficulties in reporting and resolving complaints about poor care (Harding, 2017a). While successive Care Quality Commission (CQC) 'State of Care' reports appear to show improvements in the sector, the most recent figures still report four times as many adult social care services rated as 'requires improvement' (15 per cent, n=3373) or 'inadequate' (1 per cent, n= 285) as those rated 'outstanding' (4 per cent, n=887).[18] Abuse and neglect of adults in residential care settings continues to be a problem, with scandals like those exposed by BBC Panorama's *Undercover Care: The Abuse Exposed* (2011) emerging with depressing regularity. Sexual abuse is also a problem, with a CQC report outlining analysis of 899 incidents of sexual abuse in adult

---

[18] Care Quality Commission (2019) *The State of Health Care and Adult Social Care in England 2018/19*, https://www.cqc.org.uk/sites/default/files/20191015b_stateofcare1819_fullreport.pdf (accessed 24 November 2020).

social care notified to them in a three-month period in 2018, including 47 allegations of rape.[19]

Workforce issues are a major source of difficulties in both quality and sustainability in the adult social care sector. The Health Foundation estimated that there was a workforce gap of 122,000 in November 2019, with around a quarter of adult social care staff on zero-hours contracts.[20] This workforce gap creates a reliance on agency staff, which in turn was blamed for some of the spread of COVID-19 in care homes. It is also likely to be made worse by Brexit, with care work unlikely to pay well enough to facilitate future economic migration under current proposals. This, in combination with an ageing population, means there is likely to be an even more significant care gap in the future. High staff turnover is also a major problem in the care sector, with around a third of the workforce leaving the care sector every year. This compounds problems with care quality: the small minority of providers rated as 'outstanding' by CQC had much lower staff turnover; those with high staff turnover also have high vacancy rates, and therefore existing staff are under more pressure, and given less time to undertake their caring tasks, which can lead to poor-quality care.

Chronic underfunding of adult social care is often cited as the reason for these problems, and funding constraints, particularly during the period of significant local authority funding cuts from 2010–15 certainly had an impact. The adult social care sector is funded through a combination of public funding distributed through local authorities (currently in the region of £22 billion annually, which is in real terms slightly lower than the levels of funding in 2008–09), alongside contributions to care from those who are partially or fully self-funding because they do not qualify for local authority support, and a huge contribution from unpaid, informal care. Local authorities pay, on average, £636 per week for adults over 65 and £1,320 per week for care for working age adults. The Competition and Markets Authority estimated in 2017 that self-funders pay, on average 41 per cent more for placements than local authorities.[21] This fact, coupled with the

---

[19] Care Quality Commission (2020) *Promoting sexual safety through empowerment: A review of sexual safety and the support of people's sexuality in adult social care*, https://www.cqc.org.uk/sites/default/files/20200226_asc_sexual_safety_sexuality_summary.pdf (accessed 24 November 2020).

[20] Gershlick, B. and Charlesworth, A. (2019) *Health and Social care workforce: Priorities for the next government*, https://www.health.org.uk/publications/long-reads/health-and-social-care-workforce (accessed 24 November 2020).

[21] Competition & Markets Authority (2017) *Care Homes Market Study: Final Report*, https://www.gov.uk/cma-cases/care-homes-market-study#final-report (accessed 24 November 2020).

uneven burden of care where around half of people over 65 may spend over £20,000 on care costs, and a minority will spend over £100,000, creates a particularly unfair system (Harding, 2017b).

The vast majority of care providers are private (for-profit) companies, though a small proportion are voluntary sector organizations. At present, three of the 'big five' social care providers (HC-One, Barchester and Four Seasons) are owned by private equity firms, one (BUPA) is an international not-for-profit company, and one (Care-UK) is a publicly listed company. Provider failure is a significant concern in the sector – Southern Cross used to be the largest player in the market, but folded in 2011, with many of its services being bought by HC-One; Four Seasons collapsed in 2019, and the administrators put the business up for sale. Brexit is expected to contribute directly to further provider failures, particularly of smaller providers, which operate on small margins, as a consequence of anticipated rises in food costs and difficulties recruiting staff.

High-profile provider failures may suggest that adult social care is an unsustainable business proposition. Yet HC-One reportedly paid out £48.5 million in dividends in 2017 and 2018, while declaring a loss each year, paying no UK corporation tax since its formation in 2011, and receiving £6.5million in net tax credits since 2014, which suggests that the overall picture is rather more complex.[22] The value and contribution of informal, familial, care also adds complexity to the system. In the face of poor-quality provision, lack of funding for private care or a lack of the right kinds of care in a person's area, a significant portion of adult social care is taken on by family members and friends, rather than by formal care services. Reform of adult social care needs to tackle all of these intersecting and overlapping issues, rather than finding ways to fund the existing system if we are to build a fair care system for the future.

Reforming adult social care

There have already been several attempts at reform of adult social care. The 1999 Royal Commission led to free personal care in Scotland, but was never implemented in England. In 2009 the Labour Government published a Green Paper proposing a National Care Service, free at the point of use (like the NHS). The 2011 Dilnot Commission proposed a lifetime care costs cap, with a higher floor for state support than under the present system. The

---

[22] Plimmer, Gill. (2019) 'Care home group paid £48.5m in dividends while warning of cuts', *Financial Times*, 10 May, https://www.ft.com/content/c0e37072-7243-11e9-bf5c-6eeb837566c5 (accessed 24 November 2020).

Care Act 2014, passed under the Conservative-Liberal Democrat coalition government, legislated for this system but this part has not been implemented. A new Green Paper was promised in 2017, but has not yet been published despite repeated promises from successive governments. In their report into 'Readying the NHS and Social Care for the COVID-19 Peak', the Public Accounts Committee recommended that the DHSC set out 'what it will be doing, organisationally, legislatively and financially, and by when, to make sure the needs of social care are given as much weight as those of the NHS in future'[23] by October 2020. That deadline was not met.

The number of failed attempts at reform of adult social care suggests that there is little political consensus about how to build a sustainable, affordable, high-quality adult social care system. Many of the opportunities for social care reform have, ultimately, failed because they are seeking to add extra funding to a system that is fundamentally dysfunctional. There is a danger that any additional funding that is pushed into care without a wider review of the sector will be consumed by servicing the debt within the system, and rising labour and other costs, rather than on improving services. In the remainder of this chapter, I suggest a way forward out of this conundrum, by proposing five concepts that could underpin reforms to adult social care. These are that care needs to be relational, responsive, rights-oriented, valued, and above all, fair.

Relational

I have argued earlier that solving the social care crisis requires a relational approach (Harding, 2017b). By relational I mean that we need to keep in mind the ways that individual experience, and the choices available to us, are shaped by our personal relationships, social norms and legal rules. For example, care needs are often met by informal care provided by family members, particularly if the person with unmet care needs is ineligible for state funded support. Yet informal care from family members may lead that carer (most often women, often of working age) to opt out of the labour market for a period of time. There can be a multitude of consequences for a decision to provide care: interruptions in the carer's national insurance record; challenges returning to the labour market later in life due to age discrimination; the potential for poverty in older age; stress and isolation that may catalyze mental and physical ill health; or housing insecurity (Harding,

---

[23] Committee, House of Commons Public Accounts (2020) *Readying the NHS and Social Care for the COVID-19 Peak*, https://committees.parliament.uk/publications/2179/documents/20139/default/ (accessed 29 September 2020).

2017a). Regulatory systems are also part of this relational system; if the regulatory environment for care enables private equity firms to run care providers with a view to financialization (for example from selling capital assets and leasing them back to care providers) then care fees will be used to finance debt repayments rather than quality care. In times of economic downturn, this places providers at risk due to falling income and rising prices.

Responsive

Care also needs to be responsive. In some areas (particularly London) there has been a move away from the care home model towards a preference for in-home (domiciliary) care. This is unsurprising given consistent social gerontological research findings that older people generally prefer to 'age in place', rather than moving into a formal care setting. The COVID-19 catastrophe in care homes has the potential to accelerate this move from care homes to care provision in the community. There are many positive elements of this shift, primarily the way that it can enable support for people to live in their local community rather than segregating the old and disabled from society. Yet during the first wave of COVID-19 in the UK, domiciliary care providers were essentially ignored by government and policy makers until well into the pandemic peak. Anecdotal evidence suggests many people who rely on domiciliary care services had these withdrawn during lockdown and had to rely on unpaid family carers instead.

Rights-oriented

Person-centred care has been a staple of adult social care for many years now, and there is a general consensus that person- (rather than task-) centred approaches are at the heart of good care. Yet there is relatively little awareness of human rights by care professionals and in care contexts (Harding and Taşcıoğlu, 2017). A rights-oriented approach to adult social care would hold human rights at the centre of its regulatory framework, including both the European Convention on Human Rights (ECHR) incorporated into domestic law through the Human Rights Act 1998, and the rights stemming from other international obligations including the UN Convention on the Rights of Persons with Disabilities (CRPD). Key rights that cut across both of these frameworks include the right to be free from torture and inhumane and degrading treatment (Article 3, ECHR; Article 15, CRPD), rights to respect for private, family and home life (Article 8, ECHR; Articles 22 and 23, CRPD), and rights to liberty and security of the person (Article 5, ECHR; Article 14, CRPD). The CRPD goes further than the ECHR in many respects, as it recognizes the profound social disadvantage that disabled people experience, and also protects: the right to enjoy legal capacity (Article 12), to live independently and be included in the community (Article 19), to adequate standards of living and social protection (Article 28), to participation in political, public (Article 29) and cultural life (Article 30). Holding these multiple rights at the heart of care, and designing a care system that explicitly and deliberately seeks to uphold them, would lead to a very different approach than the current system, where disabled people and older people with care needs, including dementia, are segregated from society for the convenience of care providers.

Valued

Care is an essential component of society. Everyone requires care at some point in their lives; everyone is likely to provide care at some point in their lives. Yet those who provide care in paid employment are consistently undervalued and low-paid, with an over-reliance on zero-hours contracts, insecure employment and high staff turnover (Hayes, 2017). The social de-valuation of care is connected to the gendered assumptions that sit at the heart of social and cultural understandings of care, and of the liberal, autonomous, independent individual. If we assume that we are all interconnected, relational persons who rely on caring and connection with others to live our version of the good life, instead of assuming that we are all independent individuals, then care will necessarily take on a different set of values. Those who provide care should be rewarded for the essential services that they provide to others, so they in turn can receive the care they need and desire from others. In short, we need to re-value care so that the cycles of connection, care provision and care receipt are made visible, responded to and recognized as a social good.

Fair

Care as it is currently regulated and funded in England is unfair. Those who have high care needs as a consequence of a health problem that has a medical need at its heart are provided fully funded care by the National Health Service (NHS) through Continuing Healthcare funding. Those whose key care needs are assistance with the activities of daily living as a result of dementia or frailty in older age are often given no financial assistance with their care costs, and left to fund care themselves or rely on informal care from family members. Many people will be exposed to relatively low care costs throughout their lives, others will be all but bankrupted by the care they or a close family member require (Harding, 2017a). People whose impairments stem from, for example, acquired brain injuries that are the fault of an insured other often have access to far greater levels of care and support than those who sustain injuries that are their own, or nobody's fault (Harding and Taşcıoğlu, 2017). Self-funders who require residential or nursing care cross-subsidize the costs of those whose care is paid for by the local authorities. A fair care system would remove these sources of inequality, enabling all those who need care to access it while spreading risk across society. The challenge of finding a popular funding mechanism for adult social care is, however, one of the key reasons for the overall lack of a solution to social care crisis.

There is, so far, little political consensus on how to fund a fair risk-spreading scheme for social care. A number of alternatives have been floated in the years since it became apparent that there was a need for a fairer approach to funding social care. One proposal would be an insurance-based system for social care, though this would require either a private care insurance marketplace (which the insurance industry has expressed little appetite for, as only those who consider themselves to be at higher risk would be likely to voluntarily take out long-term care insurance), or a compulsory public insurance system. Many recent proposals for funding social care have looked to wealth taxation, in the form of an additional inheritance tax charge through cap and floor systems like the unimplemented system at the heart of the Care Act 2014, or through a one-off charge which recognizes the intergenerational asset inequality in contemporary society. Wealth taxation is often preferred because it is considered more progressive than income-based taxation (which the wealthiest often find ways to avoid). Recent proposals (floated through the media in summer 2020) suggest age-graded additional taxes may be the solution, with those over the age of 40 paying an additional tax. This approach is currently used in Germany and Japan. Again, though, this is unpopular as it would require working age people to fund the care of older adults in the 'baby boomer' generation who have already been net recipients of extensive public subsidy. Paradoxically, of course, the direct taxation, publicly funded, free-at-the-point-of-use NHS achieves cost risk spreading in an uncontroversial manner for health care in the UK, even though some will be far greater users of NHS resources than others.

Conclusion

Whatever approach is ultimately taken to reforming social care, fairness must be at the heart of any future reforms. Fairness, in combination with a rights-oriented, relational, responsive approach that truly values the contribution of care in society is essential to any reform of the care system. Fundamentally, care is a human, rather than a capital enterprise that in my view is, at heart, essentially not-for-profit. Whenever profit enters the system of care provision, individuals lose out. Avoiding debt-fuelled speculation is essential for a well-functioning care system that provides high-quality care for all. This is not to say that a centralized national care service would be the best approach; we do not want to revert to the days of asylums, long-stay hospitals, and locked wards. Instead, we need to recognize and support the intrinsic value of care. Instead of thinking of care as low-skilled, low pay, low status, 'women's work', we need to recognize its importance as a fundamental building block of society.

References

Harding, R. (2017a) *Duties to Care: Dementia, Relationality and Law*, Cambridge: Cambridge University Press.

Harding, R. (2017b) 'A relational (re)view of the UK's social care crisis', *Palgrave Communications*, 3: 17096, https://www.nature.com/articles/palcomms201796

Harding, R. and Taşcıoğlu, E. (2017) *Everyday Decisions Project Report: Supporting Legal Capacity through Care, Support and Empowerment*, www.legalcapacity.org.uk/research-findings/ (accessed 1 December 2017).

Hayes, L.J.B. (2017) *Stories of Care: A Labour of Law*, London: Palgrave.

Vlachantoni, A. (2019) 'Unmet need for social care among older people', *Ageing and Society*, 39(4): 657–84. doi:10.1017/S0144686X17001118

10

Housing, Homelessness and COVID-19

Rowan Alcock, Helen Carr and Ed Kirton-Darling

Introduction

This chapter examines what COVID-19 and the response to it has revealed, in the context of housing and homelessness. Our argument is that responses have been limited by what is deemed possible by current housing politics. It goes on to consider the possibilities for a different housing politics, post-pandemic, suggesting that we need to find something new, something between the promotion of the entrepreneurial individual and a collective response characterized by uniformity, exclusion and authoritarianism. Perhaps the description of classical music's response to COVID-19 restrictions may provide a useful metaphor. Socially distanced performances and reduced numbers of instrumentalists produce what has been described as an 'orchestra of soloists'. Applied to housing, this suggests a possibility of combining the individual expression of identity through home and housing simultaneously with a collective effort to achieve a minimum standard of provision. The method may be as important as the goal. We should not be afraid to explore alternatives, to trial messy and slow interventions as long as they reflect an inclusive, democratic and accountable politics as we search for an alternative to the current failed model of marketized housing provision and a discredited albeit collective past.

Housing, homelessness and COVID-19

COVID-19 ratchets up the cruel consequences of the poor-quality housing and homelessness provision that have been a long-standing feature of England's housing settlement. Mortality statistics suggest a correlation between likelihood of death from the virus and overcrowded, shared or temporary housing, a correlation with particularly devastating implications for BAME people who are disproportionately poorly housed. Housing conditions make it difficult to self-isolate, shared facilities enable the spread of the virus, and a lack of access to outside space exacerbates poor mental and physical health. Living on the streets puts those whose life expectancy is already dramatically reduced – pre-pandemic a street homeless man could expect to live to 47 and a woman to 43 – at increased risk from the virus and increases the vulnerabilities of those front line services which work with them. While a £3.2m initiative to provide emergency accommodation provided shelter for 15,000 street homeless people, the accommodation did not work for many rough sleepers; meanwhile new populations of street homeless have emerged, stimulated by job losses, relationship breakdown, and the intensification of domestic violence and mental health issues that have been a feature of lockdown.

The deleterious consequences of insecure and unaffordable housing in a global pandemic are equally catastrophic, although they have to a large extent been obscured, delayed by government action. Schedule 29 of the Coronavirus Act 2020 introduced three months' notice periods for possession periods and action was taken to stay proceedings until 23 August 2020. The stay was subsequently extended for four weeks, until 20 September 2020, and on 7 September 2020 notice periods were further increased to six months for a temporary period until 31 March 2021 (see Cowan, this volume). But, some of the most vulnerably housed, those excluded from the Protection from Eviction Act 1977 (because they share accommodation with their landlord for instance, or have no right to rent) have not been protected, so local authorities have had to manage a steady stream of applications for housing.

A desperate desire on the part of government to return to some sort of normality – which in this context equates to reactivating property rights – means there is to be no further extension to the stay on possession proceedings: 'It's right that we strike a balance between protecting vulnerable renters and ensuring landlords whose tenants have behaved in illegal or anti-social ways have access to justice', said Secretary of State for Housing Robert Jenrick in a rhetorical move that obscures the reality. Vulnerable or not, the reinstatement of the pre-pandemic status quo particularly in the private rented sector means that property rights will once again trump the need for tenants to keep their homes.

On the eve of the lifting of the eviction moratorium, the predictions were of crisis. Shelter, the UK's leading housing charity, warned that 322,000 private renters had fallen into arrears since the pandemic started, district councils predicted as many as half a million private sector renters were in danger of being made homeless and *The Guardian* reported that Newham Council in London was concerned that up to 20 per cent of its private renters were in arrears (Collinson, 2020). And the continuation of the pandemic means there is little prospect of avoiding further arrears. However, from the landlord's perspective, the eviction moratorium has proved a crude strategy. Some tenants, they allege, have used it to avoid paying rent they can afford, they have been unable to evict violent or anti-social tenants, and landlords, unlike tenants, have received no government assistance. Many landlords have suffered severe loss of income.

At the same time the arrangements made to take the homeless off the streets during lockdown are beginning to break down. Local councils are struggling to find move-on accommodation for those whose temporary housing is coming to an end. Social distancing means that winter shelters cannot operate as usual. It's difficult to believe that death rates among the street homeless are not going to rocket over winter.

The government points to the unprecedented scale of its interventions to demonstrate its concern to keep renters in their homes and to avoid homelessness. In addition to taking homeless people off the streets and banning evictions, it has increased Housing Allowance (LHA) rates for housing benefit to match the 30th percentile of rents in each local area, it has increased funding for Discretionary Housing Payments designed to meet the shortfall between housing benefit and rent, and it has made amendments to the Homelessness Code of Guidance ensuring that the housing needs of those who are at high risk from COVID-19 because of age, obesity or chronic illness are carefully considered by local authorities.

What it is unwilling to do is abolish s.21 of the Housing Act 1988, which provides landlords with a quick and non-litigious means of evicting tenants. Once the appropriate notice has been served and the prescribed time has elapsed (now six months), the landlord can obtain a possession order from the court. Evictions following section 21 notices are the primary cause of homelessness. Promises were made by the current government to end this no fault means of eviction in its manifesto in 2019. Its reluctance to implement its promise suggests that it was always conditional on speeding up evictions for rent arrears – there had to be a pay-off for landlords.

Nonetheless the courts are doing an extraordinary amount of 'heavy lifting' to manage the anticipated evictions challenge. Recognizing the problem of accrued demand resulting from the moratorium, the likely increase in demand caused by the economic consequences of the pandemic and the reduced court capacity because of social distancing, the Master of the Rolls set up a Working Group on Possession Proceedings. Its report indicates that the ending of the moratorium will not signal a return to business as usual (MR Working Group, 2020). Instead arrangements have been developed to respond to the new circumstances. There is a greater emphasis on early legal advice and increasing opportunities for compromise, courts will require (and take account of as much as possible within the legal framework) information about the impact of the pandemic on all parties, and there will be new case management and listing arrangements, including a scheme of prioritization.

Cases involving anti-social behaviour and domestic violence will take priority alongside cases of extreme alleged rent arrears, more than 12 months' rent or nine months where that amounts to more than 25 per cent of a private landlord's total annual income from any source. Nor will evictions start on day one. Case listing started on 21 September but requires a 'Reactivation Notice' and, even in the most urgent cases, 21 days' notice will be given of a Case Review. Given that substantive hearings will not take place until at least 28 days after the Review and the limited number of hearings that can take place on any one day – hearings are to be in person, individually listed in 15-minute slots and cleaning will take place between hearings – it is unlikely that many possession orders will be made before the end of the year. Commitments from the courts that hearings will be adjourned unless pre-action steps are complied with and legal advice made available to defendants, and from the Housing minister that there will be no evictions over the Christmas period, suggest that evictions may be even further delayed. But there are limits on what can be achieved. As paragraph 59 of the Working Party report sets out:

> All concerned need to keep in mind that the court's discretion at the point of decision or order is currently limited by statute. In the result, as the law stands there are material cases where the judiciary may not have discretion, or may have only very limited discretion, to take into account the effect of the pandemic on a defendant. (MR Working Group, 2020; also see Chapter 1, this volume)

Where proceedings are issued under s.21 of the Housing Act 1988, and in particular in claims under the paper-based accelerated possession procedure, there is little that can be done to delay possession, despite the judicial commitment to forensic scrutiny of the paperwork.

Despite the efforts of everyone, including government, accepting the constraints of the pre-pandemic status quo means that housing hardship cannot be avoided. Evictions may be drawn out, but they are inevitable while intervention is limited by the contemporary political imaginary. Those in the most vulnerable situations are going to be hit hardest, and the most likely outcome is a deterioration in housing conditions, increased overcrowding and increased street homelessness. Illegal evictions are likely to escalate, as the government expectation that landlords wait at least 12 months to recover arrears tries the patience and resources of many landlords. And even where landlords don't illegally evict, mediation might be used to pressure tenants to leave, with one landlord organization suggesting it as a way to 'get your property back without court action'. The consequence of the pandemic is the intensification of the very conditions which cause the virus to thrive as well as a further exacerbation of the already shocking housing disparities between rich and poor, and White and BAME populations.

The voluntary sector is also working hard to alleviate homelessness. While many day and night shelters closed or radically reduced support and a great deal of rough sleeper outreach work was stopped, organizations have sought to continue work where they can, supported by umbrella programmes. In a context of swiftly changing advice, guidance and regulations relating to social distancing, as well as regional variations, such work has been very difficult, and homelessness organizations have criticized the narrow focus on rough sleepers.[1] At the same time, many charitable organizations are witnessing reduced income and are having to reconsider their ability to run programmes.

Legacies

Perhaps if the pandemic had hit during the 1970s, before council house building was ended, before the introduction of the Right to Buy in the Housing Act 1980, before the deregulation of the private rented sector in the Housing Act 1988 and before the deregulation of mortgage finance made not only owner-occupancy but also buying-to-let the norm, then the infrastructure would have been sufficiently robust to manage the crisis better and anticipate and provide for housing need. We are not romantic about council housing and Rent Act protections – their exclusions, limitations and disciplinary overtones have been well documented. However there was an infrastructure that provided affordable housing, that controlled rents and that could respond (however clumsily) to emergency housing needs, as the construction of over 150,000 prefabricated houses within six years of the end of the Second World War demonstrates.

While housing in England and Wales has been in crisis since the industrialization and urbanization of the late 18th century, the dismantling of the 20th-century welfare protections from the 1980s onwards represented a shift in housing politics, one intimately connected to the increased

---

[1]   See, for example, the Museum of Homelessness' submission to the MHCLG Select Committee investigation, https://museumofhomelessness.org/wp-content/uploads/2020/05/MHCLG-response-corona-and-homelessness-inquiry-30.04.pdf

dominance of a neoliberal form of capitalism. It has valorized housing as a financial asset (particularly for later life) rather than as a home, and operated to deny and undermine state responsibility for the housing of its populations. That political shift and the dismantling of state provision has been a global phenomenon. However, it is the contours of the contemporary housing crisis in England that concern us, and, we argue, makes it so difficult for a coherently social response to the COVID-19 intensified housing crisis to be implemented. The role of local government as the provider of homes has been eroded, and housing associations have become commercial and competitive entities, with a growing emphasis on providing for-profit private rental homes at market rents. England is edging towards a post owner-occupancy society, one where, particularly following the global financial crisis of 2008, and paradoxically as a consequence of its promotion, home ownership becomes inaccessible to huge sections of the population, particularly the young and the precariously employed.

Renting in the private rented sector is becoming the new normal, even for families, and high demand has pushed rents sky-high. Housing wealth is increasingly concentrated in the hands of fewer and older people, and it seems that housing wealth rather than income is what provides people with increasingly elusive security. There is a new politics emerging in response to the crisis of affordability and availability of housing, one that has responded to the increasing number of voters who appear to be at the very least semi-permanent renters and which has led to the introduction of new controls on private landlordism and sanctions on those landlords who behave like 'rogues'. But there appears to be an ideological paralysis built into this new politics, one that is unprepared to control rents, forgive arrears or move away from the dominant free market culture of private renting. This paralysis favours large property owners and developers, as the reluctance for instance to implement s.38 of the Building Act 1984 (which would enable those who breach building regulations to be sued for damages), or to instigate dramatic action to solve the difficulties of long leaseholders who cannot sell their homes as a result of doubts about the fire safety of their property, or properly to protect residents from any possibility of a replay of the fire at Grenfell Tower.

This paralysis flows from a continued utopian belief in the self-regulating market. The belief is that society can 'get back to normal' – a self-regulating market normal that exacerbated the COVID-19 catastrophe. It is difficult to see how this 'normal' can be sustained once the housing consequences of COVID-19 become clear and evictions stack up. COVID-19 draws attention to the crises of land, labour and money that are at the core of the self-regulating market utopia and which are made material in insecure renting and zero-hours contracts. This diagnosis is radically critical of a society which commodifies these social spheres, arguing that they have value far beyond that which atomized monetary transactions can calculate. The COVID-19 catastrophe has legitimated state intervention into these spheres, previously perceived as economic silos, as the utopian belief in homo economicus has been shaken by the fact of community transmission.

The breakdown of the self-regulating market utopia during the COVID-19 pandemic, the acceptance of state intervention, and the implicit acknowledgement of the existence of an interconnected society, does not inevitably lead to something progressive. Interventions, such as postponing evictions or housing the homeless, while respite to help resolve the catastrophe, may result in a more authoritarian 'normal' in COVID-19's long shadow as people are blamed for their failure to take advantage of the help. The state is unlikely to give up the powers it mustered to bring the pandemic under control and deployed to reinstate the 'normal' crisis. More pertinent may be the social expectations intervention creates as authoritarian intervention becomes the monopolistic logic of societal protection.

COVID-19 demonstrates starkly that for the protection of any individual within society we must protect all. If any individual is left homeless, or in cramped and unsanitary housing, it poses a health risk to all of society. The NHS embodies this revelation of the reality of society as its existence is predicated on the fact that a decent standard of health care must be open to all. The collective understanding of housing, however, has failed to come to this conclusion as the exploitation of property for private financial gain is accepted at the same time as much of the lived experience of the home is silenced, from insufficient investment in housing conditions, to widespread overcrowding and fuel poverty. This is the normal to which some hope we return.

Authoritarian intervention appears to provide an efficient mechanism to control the virus. But such a suggestion is deeply flawed. Authoritarianism was unable to prevent the first animal-to-human transmission and it was not authoritarianism which limited the spread in higher-income households. It was the reality of our society which increased the spread in less prosperous areas, the reality of housing inequality, cramped and poorly maintained housing stock, poor working conditions and limited sick pay. COVID-19 has demonstrated we need government intervention; once the catastrophe subsides, we must demand the intervention continues to suppress the crisis. Such intervention must be as democratic and accountable as possible, and fully conscious that 'back to normal' is not good enough. We must articulate an alternative in which society is set up in order to protect everyone, not to enrich a few. This democratic intervention is, almost by definition, a call for slower or more messy intervention than an authoritarian may produce. It is intervention that is easily attacked as inefficient newt-counting, getting in the way of a mythical end point where the country will have built back better.

A new social politics of housing and homelessness

An emphasis on slow and messy change might sound like we advocate incremental, piecemeal reform, but that is not our claim. This is not to say technical legal reform is not urgently needed – for example, we would support reform focused on clarification of tenant rights and responsibilities, and reform of obviously dysfunctional parts of the law such as the unnecessarily arcane rules about housing conditions. Similarly, Section 21 should be abolished, and protections from eviction where tenants have complained about standards (retaliatory evictions) should be made more robust. We also support the need to build more good-quality homes, available for people who lack the means to purchase them, while homes which currently exist need to be made safe, healthy and environmentally sustainable.

However, such responses can sit comfortably within the broken paradigm we have outlined, and which has been so brutally exposed by COVID-19. More radical versions of them, which might be seen in plans to create urgently needed homes by overriding local objections to planning consent and giving freeholders the ability to add extra floors to existing buildings, fit most closely with an authoritarian intensification of market responses rather than a democratic response to the crisis. Instead we suggest that democracy, accountability and protection form the basis of a powerful and vital agenda. Our claim is that these values need to be at the foundation of a set of responses to the crisis in our collective homes, and further, that these values require the state to take on responsibility. More specifically, it is democratic institutions that have to take collective responsibility. Debates about what to do have to be founded in the core principles of accountability and protection, and a shared acknowledgement of the need to address problems created by the commodification and financialization of the home and the home provider.

In those debates, a key question which underpins state responsibility – and arguably, has enabled evasion of responsibility – is, if the state is responsible for ensuring safe, secure, sustainable homes, how ought we to envisage, describe or frame the relationship between the state and those people in those homes?

States exclude, citizenship excludes, and an emphasis on protection of citizens slips easily into exclusion – protection for some and not for others. This might lead to a rejection of protection by the state, and a call instead, for example, to embrace collective vulnerability and emphasize mutual aid. Such communities, and bottom-up responses to the problems we identify, are essential, standing in solidarity with those who otherwise would be excluded and providing a provocative critique of the flaws of the state. However, we suggest they are made stronger when supplemented by a capable state. In addition, communities, even the most radical and apparently inclusive, can exclude, and when it comes to basic questions of shelter, the resources, structures of accountability and objective distance of the state mean it has a critical role to play.

However, citizenship cannot be the basis of this relationship; as a social and democratic response includes taking collective responsibility for those whose participation is more limited, whether because of their age or capacity, or those who are excluded from the opportunities of citizenship. Rather than the negative 'right to rent' which exists to exclude those who have come to the UK from abroad, there needs to be a positive right to housing.

Such a suggestion highlights the need for rights as a counterbalance to the risk of paternalism in a shift to emphasize protection. After the fire at Grenfell Tower, in work for Shelter on the law relating to housing conditions, we supported a rights-based consumer framing, that 'no longer should occupiers be treated as posing health and safety risks; instead they should be treated as consumers of housing with enforceable rights to ensure minimum standards are adhered to. The state needs to accept its role as the primary enforcer of those standards' (Carr et al 2017:1). The consumer, as a way of understanding this relationship between the occupier of a home and the state, is powerful, with a coherent set of rights and broader associations under which the state backs the individual up with clear lines of support, some fundamental safety protections and an emphasis on transparency and fairness. But it also has less appealing associations. Consumers pay for a commodity, and consume a product, a relationship which reasserts a different but nonetheless potentially limiting set of individualized and individualizing property rights, as well as embedding a problematic relationship with environmental sustainability. In contrast, occupier or resident has the advantage of tenure neutrality, enabling a shift away from an initial focus on property relationships, but, consequentially, lacks an association with rights.

Perhaps a new concept is needed. Someone who lives in a place as their home, and whose relationship with that place and with the other people in it and around it ought to be taken seriously, protected, upheld, and that should be the responsibility of the state. Someone who is a soloist in an orchestra of soloists, if you like, someone who has individual rights and responsibilities but is also enmeshed in a collective and sustainable entity. The current approach is replete with refusals to take responsibility. The s.21 possession procedure is the state opting out of the consequences of market failure in housing, as are the structures and policies in social housing which have acted to restrict local authorities and promote others, including large housing associations. These amount to a claim that these are areas the state ought to step away from, to – on the most benign reading – allow others to provide a better service. The failures of this approach are plain.

However, responsibility has not been at the centre of interventions to date. Housing policy has focused on getting the housing market moving again, with short-term cuts to stamp duty to encourage sales. This financial stimulus is not about homes but is instead about the wider economy, in which house sales are a vital part of economic growth. It pays little attention to the risks of negative equity faced by those purchasing property in an artificially induced boom. The safety and security of homes is also a secondary issue, as is clearly illustrated in the failure to respond to the cladding crisis and the growing scandal relating to external wall surveys and insurance in leasehold properties.

Instead of acting to stimulate a market to fuel the wider economy, the state needs to put society first, providing a basic right to a safe, healthy and sustainable home, and only permitting a market where that approach met the needs of society. The methods must be democratic; processes which are based in the aforementioned fundamental principles, and while we do not have all the answers, they might include, for example, measures to ensure that any markets which do exist are as fair as possible for everyone, distributing rent arrears caused by COVID-19 more equitably between landlords and tenants, reducing capital gains and regulating home construction. Such moves would include ending the market in building control and returning responsibility for building safety to the state, and reversing the cutbacks which led directly to the fire at Grenfell Tower. As with much other needed reform, none of this can be done without careful reflection on the relationship between the market and society, significant investment and a renewal in understanding of the vital role of investment by the state in our collective physical and social infrastructures.

Conclusion

COVID-19 is a disease of the poor and the vulnerable. It has laid bare the inequalities in our society, just as the bombings of urban areas during the Second World War did. The immediate post-war years saw an acceleration in the building of affordable homes which had some aspirations for decency and made gestures towards equality and community. Something needs to emerge from this crisis. The pre-pandemic normal was not sustainable, and the virus has ripped through an ideology which understands humans as atomized and isolated from one another and who make independent rational decisions prompted by market realities. COVID-19 clearly demonstrates how our lives are all now connected to 'patient zero'. Yet at the same time social isolation challenges conventional understandings of community and collective responses. Just as classical music has responded by performing in orchestras of soloists, we need to reconfigure our understandings of social and individual and market relationships.

Our suggestions should not be read as reflexive returns to an interventionist pre-Thatcher state. We do not romanticize the state – now or then – and are all too aware of the deep flaws in our democratic systems. Nonetheless, society's ends are not achievable without a safe and secure home, and a reallocation of risk between those with property and those without. A messy, slow, inclusive, democratic and accountable response to the catastrophe is essential. Such a response needs to be initiated by the state, and needs to be initiated urgently.

References

Carr, H., Cowan, D., Kirton-Darling, E. and Burtonshaw-Gunn, E. (2017) *Closing the Gaps: Health and Safety At Home*, https://www.housinglin.org.uk/_assets/Resources/Housing/OtherOrganisation/Closing-the-Gaps-Health-and-Safety-at-Home.pdf (accessed 28 April 2021).

Collinson, P. (2020) 'Calls for Covid evictions ban to be extended in England and Wales', *The Guardian*, 18 September, https://www.theguardian.com/money/2020/sep/18/covid-evictions-ban-england-wales-coronavirus (accessed 28 April 2021).

Master of the Rolls Working Group (2020) *Overall arrangements for possession proceedings in England and Wales 'The overall arrangements'*, 17 September, www.judiciary.uk/wp-content/uploads/2020/09/Possession-Proceedings-Overall-Arrangements-Version-1.0-17.09.20.pdf (accessed 28 April 2021).

11

Education, Austerity and the COVID-19 Generation

Alison Struthers

Introduction

> COVID-19 has exposed and then amplified existing inequalities
> facing children, meaning those children already facing the worst
> life chances have felt the greatest burden from the virus and our
> response to it. (Children's Commissioner for England, 2020: 27)

As mentioned in the introduction to this book, COVID-19 has been
described as a great leveller; a virus that cares not about the colour, creed or
bank balance of its hosts. While there has been recognition at government
level that COVID-19 is more likely to affect certain groups – Black, Asian
and minority ethnic communities, older people, and those with underlying
health conditions in particular – there nevertheless remains something of a
whimsical notion that we are all in this together. The great leveller rhetoric
has perhaps been utilized in an attempt to create something of a sense of
community and unity at a time of national crisis, but the reality remains that
COVID-19 is far from a great leveller. It is instead an amplifier of existing
inequalities underlying not only the sectors discussed in the various chapters
in this book, but across almost every facet of society. With schools closing
early in the pandemic and re-opening for the vast majority of pupils only after
a variety of other businesses and services such as non-essential shops, pubs
and hair salons, the already widening attainment gap between disadvantaged
pupils and their wealthy peers in England has expanded further, and the
effects of this are likely to be both profound and enduring.

This chapter will discuss the stratified effects of COVID-19, and the responses to it, within the formal education sector in England based principally on socio-economic factors, with other social categorizations, including ethnic origin and disability, being discussed where relevant. It begins by considering the impact of the 2008 economic crash upon the education sector. How did the age of austerity affect schools more generally, and pupils from disadvantaged backgrounds in particular? Consideration will then be given to why this matters during the current global pandemic, and how the responses to COVID-19 are likely to have entrenched and exacerbated existing inequalities. In the concluding section, the important question of how these injustices might be remedied is addressed. Is there a way to ensure that the UK's economic recovery from the pandemic is handled in a sustainable and equitable way, with the burden of debt repayment falling not just on the poorest and most vulnerable sectors of society?

Education and the age of austerity

Various chapters in this book have discussed the significant adversity and suffering caused by the UK's response to the global economic crash of 2008. The perfect storm of falling incomes, rising living costs, economic stagnation, public spending cuts, benefit cuts, a housing crisis and weakened labour rights caused particular hardship to already marginalized groups, including lone parents, people with disabilities, vulnerable children and those already living below the poverty line (Oxfam published some startling statistics in 2012, including that austerity spending cuts hit the poorest tenth of the population 13 times harder than the richest tenth).[1] Treating budgets and spending cuts as neutral government functions during austerity resulted in those who were already vulnerable being further targeted, with cuts to government-sponsored services impacting spectacularly on the lives of disadvantaged children across the UK. For example, government spending on early years education, the Sure Start programme and the childcare element of the Working Tax Credit decreased by a significant 21 per cent between 2009–10 and 2012–13, with real-term government spending per child falling by around a quarter over the same period.

And the lasting impact of austerity measures on the education sector cannot be underestimated. While there was no one policy measure affecting schools that hit the headlines and attracted reproach and opposition to quite the same degree as the bedroom tax (though public outcry following significant cuts

---

[1]   https://oxfamilibrary.openrepository.com/bitstream/handle/10546/228591/bp-the-perfect-storm-uk-poverty-140612-summ-en.pdf;jsessionid=E4EC1A6FC11015729CE72B2C25628E13?sequence=1

to special educational needs and disabilities (SEND) funding did ultimately result in a government U-turn), existing inequalities exacerbated by a gradual series of cuts and structural changes in this sector have been enduring. The direct policy decisions of the coalition and then Tory governments have progressively eroded the funding, support and services that local authorities were able to offer to schools, which in turn have impacted most profoundly on those already struggling within the education system. The detrimental effects of austerity in this sector have become more apparent with the passage of time.

While successive governments in the UK have sought to ringfence expenditure on schools since the 2008 crash, the Institute for Fiscal Studies (IFS, 2020: 2) has recorded real-terms cuts amounting to 9 per cent per pupil between 2009–10 and 2019–20. Cuts to public spending were considered necessary to reduce the national debt and, as part of this process, local authorities experienced significant cuts to the grants they had been receiving. Although ostensibly impacting upon all local authority-maintained schools and pupils, the burden fell most heavily on the poorest and most vulnerable school attendees who were principally benefiting from the additional support services available through the local authorities. For example, staffing costs became the principal target for cuts because they represented the bulk of school spending. This resulted not only in larger class sizes and fewer subjects available, but also a reduction in additional support staff, including those involved with well-being, special educational needs (SEND), early intervention and family support.

The sweeping changes to the structure of the education system in England introduced by the coalition government in 2010 also had a bearing on funding and attainment gaps. With schools encouraged – through the promise of a significant front-loaded sum of money – to convert to academies, funds that would previously have been routed through local authorities were channelled straight to these 'new' schools. Although this process of syphoning money away from local authorities (perhaps we ought to call a spade a spade and refer to this as the commercialization of education) had started in the 1990s, it was significantly accelerated during austerity. Schools that had been maintained by local authorities began to be run like individual businesses, resulting in an effective dismantling of local authority oversight of the state school system. Where money was previously sent directly to local authorities for distribution to schools in their areas on the basis of need (with additional funds allocated based on the number of disadvantaged and SEND pupils), schools themselves were now in charge of their budgets and were expected to use this money to support services previously funded by local authorities.

The role of the local authority in providing advice, help and support to schools also diminished, and significantly, funds were routed away from schools catering for young people with SEND. In this climate of fewer available intervention services, combined with increased financial pressures on families, it is perhaps unsurprising that referrals of children to social care services saw a significant rise (a staggering 70 per cent increase between 2007 and 2013–14). This was not matched by a rise in social workers to deal with the extra workload, meaning that schools, themselves under the restraint of tightening budgets and reduced local authority support, ended up subsuming a significant amount of early intervention work with children.

Despite the introduction of measures aimed at tackling inequality in the wake of the 2008 global recession, including the Pupil Premium per capita grant to schools for pupils eligible for free school meals, deep divisions in educational attainment remained. Even before the COVID-19 pandemic, the attainment gap between disadvantaged pupils and their wealthier peers had stopped closing for the first time in a decade (Education Policy Institute (EPI), 2020a: 10–11). The report also highlighted a wider attainment gap for pupils from specific ethnic groups (particularly Gypsy/Roma and Black Caribbean pupils), for pupils with SEND, and for children in the care system and those receiving support from children's services (EPI, 2020a: 18–26). And the EPI researchers further identified the increasing proportion of disadvantaged children in persistent poverty as a significant cause of the lack of progress in narrowing the attainment gap (EPI, 2020a: 35); a finding that likely signifies the lasting impact of austerity cuts on educational equality. Where persistent poverty rates are higher, the disadvantage gap is wider: pupils on free school meals for over 80 per cent of their time at school are on average 22.7 months behind their more affluent peers, and those on free school meals for less than 20 per cent of school life are 11.3 months behind (EPI, 2020a: 18).

Clearly, even before the global pandemic and ensuing lockdowns, the lingering effect of austerity was still being felt across the UK education sector. Indeed, the EPI reported that, since 2017, the proportion of pupils with a high persistence of poverty has in fact risen from 34.8 per cent to 36.7 per cent (EPI, 2020a: 18). And the IFS (2020: 3) has noted that the additional funding given to more deprived schools in an effort to narrow the attainment gap between wealthier and poorer children has decreased from 35 per cent per pupil in 2010–11 to 25 per cent in 2018–19. It seems rather too obvious to state that significant cuts to relevant budgets and services in the wake of the 2008 crash, combined with escalating poverty rates and increased pressures on schools' already limited resources to support struggling families, would have a drastic impact on educational attainment. And it is certainly not a stretch to suggest that the burden of austerity fell most heavily on those children and young people at the lower end of the educational attainment spectrum. So what, then, has been the impact of COVID-19 on these already worrying trends?

Education and the COVID-19 generation

The economic fallout from COVID-19 is likely to result in a public debt far exceeding that of the 2008 global recession. And, as shown earlier, the period of austerity ushered in following the 2008 crash resulted in substantial cuts to spending in the education sector; cuts which disproportionately affected already disadvantaged groups. COVID-19 has lifted the lid on austerity and its lasting impact. The harmful effects of austerity measures upon various different sectors, education included, had been overlooked, slipping out of the public consciousness as debates and wrangling around the finer details of Brexit continued apace. 2020 has turned this on its head. Brexit (with all its accompanying potential for inequality and injustice) has slipped down the list of talking points, and the hardships being visited upon the most disadvantaged in our society as a result of the global pandemic have taken centre stage in the media. What, then, has been the impact of COVID-19, and the responses to it, on these groups: is COVID-19 anything close to a 'great leveller' or has it served only to exacerbate existing disparities around wealth, class, disability and ethnicity?

The Children's Commissioner for England (2020: 12, 27) pronounced in September 2020 that some of the most vulnerable children have seen their rights actively downgraded, at a time when protections should be strengthened, not undermined. It has been widely reported that schools in the most deprived areas of England will struggle to a greater extent than their more affluent counterparts to help pupils catch up after lockdown, with data suggesting that the learning gap between rich and poor pupils grew by almost half between March and July 2020 (National Foundation for Educational Research (NFER), 2020: 18–19); 53 per cent of teachers in the most deprived schools considered their pupils to be at least four months behind in their learning, compared to just 15 per cent of teachers in the wealthiest schools (NFER, 2020: 21). And, 60 per cent of private schools and 37 per cent of state schools in wealthy areas had access to an online learning platform during lockdown, in comparison with only 23 per cent in the most deprived state schools (Children's Commissioner for England, 2020: 4). Even where remote learning was available in more disadvantaged schools, many pupils had neither the technology nor home environment necessary to access it, with Ofcom (Office of Communications) estimating that between 1.14m and 1.78m children in the UK have no home access to a laptop, desktop computer, or tablet (Ofcom quoted in Children's Commissioner for England, 2020: 5).

Children and young people with SEND have arguably been particularly disadvantaged by the responses to COVID-19, and those with the most serious and complex needs have been hardest hit by emergency powers introduced under the Coronavirus Act 2020. Children on an Education, Health and Care Plan (EHCP) would normally have an absolute entitlement to special educational support in the classroom and access to relevant health services. Under the terms of the Coronavirus Act, however, from May until August 2020 councils and local health bodies only had to make 'reasonable endeavours' to deliver these crucial services, resulting in a significant decline in support for children with complex needs. Other schemes to assist families who had been receiving help from social care services were also side-lined during the pandemic, with 76 per cent of affected families reporting that the support they had been receiving for children with complex needs had essentially dissipated and they felt utterly abandoned by the state (Children's Commissioner for England, 2020: 8).

While the full effect of COVID-19 upon the educational attainment gap is not yet known, early indications suggest that, as with austerity, the heaviest burden has been placed upon the shoulders of those least able to bear it. Pupils who were already falling behind following substantial cuts to budgets and services after 2008, as well as those with SEND and additional complex needs, have been hardest hit by the pandemic. Schools in wealthier areas had the technology and resources to provide effective online learning platforms during lockdown, and their pupils largely had the equipment and home environment necessary to take advantage of this. As a result, the attainment gap has widened further than perhaps anyone could have imagined at the beginning of 2020.

Education and a post-COVID-19 future

With the lasting effects of austerity and the significant additional hardships brought about by the global pandemic in mind, it is important to consider what a fair, just and proportionate government response ought to look like. Should such a response endeavour to place significantly greater emphasis on tackling existing inequalities in education? Given the startling statistics outlined in the previous section, there only seems to be one reasonable answer to this: during the UK's economic recovery from COVID-19, the government simply must prioritize support for the most disadvantaged pupils, who are likely to have fallen behind to the greatest extent as a result of the pandemic. For such an approach to be successful, the notion that one can use a neutral version of the law and economy when developing education policy and practice would need to be dispelled. The government simply cannot throw money up in the air and expect it to land in the most appropriate places for redressing the ever-increasing attainment gap. There must be significant and targeted investment for the most disadvantaged families, from early years onwards. Despite evidence that children from poorer backgrounds already have lower educational outcomes than their wealthier peers by the age of five, no government funding has been made available for these early years settings. This is despite the startling statistic that one in three children under the age of five in the UK are living in poverty. Change must start with the youngest children, and any suitable recovery package must tackle the 'rising tide of childhood vulnerability', as the Children's Commissioner for England (2020: 27) put it.

In September 2019, the government announced that it was to allocate an extra £7.1bn in funding for schools up to 2022–23 and that this would particularly assist schools in the most disadvantaged areas. This funding will increase spending per pupil by 9 per cent in real terms between 2019–20 and 2022–23 and effectively reverse past spending cuts in this sector (though when expected increases in teacher pay are taken into account, the real-term increase for spending per pupil is likely to be closer to 6 per cent (IFS, 2020: 2)). In the shorter term, a £1bn COVID-19 package to fund catch-up support for children was also announced which, according to the Department for Education, 'will tackle the impact of lost teaching time, including targeted funding for the most disadvantaged students'.[2]

However, while the National Funding Formula[3] (introduced in 2018) purports to make the system fairer by allocating funding on the basis of need – and by seeking to ensure that pupils with the same characteristics get the same level of funding, regardless of where their school is located – the IFS reports that the formula will deliver funding increases of 3–4 percentage points less to schools in more deprived areas up to 2021. This anomaly has come about as a result of the goal to 'level up' budgets and boost the amounts received by schools in areas with lower funding rates. Where schools have fewer pupils from disadvantaged backgrounds, and thus where they have less entitlement to existing funding pots, they will nevertheless receive a disproportionate amount of funding to 'level up' their budget despite having fewer pupils in need of extra financial support.

---

2   Burns, J., 'Coronavirus: Lockdown pupils are three months behind, say teachers', *BBC News*, 1 September, www.bbc.co.uk/news/amp/education-5394798

3   Department for Education (2019) *The national funding formulae for schools and high needs (2020-21)*, https://assets.publishing.service.gov.uk/government/uploads/system/uploads/attachment_data/file/838394/National_funding_formula_policy_document_-_2020_to_2021.pdf

The EPI also reports that by the school year ending in summer 2022, funding for poorer pupils will have increased at just two thirds of the rate for their wealthier peers, and that Black and minority ethnic pupils will be even harder hit, with funding rises worth around half those from White British backgrounds (EPI, 2020b: 3–4). In other words, the most disadvantaged pupils will be receiving smaller funding increases than their wealthier counterparts. Although the government claims that schools with higher numbers of pupils from disadvantaged backgrounds remain a priority, the aim of the National Funding Formula is being distorted; and although pupils from lower-income backgrounds continue to attract more funding overall, the connection between school funding and pupil need is beginning to unravel (EPI, 2020b). Schools in more deprived areas will therefore gain less percentage-wise than their more affluent counterparts, despite the strong likelihood that their pupils will be significantly further behind in their learning. This finding not only runs counter to the objective of using school funding to 'level up' disadvantaged regions, but is also likely to entrench and intensify existing inequalities, where poorer pupils' families are already at a greater risk of poverty, food insecurity and job losses.

Some parts of the government's COVID-19 recovery plan are specifically targeted at more deprived schools. The first is the National Tutoring Programme for five- to 16-year-olds. There have been concerns, however, around whether the scale of the programme will be sufficient to meet the high demand for those who are in need of intensive catch-up support. The IFS (2020: 3) has noted, for example, that 'whilst the focus on tutoring is well aligned with empirical evidence, the plans are modest compared with the likely reductions in skills'. And another initiative targeting disadvantaged pupils has been the provision of laptop and internet connections for disadvantaged Year 10s, children with social care workers, and care leavers. While this initiative has been roundly welcomed in the education sector, it has been reported that many more devices are needed to meet demand, with an accompanying swifter dispatch and more training for teachers. It is nevertheless positive that the government has sought to address an area of considerable disparity between disadvantaged pupils and their wealthier peers, and it should be accompanied by a guarantee that schools will be able to provide comprehensive remote education for all children should they be required to remain at home due to class or school closures.

So, how might the government's recovery plan be improved? Perhaps at the most rudimentary level, schools and the range of services which protect children, for example children's centres, must be the last to close and first to re-open in the event of further lockdowns. Children's education must be prioritized, or we risk a lost generation of young people lacking the knowledge and skills necessary to follow their chosen paths. And the share of the economic recovery package for schools simply must prioritize vulnerable and disadvantaged children who have been hit hardest during the pandemic. While the government claims that the National Funding Formula achieves this aim, it has been shown that the formula does not deliver fully on this front. The data in this chapter around not only the diverging attainment gap, but also the basic access of some pupils to fundamental learning tools, has been startling. Making token concessions to increased spending for disadvantaged pupils is not sufficient. There is evidence to suggest that teachers in the most deprived schools are almost twice as likely to believe that their pupils are in need of intensive catch-up support than those in wealthier schools (NFER, 2020: 23). There must be a concerted effort to channel funding into the schools and regions where children have fallen further behind, and where they are least likely to be able to catch up.

Simply allocating schools in more deprived regions additional money is perhaps not enough, however. Schools are currently facing greater overheads relating to hygiene and safety in the wake of the pandemic. Costs for extra cleaning and additional staff required to maintain appropriate ratios for pupil bubbles have escalated and this must be taken into account when funds are being allocated for the purpose of redressing educational disadvantage. Any extra funds given to disadvantaged schools should not be subsumed within expanding cleaning bills or extra Personal Protective Equipment (PPE) provision, but rather should be spent on the vulnerable children whose education has suffered to the greatest extent throughout this crisis.

It has not been possible within this chapter to delve into the hugely significant issue of how the pandemic, and lockdown in particular, has impacted upon children's mental health. In this concluding section on the ways forward, however, this issue is too important not to be mentioned. The Children's Commissioner for England (2020: 28) has emphasized the importance of a greater focus on pastoral care, supported by accelerated implementation of the government's Green Paper on mental health, with the intended outcome that every child is able to access counselling at school. And on a more general level, schools should have an increased focus on children's mental health and well-being, rather than a singular focus on academic attainment. The government should seek to ensure that funding and appropriate support measures are available to schools to prevent a spike in exclusions, persistent absence and pupil withdrawals in the fallout from the pandemic.

It is clear that significant change is needed within the education sector to right the wrongs not just of 2020 – where disadvantaged children who were already struggling to keep pace with their wealthier peers have fallen further behind with little by way of additional funding or other support measures offered to enable them to catch up – but also of the past decade since the collapse of the global economy. It was predicted by the EPI in 2019 that it would take 500 years to close the attainment gap, but at least it was closing. This seemed to be a step in the right direction. Now the gap is not closing at all and, because this trend started before the global pandemic, COVID-19 cannot exclusively shoulder the blame. Something was already awry in the government's response to the widening attainment gap, and the latest COVID-19 recovery package seems unlikely to remedy these shortcomings.

I have heard it being said recently that the NHS was introduced in the UK at a time when we as a nation could least afford it. It was not a question of cost, but rather one of need. With this in mind, the current government must decide where its priorities lie. COVID-19 has shone a spotlight on an education system that is failing not through the endeavours of dedicated staff, pupils and additional service providers, but rather through a constant and stifling squeeze on finances, time and resources. If this situation is to be reversed, the only solution is for money to be spent where it is most needed. In order to support those who have fallen behind to the greatest extent as a result of multiple lockdowns, the funding being made available for schools simply must target disadvantaged schools in deprived communities. Narrowing the attainment gap should be central to the government's 'levelling up' agenda.

It goes without saying that education is crucial for inter alia job prospects, social mobility and quality of life, and the government has got away with side-lining it for too long, often in favour of spending on vanity projects such as HS2 (High Speed 2). It appears, however, that one of the only silver linings of COVID-19 is that there is now an appetite for change. The very real hardships exposed by the pandemic have served somewhat to blow the ideological dogma of the government's position out of the water – the attainment gap cannot be closed simply by allocating small amounts of additional funding to schools in deprived areas. Systemic change is needed. Serious and careful consideration must be given to intersectional disadvantages and the lingering detrimental effects of austerity measures in order to tackle society-wide inequality and its impact upon educational attainment. The government's response to the current crisis must not simply focus on how to return us to our pre-COVID-19 position, but rather this re-building ought to tackle the structural inequalities that saw disadvantaged families being the most susceptible to adversity during this national crisis. This, of course, involves change across all sectors of society (many of which have been addressed in other chapters in this volume), but perhaps education ought to be viewed as the cornerstone for such change. To come full circle and return to the words of England's Children's Commissioner, 'the true measure of a society is in how it treats its most vulnerable members' (2020: 3). It is time for the government to prove that they are willing to prioritize those most adversely affected by the ills of this pandemic by providing schools with the funding, resources, staffing and time necessary to allow the COVID-19 generation a genuine chance to reach their fullest potential.

References

Children's Commissioner for England (2020) *Childhood in the time of Covid*, London: Children's Commission for England, www.childrenscommissioner. gov.uk/wp-content/uploads/2020/09/cco-childhood-in-the-time-of-covid.pdf (accessed 26 October 2020).

Education Policy Institute (EPI) (2020a) *Education in England: Annual Report 2020*, London: EPI, https://epi.org.uk/publications-and-research/education-in-england-annual-report-2020/(accessed 26 October 2020).

EPI (2020b) *Analysis: School Funding Allocations 2021–22*, London: EPI, https://epi.org.uk/publications-and-research/school-funding-allocations-2021-22/#:~:text=In%202021%2D22%2C%20total%20Schools,cent%20after%20allowing%20for%20inflation (accessed 26 October 2020).

Institute for Fiscal Studies (IFS) (2020) *2020 Annual Report on Education Spending in England: Schools*, London: IFS, www.ifs.org.uk/uploads/2020--annual-report-on-education-spending-in-England-schools.pdf (accessed 26 October 2020).

National Foundation for Educational Research (NFER) (2020) *The challenges facing schools and pupils in September 2020*, London: NFER, www.nfer.ac.uk/media/4119/schools_responses_to_covid_19_the_challenges_facing_schools_and_pupils_in_september_2020.pdf (accessed 26 October 2020).

12

What Have We Learned about the Corporate Sector in COVID-19?

Sally Wheeler

Introduction

The most obvious story about business that could come from lockdown is one of the severe economic strain that will be experienced as a result of the drop in consumer demand that occurs when people are no longer able to move freely. Short-term government intervention will postpone insolvency. The employee furlough scheme aside, this intervention has taken the form of the cancellation of business rates for particular industries (retail, hospitality and leisure) with a cash grant scheme targeted at smaller businesses in those sectors. Other industries, such as fishing, have been similarly supported. Businesses occupying low-value properties have been given small business rates relief. Small- and medium-sized enterprises have been reimbursed for 14 days of employee sick pay if the absence is COVID-19-related to include employees who were self-isolating as well as those who were sick.

However, this support has been insufficient for some businesses. As lockdown has eased there have been numerous announcements of businesses, particularly in the retail, hospitality and consumer goods manufacturing that will not resume trading – for example, Harvey's Furniture, Victoria's Secret, Antler Luggage, Quiz and Debenhams have all announced that they are in difficulties. Large concerns like these will be able to sell their brand name or continue to trade while in administration or under a voluntary agreement as they search for a buyer or reach a settlement with some key creditors; others have announced that they will restructure and trade only in some markets, using particular channels, for example Feather & Black will move to a concession and online business only, and Cath Kidston will be online-only in the UK with stores in Asia. Some smaller corporations will continue as 'zombie' companies unable to increase productivity because of the cost of servicing their debts but still crowding out of the market healthier and more innovative rivals.

Business failure on this scale usually offers an opportunity to critique the adoption or not of innovation, the adaptation or not to changing markets and consumer preferences, the ratio of loan to equity capital, the quality of management decisions and so on. However, the light shone by the UK lockdown which required all non-essential businesses to close by 26 March 2020 and its staggered reopening by mid-June illuminated the practices of an apparently successful business. This chapter focuses on Boohoo, a publicly listed company on the Alternative Investment Market (AIM); and the rise of fast fashion and the credibility of Environmental, Social and Governance investing. It exposes the fault line that separates workplace conditions and environmental degradation from monetary return on investment. The chapter ends by offering some thoughts on the behaviour of those who enable industries such as fast fashion to take hold and thrive – consumers and investors. It suggests what a post-COVID-19 future for corporate accountability might look like.

Lockdown and Leicester

Retail trading and COVID-19

Non-essential retail businesses trading from fixed physical locations were required by the UK government to close by 26 March 2020 under regulations derived from the Public Health (Control of Disease) Act 1984. Included in the list of retail business considered non-essential were shops selling clothing. Excluded from the list were storage and distribution centres including those that serviced online retailers. The government's organizing idea for this part of the economy was that businesses could and should trade *if* it was safe (*read*, they could and would make a safe workplace for employees) for them to do so. Manufacturing premises were also excluded from the closure order provided that the workers were not able to work from home, were fit to work, were not part of a household where anyone was ill or self-isolating and were able to observe public health guidelines in relation to hand-washing and physical distancing.

The rationale for retailers wanting to continue to trade online was to maintain some cash flow and in the words of a statement from ASOS (an online-only clothes retailer) '[to do] the responsible thing ... when you consider our suppliers and all those employed within the supply chain' (ASOS, 2020). This concern for the welfare of workers in the supply chain echoes the promises and policies contained in the corporate social responsibility (CSR) reports of nearly all listed corporations. However, in reality, clothing retailers moved very quickly after states began to impose lockdowns to push risk down the supply chain by cancelling orders for clothing; relying on force majeure clauses in contracts to allow them to do so; and refusing to honour outstanding payments for already delivered stock, inviting suppliers to collect it instead. Thousands of workers in developing countries who are employed at the bottom of the garment supply chain have found themselves laid off indefinitely, with credible accounts of labour activists and unionized workers being disproportionately targeted. This abandonment of previously much vaunted CSR policies by large corporations, which in many cases have continued to pay shareholder dividends and executive bonuses, mirrors what occurred during the 2008 global financial crisis. If CSR is to have any credibility it must work for the most vulnerable. This quiet abandonment of CSR policies has not resulted in any outcry from investors.

Unsurprisingly, there was pressure from warehouse and distribution centre staff and their unions to close their workplaces as safe working conditions could not be created. Postal workers complained that they were taking health risks in delivering non-essential items ordered online. Some businesses such as Paul Smith, Next and Net-a-Porter did cease online trading. However, others, for example clothing retailer Boohoo, did not. Online sales recorded an 18 per cent increase in April 2020 to form 30.7 per cent of all retail sales which recorded a drop of 18.1 per cent (Office for National Statistics (ONS) 2020).

In early May a three-phased plan to ease the lockdown restrictions in England was announced. Phase one began on 11 May with those who could not work from home being encouraged to return to their workplaces. Phase two began on 1 June. Retail premises that were still subject to the March closure order were allowed to reopen. Phase three, which started on 4 July, allowed places where indoor gatherings would obviously occur to open (such as gyms, hotel accommodation, museums and galleries).

The re-closure of Leicester

Leicester, a city of 330,000 people, and its immediate environs in the East Midlands did not progress to phase three opening. Instead, on 29 June the area became the first large-scale site in the UK to experience a 'local' lockdown – previously, additional lockdowns had been of single use, individual facilities (for example a meat-processing factory in Yorkshire). Schools and non-essential shops were ordered to close again. Vulnerable individuals were told to recommence or continue shielding themselves and the remaining population asked to stay at home as much as possible and undertake only essential travel within Leicester. The rest of the UK was asked to avoid the lockdown area. The reason given was that, in the preceding two weeks, 944 COVID-19 cases had been reported in the area, giving the city an infection rate of 135 cases per 100,000 people. Leicester accounted for 10 per cent of all COVID-19 cases reported in the UK in the previous week. Taken together this gave Leicester three times the volume of infection enjoyed by the next most highly infected area.

Lockdown began to be eased in mid-August with some retail functions allowed to reopen. At the time of writing (October 2020) restrictions remain in the city centre and its immediate urban environs; individuals are still prevented from overnighting away from their usual place of residence or meeting other individuals within their private gardens. This last restriction echoes much of the cultural disconnect evident in the UK's COVID-19 planning; inner city Leicester is a relatively poor and densely populated area, consequently few of the families and individuals affected by the lockdown would live in accommodation that had access to a shared, never mind private, garden.

What was not made clear and remains, even now, unclear was the reason or reasons for COVID-19 cases spiking in Leicester. Amid claims and counter claims from central and local government about the evidence that could be derived from different test settings, the need for more granular geographic information about exactly which area was returning high numbers of cases and calls for more public information to be available in a multilingual format (70 languages are spoken in Leicester, the most popular after English is Gujarati which 16 per cent of the population report as their first language), it became apparent that there were a number of competing narratives that sought to explain the rising number of cases. It is the contestation in this narrative space that exposes Boohoo PLC, the alleged working practices of the subcontractors in its supply chain, and the mechanics of fast fashion to the public gaze.

According to a statement released by Public Health England on 2 July there were 'no explanatory outbreaks in care homes, hospital settings, or industrial processes' (BBC News, 2020). Instead most of the positive tests were to be found in the under-19 age group and this required investigation. However, a statement from Health Secretary Matt Hancock made on 29 June suggested that the rise in cases came as a result of the failure of 'targeted action'[1] at factories and workplaces with the situation exacerbated

---

[1] Hancock, M. (2020) 'Plans for managing the coronavirus (COVID-19) outbreak in Leicester', Oral statement to Parliament, https://www.gov.uk/government/speeches/local-action-to-tackle-coronavirus (accessed 19 April 2021).

by poverty, higher ethnic diversity and higher density housing. In the same time frame a UK-based not-for-profit co-operative, Labour Behind the Label, which campaigns for the rights of workers in the global garment industry released a report entitled *Boohoo and COVID-19: The people behind the profit* (LBL, 2020). The report attributed blame for Leicester's COVID-19 spike to clothing factories operating in the city; factories, it alleged, which had not shut down during the lockdown despite not being able to provide socially distanced working conditions or Personal Protective Equipment (PPE) and had required workers to carry on working even if they were sick, had tested positive or were members of households where vulnerable people were shielding. These factories were working exclusively as subcontractors on orders for Boohoo and its brand names, PrettyLittleThing and Nasty Gal.

An undercover reporter working for *The Sunday Times* supported these allegations in an exclusive that ran the following Sunday 5 July 2020 (Matety, 2020). The reporter also drew attention to the wages that were being offered by Boohoo's subcontractors: a maximum of £4.50 an hour against a national minimum wage for workers aged over 19 of £8.72. To add to low wages and unsafe working conditions, these subcontractors were also accused of encouraging benefit fraud among their workers and making furloughed workers carry on working. Boohoo and its subcontractors have become, ex post facto, responsible for the community transmissions that created the conditions for the re-lockdown in Leicester.

Boohoo and fast fashion in Leicester

Introducing Boohoo

Boohoo is a Manchester-based company founded as an owner-run enterprise in 2006 that sells clothing online, largely sourced from UK manufacturers. It had an IPO in 2014 with its shares priced at 50p. Its business signature is the very low retail price of its products; dresses that retail at less than £18 and bikinis at less than £4, promoted almost exclusively through social media 'influencers'. Despite this business model it has acquired in the last two years the relatively upmarket brands of Coast, Karen Millen, Oasis and Warehouse. In January 2020, its share price was 333.7p and its market value was £3.89bn (higher than Marks and Spencer PLC). Its sales figures have risen from £195m to £1.2bn and its pre-tax profits from £16m to £92m. Until the events of the Leicester lockdown Boohoo had been able to drive its sales and profits up year on year from its initial listing while other clothing retailers such as ASOS, Next and Debenhams saw their profits from clothing ranges fall dramatically. It is a phenomenal success story in terms of return on investment.

The combined effect of the Labour Behind the Label report and *The Sunday Times* exclusive was a 50 per cent drop in Boohoo's market value in the week 6–10 July (see Figure 12.1). Share prices go down when investors sell their shares. According to efficient market theory, share prices move (up and down) when new information becomes available to investors and they act on it. Here, investors were signalling that they did not want to be associated with a company that had been very publicly accused of acquiring its stock from manufacturers offering extremely poor working conditions and employee remuneration. That suggested Boohoo either conducts very poor stewardship of its supply chain or was indifferent as to how its products are made, or both. Both, it seems, was the answer. Boohoo took the unusual step of commissioning an independent review of its supply chain conducted by Alison Levitt QC (Levitt, 2020). She reported in September 2020 that the supply chain was indeed poorly governed and that senior members of the Boohoo Board had known specifically, from December 2019 at the latest, of poor working conditions and low pay.

Following inspections in July, it was announced that Boohoo's subcontractors had not committed any offences under the Modern Slavery Act 2015 (MSA 2015). This tells us something about how bad working conditions and practices have to be before liability under the legislation occurs. Boohoo's (2019) Modern Slavery Statement (the latest available) sets out a variety of policies that it applies to subcontractors and expectations that it has of them, but it is very short on how these policies have been implemented and then evaluated. There is almost nothing on the results of actual engagement with subcontractors in the UK or overseas. While the Statement is required, its content is not regulated or evaluated in any way except by actors in the investment market. Legislation apart, there are numerous voluntary guidelines and multi-stakeholder initiatives that are focused on preventing exactly the sort of abuse of employees that has occurred in the Boohoo supply chain by pushing requirements of transparency and traceability up the chain to the lead manufacturer and the retailer on foot of their moral responsibility.

At least 20 sustainable investment funds held shares in Boohoo prior to *The Sunday Times* report, despite presumably knowing that the fashion industry was notorious for issues of bad practice in its supply chain around pay and working conditions, union representation and other breaches of human rights (for example the practices revealed by the Rana Plaza building collapse in Bangladesh in 2013). In 2018, the *Financial Times* ran a story about small garment factories in Leicester that acted as subcontractors to Boohoo paying less than the minimum wage and operating in unsafe conditions (O'Connor, 2018). A subsequent House of Commons report in January 2019 (House of

Figure 12.1: Boohoo share price movement in 2020

Boohoo group plc (BOO.L)
Share price movement in 2020

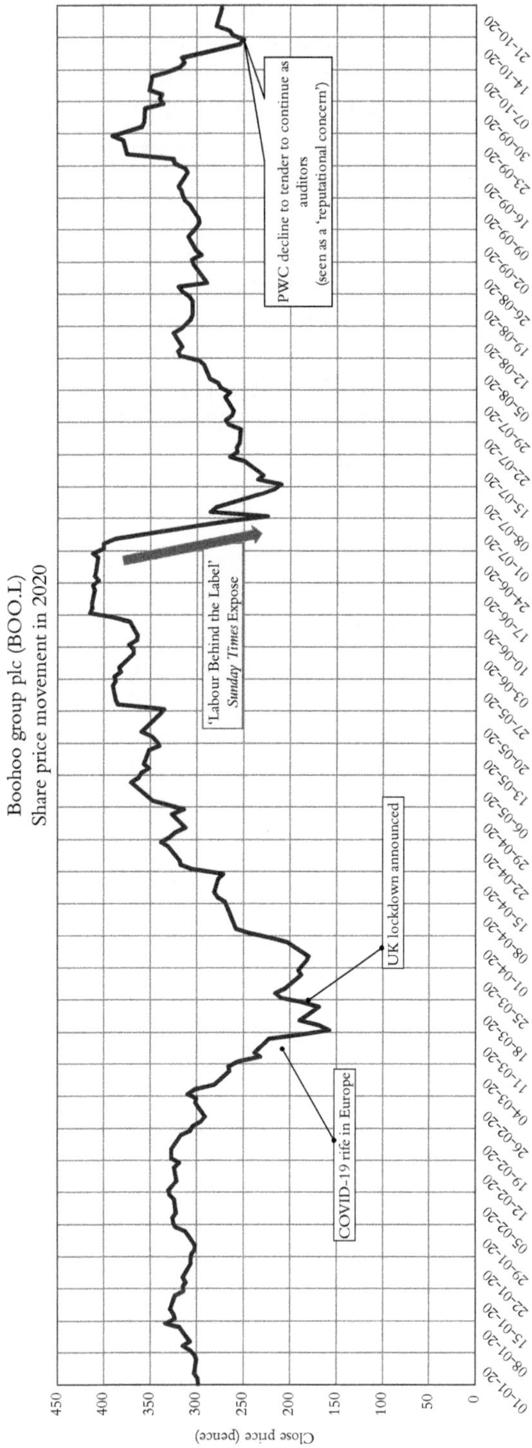

Commons, 2019) also voiced concerns about Boohoo's position on trade union membership for their employees and their policy on subcontractors paying less than the minimum wage. The report identified Boohoo as one of the 'less engaged' (its lowest category) retailers that it had taken evidence from. Neither of these negative reports appeared to impact on Boohoo's share price (see Figures 12.2 and 12.3). The news that PWC was not tendering for Boohoo's audit work was of more concern to investors (see Figure 12.1). Recent literature suggests that the determinative factors in garnering the interest and action of investment fund managers seems to be the media source of the information, the style of reporting (sensationalist or not) and the blaming of a corporation rather than specific employees. To these we might add pay walls and the performativity that occurs in the face of a global pandemic. The *Financial Times* and a Parliamentary Report are clearly not sensationalist enough!

Fast fashion in Leicester

Boohoo is a fast-fashion retailer. Fast fashion is a distinct business model within the clothing industry. It eschews physical presence in favour of online platforms and portals that offer products priced so low (and often made from non-recyclable cheap mixed-fibre fabric) that they are purchased as 'wear once and throw away' items. Clothing is one of the few items that has declined in retail price over the last 20 years. Marketing takes place through social media channels and 'celebrity' endorsement. Fast fashion relies on consumer demand identifying products for manufacture. Relatively small numbers of a large range of clothes are made up initially. The designs that sell are then reproduced very quickly to meet demand. The use of a distribution centre as the physical base has two advantages: consumer demand can be satisfied with less product investment as there is no need to keep a range of stock in geographically dispersed locations, and the availability of display space is not a constraint on new products. It is speed to market (days from first appearance to availability for the online customer) that attracts the name 'fast fashion'. Manufacturers in the fast-fashion supply chain make very small margins on contracts. Work is carried out under huge time pressure for fear of financial sanction for late delivery with no guarantee of further work. This does not encourage investment in safe working conditions or payment of the legally mandated minimum wage.

Post-Second World War, the UK garment manufacturing industry, much of which was situated in the East Midlands, went into a steep decline unable to compete with developing countries which enjoyed commercial advantages around lower labour costs, lower environmental regulation, closeness to fabric production and improved airfreight transport structures. Leading locations for

Figure 12.2: Boohoo share price movement April–June 2018

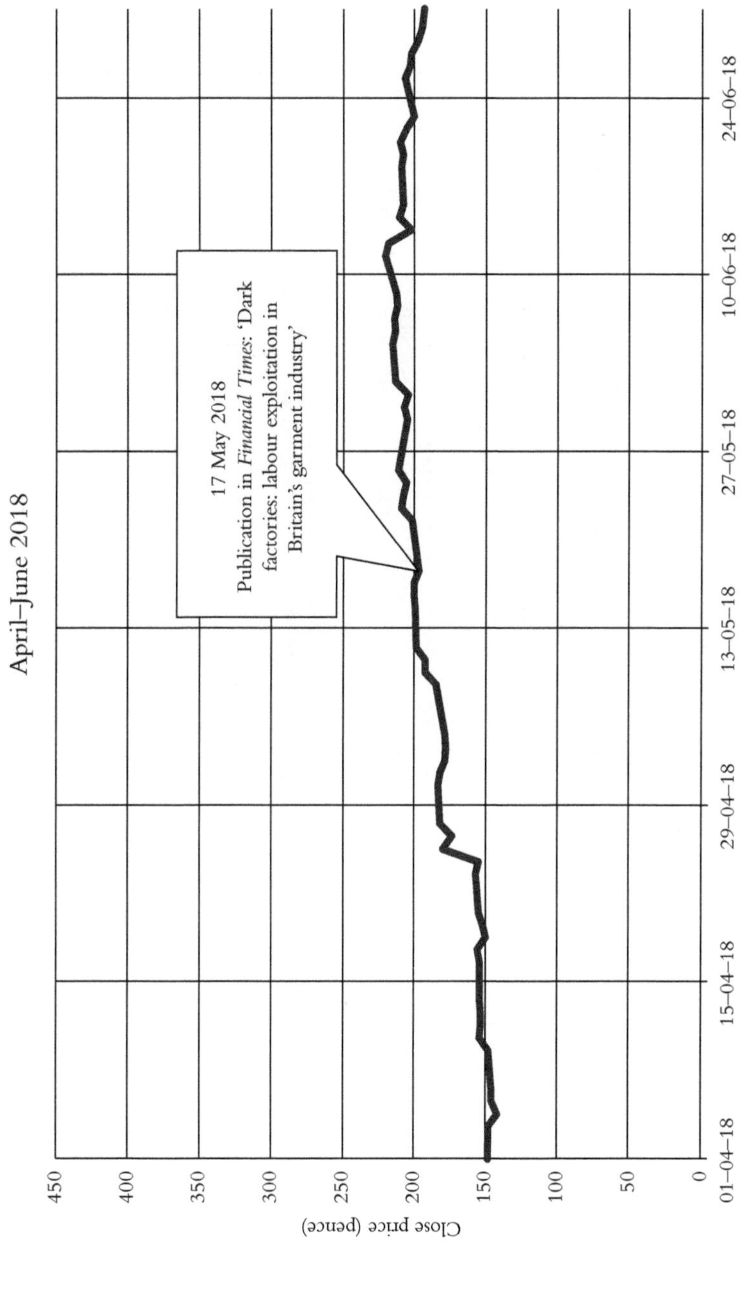
April–June 2018
17 May 2018
Publication in *Financial Times*: 'Dark factories: labour exploitation in Britain's garment industry'
Close price (pence)
450
400
350
300
250
200
150
100
50
0
01–04–18
15–04–18
29–04–18
13–05–18
27–05–18
10–06–18
24–06–18

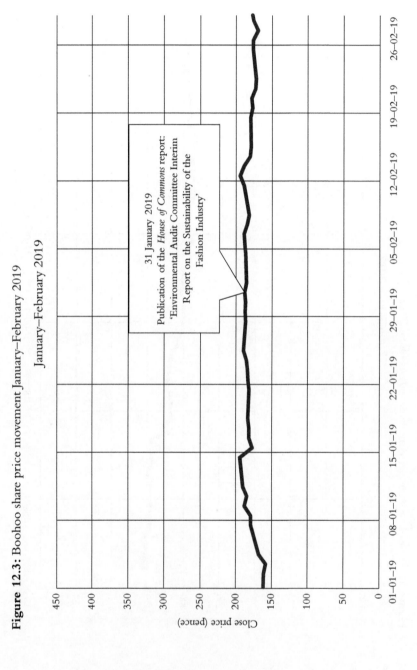

Figure 12.3: Boohoo share price movement January–February 2019

garment sourcing became China and SE Asia and more latterly Eastern Europe and North Africa. Somewhat counter-intuitively UK garment manufacture began to be reshored in the aftermath of the 2008 crisis, in Manchester and London with Leicester as the largest hub. This reshored industry is structured very differently from its predecessor. In 1978, 368,000 people were employed in the UK garment industry; in 2012, that figure was 28,000 – a huge decrease but still a sufficient number to contribute to a regional economy. Eighty-five per cent of garment firms in Leicester employ less than 20 employees, although this figure has to be understood in the context of an industry that is thought to understate the number of its employees (Centre for Sustainable Work and Employment Futures (CSWE), 2014).

Fast fashion is the driver behind the reshoring of the garment industry into the UK and into Leicester. It needs production and consumption sites to be geographically proximate if clothes are to be available for retail purchase quickly. The demographics of Leicester create the perfect storm of a vulnerable workforce and an industry that is low on technology and high on manual labour with a reputation for exploitative working practices. Wage costs are the highest cost that garment manufacturers carry. A third or so of Leicester's current residents are born outside the UK. Those identifying as Indian make up 28 per cent of the population of Leicester city with a clustering in the council wards in the east of the city (also home to many small garment factories). 2011 Census data indicates that there is a correlation between these council wards and those residents who report not being able to speak English well (Centre on the Dynamics of Ethnicity (CoDE), 2013). Family ties attract immigrants from the Indian sub-continent and East Africa. New migration routes have seen Leicester become popular with Somalis and Eastern Europeans. Indeed African is the fastest growing ethnic identity (CoDE, 2013). Issues around residency status, the right to work and an absence of language skills create key vulnerabilities, and these are all common and ongoing problems for these residents. They have limited access to the welfare system meaning they have little choice but to accept the sort of working conditions and denial of their rights that *The Sunday Times* exposed in early July. In the absence of these vulnerabilities, migrants in these groups suffer structural inequalities in the labour market securing poorer wage outcomes than Western Europeans and those from the 'White' Commonwealth.

Responsible investing and responsible consumption

Environmental, social and governance investing

Fast fashion exacerbates the problems of the fashion industry in relation to exploitative working conditions for employees and environmental degradation; excess waste, pollution and inefficient resource use are all issues. The purchase of 'more' clothing increases the environmental footprint of an industry that uses water, chemicals and energy in intensive wet processes (bleaching, dyeing and finishing). Petro-chemicals are required for the production processes of synthetic fabric with the knock-on effect of considerable CO_2 emissions. Intensive cultivation of crops such as cotton requires large quantities of pest control chemicals. Producing more clothing generates more production waste through the cutting of fabric and, most significantly for fast fashion, through the generation of deadstock; clothing that remains unsold. It is often incinerated. Online-only fashion retailers use packaging to send their products to customers. Cheap clothing encourages consumers to discard items quickly and replace them with others. Used textiles, if recyclable (and much is not), can be turned into insulation and mattress stuffing. The success of this depends on the availability and promotion of recycling as a lifestyle position. It would be more constructive to address the role of fast fashion in consumption practices.

Boohoo was very popular with ESG investment funds. ESG refers to environmental, social and governance practices within a corporation that make it attractive to those looking for positive financial returns in the context of sustainable investment. Sub-classes of sustainable investment include socially responsible investing, ethical investing and values-based investing. ESG investment funds are popular across the investment market spectrum from retail investors to pension funds where there is a desire to support and reward those corporations that are using best practices in ESG areas. There used to be speculation from the investor community about whether ESG funds could provide a viable financial return. Clearly they can, not least because of the inclusion of very profitable corporations like Boohoo. The inclusion of corporations pursuing the fast-fashion business model, particularly an individual corporation that has a track record of supply chain management as poor as Boohoo's, must place question marks around the efficacy of ESG. Boohoo appears in the lowest decile in pressure group Fashion Revolution's Transparency Index for 2020, its highest individual score is for 'policy and commitments' and its lowest individual score is, unsurprisingly, for 'traceability'; information about supply chain participants (Fashion Revolution, 2020). Boohoo has never made this public and any mention of supply chain governance is absent from its 2019 and 2020 annual reports.

Environmental, social and governance regulation

ESG investing is increasing in popularity. A decade ago it was a minority interest in Europe. Now it is worth €120bn, up 2.5 times from 2018. Between 2016 and 2019 corporations with good ESG ratings received 15 per cent more investment than those with poor ESG ratings. Some corporate activities (the 'sin' stocks) are considered to be incompatible with the values of the ESG investment market; fossil fuel, arms manufacturer, tobacco. Fund managers and rating agencies automatically exclude these areas from ESG funds and indexes. Fast fashion with its record on environmental issues and lack of supply chain governance could/should be similarly excluded. We might question how a bikini can retail for £4 *without* labour standards being breached.

Information on ESG activities within particular corporations comes to retail investors or fund managers via one or more of the plethora of ESG rating agencies that exist. Each rating agency designs its own criteria for ratings and its own scoring system. This can and does lead to vastly different results. Boohoo received high scores from some ratings agencies because it was using a UK supply chain and this was assumed to contain subcontractors that would offer higher labour standards than those in developing countries. Another example is Tesla; it appears very close to the bottom of one rating agency's table because of concerns about workers' rights but very close to the top in another agency's list because of its disposition towards the environment.

It seems no ratings agency conducted independent inspections of Boohoo's UK supply chain or asked Boohoo for evidence that it had done so. There is no underpinning definition of ESG. In addition to ratings agencies being free to gather and rate data about corporations as they wish, there is no regulation of the ESG claims for the fund they produce (Berg et al, 2020). There are suggestions that ESG funds are weighted towards corporations with few employees. There is no requirement for the claims of assessed corporations to be independently audited or benchmarked against ISO standards. When auditing or benchmarking does takes place it is up to each individual corporation to decide which parts of its operations are examined in this way and what standard is chosen. This creates huge potential for *greenwashing*; corporations are presented in a much better ESG light than their total performance would support. These regulatory and certification absences for ratings agencies, their products and corporate activities make it very difficult for investors, assuming they care about how their investment returns are produced rather than just want to be seen to care, to make either comparisons between funds or sound investment choices. The choice of Boohoo as an ESG investment fund participant and the take-up of those funds demonstrates that there are serious flaws with using ESG in its current form as a proxy for good corporate conduct.

Consuming fast fashion

The remaining actors in the fast-fashion puzzle are consumers and the social influencers who draw them to retailers like Boohoo. Consumers are likely to be price conscious. They, and the social influences that promote these products, know that an £8 dress from a fast-fashion retailer is cheaper than other similar items. It does not necessarily follow that more expensive clothing has come from a supply chain with better governance, but very cheap clothing is more likely than not to come from supply chains where profit margins do not support human rights compliant working conditions. It is important to construct an argument that persuades consumers and influencers to have an obligation not to reward fast-fashion retailers. Sometimes an appeal to localism can concentrate minds but this is problematic in the case of Boohoo, which has received a benefit from localism in its ESG ratings, as the figures discussed in this chapter demonstrate, given that it sources from within the UK. Reversing the localism argument and building a position for change based not on liability and complicity, as we do with retailers and lead manufacturers, but on connection ('this is happening in a city near me') and education is more likely to achieve results. Collective action, although usually hard to organize, might become more of a possibility during a time of limited movement.

Essentially these are appeals for fans of fast fashion to slow down and recognize that they are both privileged and powerful in relation to those who make their clothes and those who sell them.

References
ASOS (2020) 'Investors: Year in Review', https://www.asosplc.com/investors/2020-year-in-review/year-in-review (accessed 1 December 2020).
BBC News (2020) 'Coronavirus: "No obvious source" of Leicester Covid-19 outbreak', 1 July, https://www.bbc.com/news/uk-england-leicestershire-53257835 (accessed 14 July 2020).
Berg, F., Koelbel, J. and Rigobon, R. (2020) *Aggregate Confusion: The Divergence of ESG Ratings*, https://ssrn.com/abstract=3438533 (accessed 20 August 2020).
Boohoo (2019) 'Modern Slavery Statement', https://media.business-humanrights.org/media/documents/Boohoo_snapshot_2021-01-11_170205.7517440000.pdf (accessed 8 January 2020).
Centre for Sustainable Work and Employment Futures (CSWE) (2014) *New Industry on a Skewed Playing Field: Supply Chain Relations and Working Conditions in UK Garment Manufacturing*, University of Leicester and CSWE.

Centre on the Dynamics of Ethnicity (CoDE) (2013) *Local Dynamics of Diversity: Evidence from the 2011 Census*, University of Manchester and CoDE.

Fashion Revolution (2020) 'The Fashion Transparency Index 2020', https://www.fashionrevolution.org/about/transparency/ (accessed 14 August 2020).

House of Commons (2019) *Fixing Fashion: Clothing Consumption and Sustainability* (2019) House of Commons Environmental Audit Committee, 16th Report of Session 2017–2019. HC 1952.

Labour Behind the Label (LBL) (2020) 'Report: Boohoo & COVID-19: The people behind the profit', https://labourbehindthelabel.org/report-boohoo-covid-19-the-people-behind-the-profit/ (accessed 14 August 2020).

Levitt, S. (2020) 'Independent Review into the Boohoo Group PLC's Leicester Supply Chain', https://www.boohooplc.com/sites/boohoo-corp/files/final-report-open-version-24.9.2020.pdf (accessed 27 September 2020).

Matety, V. (2020) 'Boohoo's sweatshop suppliers: "They only exploit us. They make huge profits and pay us peanuts"', *The Sunday Times*, 5 July, www.thetimes.co.uk/article/boohoos-sweatshop-suppliers-they-only-exploit-us-they-make-huge-profits-and-pay-us-peanuts-lwj7d8fg2 (accessed 31 October 2020).

O'Connor, S. (2018) 'Dark factories: Labour exploitation in Britain's garment industry' *FT*, 17 May, https://www.ft.com/content/e427327e-5892-11e8-b8b2-d6ceb45fa9d0 (accessed 14 August 2020).

Office for National Statistics (ONS) (2020) *Retail Sales, Great Britain: June 2020*, www.ons.gov.uk/businessindustryandtrade/retailindustry/bulletins/retailsales/june2020 (accessed 6 August 2020).

13

Social Security under and after COVID-19

Jed Meers

Introduction

The Department for Work and Pensions' (DWP) online guidance for recipients of Universal Credit ('UC') sets out, 'the kinds of things that claimants will be required to do in return for receiving [UC]' (Department for Work and Pensions, 2020). It is, in all but name, a claimant-facing statement of the benefit sanctions regime. In the early days of the COVID-19 crisis, work search requirements and (new) sanctions were suspended for three months from April 2020. If claimants were unable to do 'the kinds of things' they are 'required to do' as a result of the pandemic, they would not be sanctioned. This guidance was updated on 1 July 2020. The change is detailed in full on the document's gov.uk page:

> **1 July 2020:** Removed the wording 'You will not get a sanction if you cannot keep to your Claimant Commitment because of coronavirus (COVID-19)'.

Those UC recipients who are shielding due to health concerns, self-isolating as a result of symptoms, or are unable to find work or increase their hours due to a decimated labour market, may be forgiven for thinking that the COVID-19 pandemic is still very much in motion. Indeed, the deleted sentence appears to be an uncontroversial statement to even the most hardened advocate of benefit sanctions: removing it implies that sanctions may now arise as a direct result of the COVID-19 pandemic. The re-instatement of sanctions and this change to guidance is illustrative of the issues facing the social security system in this ongoing crisis. Does this pandemic really herald a 'new normal' in social security support, or will the state row back quickly? As we enter a deep recession, have the lessons of the last decade of austerity been heeded? Are those same groups hit disproportionately by the austerity agenda – women, lone parents, Black and minority ethic (BME) households, and disabled people – the same being disproportionately affected now?

This chapter cuts across these questions in three sections. The first provides some brief context and an overview of demands currently being placed on the social security system. The second addresses the lessons learnt from a decade of austerity scholarship, and their resurgence in the government's response to the COVID-19 pandemic. The third looks at 'frontier problems' – issues which sit at a three-way boundary between the COVID-19 pandemic, pre-existing challenges to social security administration, and the future of the welfare state. They are all problems that pre-date the pandemic and were already part of the direction of travel in social security administration, but have been exacerbated and accelerated.

Context

In response to the crisis, the government made a series of welcome changes to social security support in quick succession. The UC standard allowance was increased across all age groups by £20 per week, housing benefit increased to cover the 30th percentile of current rents (as opposed to the 30th percentile from 2011), the 'minimum income floor' removed for self-employed claimants, an increase to tax credits, changes to statutory sick pay – to name but some. There is not space to consider all changes in detail in this chapter: for an overview, readers are better served elsewhere (Harris et al, 2020).

At the outset, however, it is worth setting out the ongoing demands placed on the UK social security system and their peak in the early days of the pandemic. The surge in applications for UC – the government's flagship working-age support for those out of work or on a low income – is the starkest example of the almost immediate impact of the lockdown on the labour market. Figure 13.1 details the numbers of UC declarations (effectively, applications for support) made between 1 March and 23 June 2020.

Applications peaked at the end of March 2020 with over 100,000 declarations in a single day. In the first two months of the pandemic, there were 2.4 million individuals newly claiming UC, taking total claimants to 5.6 million by the end of June. The biggest increase is among those aged 16–24 years old, accounting for 30 per cent of new claimants in this period.

This increase in applications is met by a parallel increase in the austerity-era reforms biting on a greater number of households. Taking the 'benefit

Figure 13.1: Declarations for UC made by individuals and households from 1 March to 23 June 2020.

Universal Credit declarations

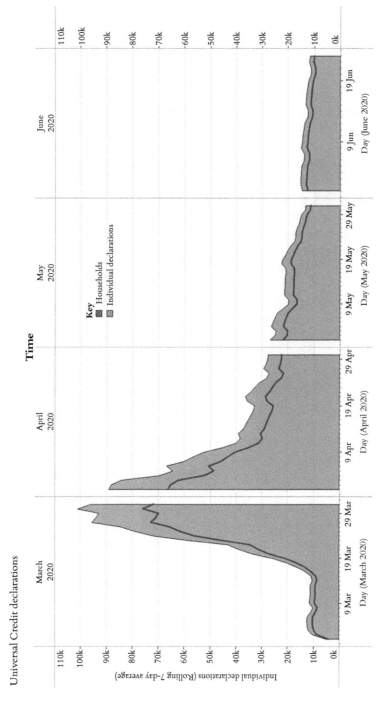

Note: Interactive version available at https://tinyurl.com/UCFigures

cap' as an example (on which more follows), the total number of households affected increased dramatically. The policy limits overall payment of support to individuals and households in receipt of some working-age benefits. Figure 13.2 details the total capped households, from May 2018 to May 2020. In January 2020 there were a total of 78,125 capped households. By May 2020 this had nearly doubled to 153,660.

These figures show that, notwithstanding some welcome increases to payments in response to the crisis, many of the same dynamics from the austerity era are in play. These austerity-era reforms are biting on these same groups most affected by the pandemic. Poverty in BME households has increased over the course of 2019–20; a BME household is now over twice as likely to be in poverty than a White household. The majority of those affected by the cap, as the Supreme Court considered in *R (DA) v Secretary of State for Work and Pensions* [2019] UKSC 21, are lone parents who are overwhelmingly women. Of the new total affected, 62 per cent are single-parent families, and Black and minority ethnic families are disproportionately impacted. Concerns about the benefit cap, bedroom tax, benefit sanctions, PIP assessments, UC transition and many more, not only still stand, but are now likely to affect far greater numbers. The next section revisits three of the lessons from the austerity era and their reflection in the government's response to this pandemic.

Lesson one: poor law echoes

The reductions to social security support in the wake of the 2008 crisis were laced with long-standing Elizabethan and Victorian concerns over relief for the poor. The ancestry of flagship policies in the Welfare Reform Act 2012 and Welfare Reform and Work Act 2015 sought in part to balance the supposed tensions that so obsessed the Victorians' response to poverty: that expenditure on relieving poverty is in danger of jeopardizing sound economic management, and undermining the virtues of self-sufficiency and work. They echoed the processes of differentiation between 'deserving' and 'undeserving' recipients of support from the state, with eligibility tied to behaviour or vulnerabilities.

One of the lessons of austerity is that these stigmas do not buckle when faced with a crisis. Beltram's analogy in the 1980s that the 'workhouse test cannot be applied' when crisis strikes and 'hundreds of workers are laid off in one city' speaks to the idea that normal service is suspended in an emergency (Beltram, 1981). However, we can see evidence of these poor law echoes persisting in the government's current response to the pandemic.

First, there is a distinction drawn between the millions of people in receipt of 'legacy benefits' – forms of support that pre-date the introduction of

Figure 13.2: Total number of households subject to the 'benefit cap' policy from May 2018 to May 2020.

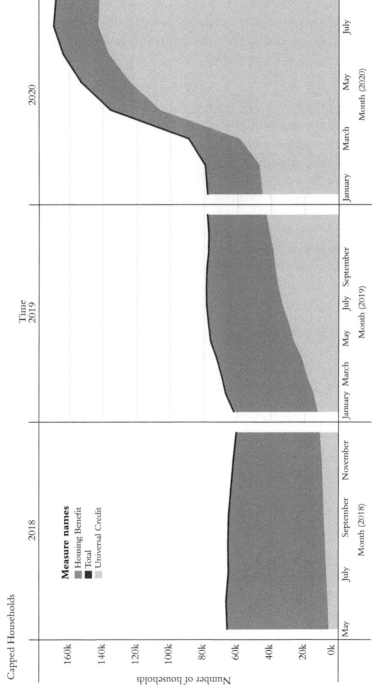

Note: Interactive version available at https://tinyurl.com/CappedHouseholds

UC, such as income-based Jobseekers' Allowance, and Employment and Support Allowance – and those receiving UC. The welcome increase to UC and Working Tax Credits of £20 is not matched for those receiving these legacy payments. New claimants, who are likely to have lost work as a result of the pandemic, are prioritized over those who were already in receipt of support. The nearly two million people receiving Employment and Support Allowance, who receive additional support by virtue of ill-health or disability, receive no uplift.

Second, this effect is compounded through operation of the 'benefit cap'. UC claimants who have been employed for 12 months prior to their claim (for the equivalent of at least 16 hours a week at the minimum wage) receive a nine-month grace period in which the cap does not bite (Harris et al, 2020). Existing claimants or those who do not meet these conditions are subject to a cap that – especially in high rent areas – can push claimants into destitution. This distinction is in danger of creating what Harris et al describe as a 'two-tier claimant hierarchy' in the social security response between those freshly out of (a particular kind of) work and those not: put another way, those deserving of increased state support and those not.

Third, the 'two-child limit', delivered through child tax credit or UC, has been left untouched. The policy limits support under the tied-payments to two children in a given family – a reduction now affecting 250,000 households. It is difficult to conceive of a policy that would do more to indulge the anxieties of an Edwardian- and Victorian-era poor law commissioner. The three key motivations behind the policy for households to face the 'same choices' as those not in receipt of benefits, to create 'more fairness' between tax payers and benefit recipients, and to save money, all view the recipients and their children as long-term dependents in need of a lesson in self-sufficiency (see O'Brien, 2018). The resilience of this policy in the face of this crisis – alongside others in a similar vein, such as the 'benefit cap' and sanctions regime – speaks to the enduring nature of these 'poor law' echoes.

Lesson two: reductions in entitlement and access to justice

In the wake of the 2008 financial crisis, the welfare advice sector faced significant challenges. First, an already over-stretched sector faced a considerable increase in demand. Those subject to reductions in support or earnings came up against the social security system's labyrinthine processes, frequent administrative errors, delays and barriers to access. Second, reductions in social security support were accompanied with reductions in provision for the welfare advice sector. Considerable reductions in public funding – most markedly reforms to legal aid in the wake of the Legal

Aid, Sentencing and Punishment of Offenders Act 2012 – led to pockets of social welfare advice deserts across the country. Indeed, over half of the population now live in an area with either just one housing legal aid provider or none at all.

In the current pandemic, demand for advice has skyrocketed. The Citizens Advice website had its busiest ever week in March 2020, hitting 2.2 million visits. The pandemic has, however, brought with it additional challenges by catalyzing the shift towards digitalization. With applications, internal appeals and tribunal processes moving online, demands on advice sector resources have increased dramatically. Just ahead of the crisis, a survey by the Administrative Justice Council found that 35–50 per cent of welfare advice service users require assistance in navigating online systems, with 34 per cent of organizations unable to meet demand and 33 per cent struggling to meet demand – just 5 per cent could meet demand for such services (Sechi, 2020).

The government's response has, in part, recognized the role played by the sector and that more funding is required. On 4 May 2020, the government announced an additional £5.4 million in emergency funding for not-for-profit advice centres, with Justice Minister Alex Chalk noting that the sector needs support to 'boost remote capability and help as many people as possible during these challenging times'.[1] This does not, however, come close to mitigating the damage done to the capacity of the advice sector over the past ten years, or allow it to meet the scale of unprecedented demand. Recent evidence from the Advice Services Alliance highlights the extent to which pre-existing gaps in capacity and shortfalls in funding are being exacerbated by the COVID-19 crisis: 75 per cent of respondents identified a shortage of access to advice in their area (Advice Services Alliance UK (ASAUK), 2020).

Lesson three: the policy process matters

Social security policy is infamously complex and changes can affect millions of households at a time. The lesson of the 2008 crisis response is that the policy process is of central importance: both the procedures and scrutiny available prior to a measure's introduction, and – as importantly when policies are introduced at speed – the capability and willingness to change approach when evidence of having harmful effects comes to light.

---

[1]   Legal Action Group (2020) 'Government announces grant help for Law Centres', https://www.lag.org.uk/article/208141/government-announces-grant-help-for-law-centres (accessed 23rd January 2021).

In the wake of the 2012 and 2015 Acts, one does not have to look far to find evidence of the policy process falling short. The 'bedroom tax' policy's exemption for children who could not share a room (but not adults), and adults who required overnight care (but not children), was derided as an 'ironic and inexplicable inconsistency' by the Supreme Court.[2] The government's closure of the Independent Living Fund had failed to have regard to the 'potentially very grave impact upon individuals in this group of disabled person'.[3] And, the principle of the UC 'lobster pot' (once you are on the new payments you cannot go back to 'legacy benefits') was derided as a policy 'to do with administrative cost and complexity [and] nothing to do with the merits of their cases'.[4]

Facing a crisis requiring an immediate response, governments must act quickly. There are, however, implications of a 'temporality of exception': where the pace at which legislation is adopted accelerates in the face of a crisis, while democratic or other scrutiny subsides. Government guidance, messaging and application processes are as important. Perhaps the best example in the course of this pandemic is the thousands of households who, in response to government advice, applied for UC, only to find that they had lost (permanently) their entitlement to tax credits. As highlighted by the Child Poverty Action Group's 'Early Warning System',[5] replacing the latter with the former can lead to a loss of monthly income of over £100 in some circumstances. The 'lobster pot' means there is no way back: tax credit payments cannot be restored once you enter the UC scheme. Although the problem was apparent immediately, it took until early May for the DWP to issue clearer guidance and incorporate a warning. By that time, the peak in UC applications had passed.

Frontier problems

Having set out these 'lessons' learnt in the wake of the austerity agenda – and the extent to which the problems that underpin them are resurfacing in the course of this pandemic – this section now looks forward. I deal here with 'frontier problems' that sit at a three-way boundary between the COVID-19 pandemic, pre-existing challenges to social security administration, and the future of the welfare state. They all pre-date the COVID-19 pandemic,

---

[2]   *R. (on the application of Carmichael) v Secretary of State for Work and Pensions* [2016] UKSC 58 [47].

[3]   *R. (on the application of Bracking) v Secretary of State for Work and Pensions* [2013] EWCA Civ 1345 [61].

[4]   *R. (on the application of TD) v Secretary of State for Work and Pensions* [2020] EWCA Civ 618

[5]   See https://cpag.org.uk/policy-campaigns/early-warning-system

but have been exacerbated and accelerated by it. I deal with three in turn, algorithmic decision-making, the connected issue of digital exclusion, and the role and use of discretionary funds.

Algorithmic decision-making

For any technically minded readers, at the time of writing the DWP is looking to appoint talented 'Robotic Process Automation Engineers' to 'deliver and deploy technology to automate routine tasks'.[6] The job posting boasts that:

> To date, DWP have developed and deployed over 44 automations processing over 7m transactions ....

It goes on to tell prospective applicants that:

> Your main focus will be Robotics Process Automation, however, many of our innovative projects will also involve OCR [Optical Character Recognition], Computer Vision, Character Recognition and Natural Language Processing. You will be a member of either the Delivery or Live Service teams within the Intelligent Automation Garage, working in a fast paced environment following agile principles to deliver and run high quality business critical automations.

This DWP 'Intelligent Automation Garage', in which the Robotic Process Automation Engineers sit, is not a new development: it has been in existence since 2017 and now employs nearly 100 full-time staff. The development of automation processes is not entirely in-house. The department has contracted heavily with UiPath – a New York-based tech company. Their company website states that they have 'deployed 50 UiPath Robots now giving a flexibility and efficiency that the DWP could not have delivered before'.[7] They point in particular to their involvement in streamlining a backlog in new pension claims, stating that:

> The process was heavily manual, and this had led to a backlog of over 30,000 claims. Shaun Williamson, Senior Product Manager

---

[6] As these were live job adverts, a link to the advert is no longer available.
[7] Unipath (2020) 'The UK's Largest Government Department Transforms Business Processes with RPA' , https://www.uipath.com/resources/automation-case-studies/dwp-government (accessed 23 January 2021).

at DWP, estimates that the department would have needed to employ thousands of people and taken several thousand hours to catch up. Instead, The Garage deployed 12 UiPath Robots – handling 2,500 claims per week – which cleared the entire backlog in two weeks ....

UiPath Robots are built from easy-to-use customizable templates so the department can create a new Robot in three minutes.[8]

These examples illustrate the pace and scale of change happening under the surface in the DWP. The greater use of digital technologies has been in train for some time; UC was itself designed to be 'digital by default', not only to digitize the claimant-facing application processes, but to facilitate greater use of automated decision-making (for instance, in the detection of fraud, the assessment of income and expenditure, and verification of identity).

This is not a development confined to centralized government. Use of algorithmic 'risk assessment' tools is widespread among local authorities to target households for preventative services or for calculating eligibility. Creative applications abound, with the Local Government Association offering a series of grants as part of their 'digital transformation fund' for innovate uses, such as the London Borough of Hounslow's efforts to 'develop a multi-agency intelligence tool for identifying the top 20 adults with complex needs and chaotic lives' in the borough.[9]

These processes have been catalyzed by the pandemic for two reasons. First, the colossal increase in demand for support creates clear incentives to open up more processes to automation or accelerate programmes that were already underway. Second, the DWP faces a significant backlog on applications that have been delayed as a result of the suspension of face-to-face assessments or the redeployment of staff to process UC claims. As of the end of April, there were 166,630 personal independence payment claimants waiting for a scheduled assessment.

Algorithmic decision-making raises a series of challenges in the context of social security administration. Decision-making becomes even less transparent, with the DWP being reluctant to release the algorithms for automation, even via Freedom of Information Requests. This lack of

---

[8]   Unipath, 2020.

[9]   Local Government Association (2020) 'Digital Transformation Programme funded projects', https://www.local.gov.uk/sites/default/files/documents/digital-transformation-pr-387.pdf

transparency has knock-on consequences for appeals. If the decision is a variant of 'computer says no', how can claimants have adequate information about the basis of the decision to challenge it effectively?

Evidence suggests that automated decision-making raises significant equity concerns. As O'Neil (2016) notes, there is a 'disturbing pattern where human discretion is used for decisions regarding wealthy people, and artificial discretion is used for decisions regarding poor people'. Using historic data to train new systems can ingrain discrimination against certain groups – the so-called 'rational discrimination' of algorithms. As O'Neil argues, this can work to reinforce existing inequalities and further embed structural racism into administrative systems.

It is also important to note that these systems do not remove human discretion. Instead, there is a transfer of discretion to IT professionals – these 'Robotic Process Automation Engineers' developing processes in the 'Intelligent Information Garage'. It is unclear the extent to which their decisions are reviewable, and there is a danger of errors in algorithms to go undetected (as was the case with Australia's Centrelink system,[10] where the algorithm made significant jurisdictional errors in the recovery of social security debts).

Digital exclusion

This long-term trend on algorithmic decision-making – accelerated further by the pandemic – goes hand in hand with the digitization of claimant-facing services and application processes. In response to the crisis, the DWP made a swathe of reforms to application processes across the social security systems, perhaps best expressed in the 'Don't Call Us, We'll Call You' policy, where 'the emphasis [is] on the department to follow up with claimants if more information is needed'.[11] The 'new style' Employment and Support Allowance is an online creature, with an online-by-default application process, and identity checks for UC have been streamlined by allowing claimants to verify their identity through the Government Gateway.

These developments and their likely staying power are set into even sharper relief by the 'digital divide'. The Government's Digital Strategy acknowledges that more than 11 million people lack basic digital skills and

---

[10] Henman, P. (2019) 'Of algorithms, Apps and advice: digital social policy and service delivery', *Journal of Asian Public Policy*, 12(1): 71–89.

[11] Department for Work & Pensions (2020) 'Don't call us, we'll call you', https://www.gov.uk/government/news/don-t-call-us-we-ll-call-you

10 per cent of households do not have access to the internet. These problems are not evenly distributed across the population. Long-standing research into 'digital inequalities' highlights that older and poorer households are by far the most affected. In the context of social security, this is not just about access to services. It is also about access to support. As advice organizations move their staff and processes online and capacity for face-to-face support becomes limited, digital exclusion is more likely both to go undetected and have greater consequences for the excluded.

For those navigating the social security system, the digitization of court hearings has been significant. The Coronavirus Act 2020 (s.55(b) and Sch 25 para.2) provides tribunals with a power to dispose of an appeal without a hearing where (1) the matter is urgent; (2) it is not reasonably practicable for there to be a hearing; or (3) it is in the interest of justice to do so. In practice, this has led to a significant acceleration in the use of telephone tribunal hearings and creates additional incentives for claimants to opt for a paper-based hearing.

Telephone hearings pose inherent disadvantages for certain groups. Early work by the Equality and Human Rights Commission has found that making reasonable adjustments for those with cognitive impairments, mental health conditions and/or neurodiverse conditions is often impossible in a telephone or online format. Applicants participating in hearings with a medical element – such as those dealing with personal independence payment eligibility – may face inherent disadvantages in outcomes. Difficulties in accessing advice or online systems may motivate more to pursue paper-based hearings, at which applicants face dramatically reduced chances of a successful outcome (data shows that nearly half of face-to-face appeals are allowed, compared to just 15 per cent of paper-based appeals).

Use of discretionary funds

In common with long-standing approaches to social security administration, some attempt has been made to plug holes in statutory entitlement through the use of discretionary payments. The Westminster and devolved governments have introduced a wide range of discretionary funds to help those who require additional support as a result of the crisis. In the budget on 11 March, the Westminster government announced a £500 million 'hardship fund' to be distributed to local authorities in England to 'support economically vulnerable people and households'. Government guidance on its use clarified that the 'strong expectation' is these funds will be used to effect a council tax reduction of £150 for those in receipt of local council tax support. Any remaining funds can be used for 'additional discretionary support'.[12]

The Scottish government announced a £350 million fund to support 'those most affected by the coronavirus'.[13] This comprises increased contributions to the existing Scottish Welfare Fund, a new £70 million 'Food Fund' to underpin local authority 'support [to] households who may experience barriers in accessing food'. In Northern Ireland, the pre-existing Discretionary Support scheme has expanded its remit to provide assistance where households have been diagnosed with COVID-19 and/ or advised to self-isolate and has increased the income threshold for those eligible for support.[14]

In total, £3.2 billion of discretionary payments has been allocated to English and Welsh local authorities to deal with the myriad of impacts of the crisis in their local area. These discretionary funds are turned to frequently by ministers in the House of Commons when responding to questions about those missing out on support. Looking at July 2020 alone, Hansard details 29 separate instances of ministers referring to the £3.2 billion un-ringfenced funding given to councils when referring to support for rough sleepers, housing services, adult social care, children's services and the 'most vulnerable' – to name but some. In response to Marcus Rashford's high-profile campaign on Free School Meals, the government's reflex was to refer to a discretionary pot: the £63 million for local authorities to 'support families with urgent needs' and 'provide discretionary financial help' (HC Deb, 21 October 2020, c1136).

Additional funding is, of course, welcome. This approach does, however, present two problems. The first is a 'frontier' problem between the effects of the COVID-19 pandemic and the legacy and continued impact of the austerity agenda. The problems these payments are tasked with helping to alleviate – access to food, housing, support for the 'most vulnerable' – are

---

[12] Ministry of Housing, Communities & Local Government (2020) 'Government confirms £500 million hardship fund will provide council tax relief for vulnerable households', https://www.gov.uk/government/news/government-confirms-500-million-hardship-fund-will-provide-council-tax-relief-for-vulnerable-households

[13] Scottish Government (2020) 'Helping communities affected by COVID-19, https://www.gov.scot/news/helping-communities-affected-by-covid-19/

[14] Department for Communities (2020) 'Minister announces further support for those affected by COVID-19', https://www.communities-ni.gov.uk/news/minister-announces-further-support-those-affected-by-covid-19

long-standing, structural and not a temporary result of the pandemic capable of being plastered over with discretionary funding. Second, local authorities were already facing a funding crisis prior to the pandemic: now the Local Government Association estimates that they face an additional £7.4 billion funding gap. Any additional support must be seen in the context of a decade of rhetoric on 'localism' being matched with the dissemination of local authority budgets.

Conclusion

Social security systems across the world are facing the huge economic shock generated by the COVID-19 pandemic. However, this is not a short-term crisis. Governments, administrators and local authorities must learn the lessons of the last decade of austerity scholarship as we head into another deeper recession. Many of those same injustices that characterized the austerity agenda are present in the government's response to the pandemic. The lessons of the austerity agenda – in particular the distinction between deserving and undeserving claimants, insufficient capacity in an under-pressure advice sector, and how poor process exacerbates poor policy making – are all evident in the government's response to this pandemic.

The COVID-19 pandemic may yet herald a revitalized debate on the appropriate level of social support or lead to current policy changes being put on a more permanent footing. However, the argument that the pandemic is universal, and therefore may lead voters to demand more in the way of social support than has been the case in the UK welfare state model, is blunted by the fact that the pandemic has not been universal at all. Much like the health impacts, the social impacts have been skewed towards those same groups adversely affected in the wake of the 2008 austerity response. Current signs point to a government likely to row back on the positive elements of their social security response and not take heed of the lessons of the austerity agenda.

References
Advice Services Alliance UK (ASAUK) (2020) *Advising Londoners: An evaluation of the provision of social welfare advice across London*, https://asauk. org.uk/wp-content/uploads/2020/07/Advising-Londoners-Report-30072020-1.pdf (accessed 21 January 2021).
Beltram, G. (1981) *Testing the Safety Net*, London: Bedford Square Press.
Department for Work and Pensions (2020) *Universal Credit and your Claimant Commitment*, www.gov.uk/government/publications/universal-credit-and-your-claimant-commitment-quick-guide (accessed 21 January 2021).

Harris, N., Fitzpatrick, C., Meers, J. and Simpson, M. (2020) 'Coronavirus and social security entitlement in the UK', *Journal of Social Security Law*, 27(2): 55–84.

O'Brien, C. (2018) '"Done because we are too menny": the two-child rule promotes poverty, invokes a narrative of welfare decadence, and abandons children's rights', *International Journal of Children's Rights*, 6(4): 700–39.

O'Neil, C. (2016) *Weapons of Math Destruction: How Big Data Increases Inequality and Threatens Democracy*, New York: Penguin.

Sechi, D. (2020) *Digitisation and Accessing Justice in the Community* (Administrative Justice Council), https://ajc-justice.co.uk/wp-content/uploads/2020/04/Digitisation.pdf (accessed 21 January 2021).

14

Maintaining the Divide: Labour Law and COVID-19

Katie Bales

Introduction

In interrupting the supply and demand necessary for global capitalism to function, COVID-19 has significantly impacted upon our working lives. It has exposed the existing inequalities present within our labour framework and drawn attention to the working conditions of 'front-line workers' who have been consistently undervalued and underpaid by UK governments and businesses. The government's response, such as the Coronavirus Job Retention Scheme ('CJRS'), further exemplifies the problematic and hierarchical nature of employment status which privileges certain groups over others. Coupled with a reduction in union representation and cuts to regulatory 'red-tape' for employers, the balance between workers' rights and business interests has been tilted in favour of the latter for decades.

This chapter begins by exploring the ways in which lockdown impacted on the workforce and the position of front-line workers. It then interrogates the existing labour framework on employment status which continues to create precarious classes of workers in the name of 'flexibility'. Finally, the chapter addresses the situation of undocumented workers who, absent the criminal law, remain abandoned by the state. Undoubtedly, the insecure immigration status of those who are undocumented creates a form of hyper-precarity which distinguishes them from our traditional understanding of the precariat. What we see then, is that a hierarchy of rights and entitlements remains prevalent under the COVID-19 labour packages which privileges those with greater security (and often income) over those who are perhaps most in need.

Locking down the labour force

Front-line workers

Lockdown meant that the majority of British businesses were told to close their premises, save for those deemed 'essential' in industries such as childcare, education, health, social care, transport, refuse, cleaning and supermarkets. Women, the working class and non-White populations are disproportionately represented among essential workers. The TUC report[1] that structural racism within these sectors means that people of colour are more exposed to the virus while at work, due to being forced to undertake riskier front-line tasks that 'White colleagues had refused to do', and through the denial of access to Personal Protective Equipment (PPE) and appropriate risk assessments. That over-representation of BAME communities, coupled with instances of structural racism and discrimination at work, are a contributing factor to the higher death rate among this group.

Occupation is a significant factor in terms of exposure to the virus and risk of death. Those working in security, transport, food production, retail, construction, processing plants, and health and social care had significantly higher rates of death from COVID-19 than those in non-front-line positions. Despite the essential nature of this work, and the increased health risks borne out by these workers, their labour is considered to be low-skilled, attracting poor working conditions and poverty wages, often below the real living wage level (£9.30 across UK and £10.25 in London). While many of these workers felt apprehensive about continuing to work during the peak of the pandemic, they were left with little other option in fear that refusal to work would result in a loss of employment. Other personal narratives recount a sense of duty in continuing to work, fostered by persistent military metaphors in the media likening workers to 'soldiers' on the 'front line' of wartime Britain.[2] Yet these workers did not enlist for these positions, nor

---

[1] Trades Union Congress (TUC) (2020) 'Dying on the Job. Racism and Risk at Work', https://www.tuc.org.uk/sites/default/files/2020-06/Dying%20on%20the%20job%20final.pdf (accessed 15 November 2020).

[2] Al Jazeera (2021) '"Worse than War": Health Workers on a Year of the Pandemic', www.aljazeera.com/features/2021/3/10/frontline-healthcare-workers-around-the-world-covid (accessed 24 March 2021); Rafferty, A.M. (2020) 'Coronavirus, Nursing and War: Action That Followed National Conflict Can Help Guide the UK Now', *The Conversation*, http://theconversation.com/coronavirus-nursing-and-war-action-that-followed-national-conflict-can-help-guide-the-uk-now-140320 (accessed 15 November 2020); Bodkin, H. (2021) 'Inside a Covid Intensive Care Ward Where Staff Are on a War Footing', *The Telegraph*, www.telegraph.co.uk/news/2021/01/07/inside-covid-intensive-care-ward-staff-war-footing/ (accessed 24 March 2021).

the heightened risks posed to themselves and their families when signing their work contracts.

The pandemic has brought the importance of front-line jobs into focus and exposed the fact that our country cannot function without 'low-skilled' nursery workers caring for our children, or supermarket attendants stocking our shelves. Yet among the claps for carers and other vacuous platitudes, demands for increased wages have largely been ignored by the government and employers alike. The intention instead is to maintain the status quo and preserve a low-paid, precarious and disposable workforce attendant to acute shortages in the labour market. This position is unsurprising given that many front-line jobs are equated with reproductive labour or 'women's work' which is considered low-value and unworthy of recognition. Despite claims that we are 'all in this together', the reality then is that front-line workers face a much greater level of exposure to the virus than others. A disproportionate number of this workforce are women or minority ethnic suffering from existing structural discrimination and disadvantage who are likely to feel the negative effects of COVID-19 more acutely.

Working from home

The remaining workforce (who were sent home) can further be divided into two camps: the white-collar workers able to work remotely from home, and those whose employers or businesses experienced a total cessation of work, with risks in terms of job security. Remote working was largely granted to middle-class workers considered to be professional who maintained relative security in terms of wages and employment. This is supported by data from the Office for National Statistics (ONS)[3] showing that employers requiring higher qualifications and more experience were more likely to provide homeworking opportunities than for those engaged in elementary or manual occupations.

Economically, the most negatively impacted workers were those for whom lockdown meant a total cessation of work, with serious ramifications in terms of wages and job security. ONS data show that the youngest workers, oldest workers and those in manual or elementary occupations were most likely to be temporarily away from paid work during this period. In order to avoid an economic crisis, the Chancellor announced an unprecedented

---

[3] Office for National Statistics (ONS) (2020) 'People Temporarily Away from Paid Work in the UK', www.ons.gov.uk/employmentandlabourmarket/peopleinwork/employmentandemployeetypes/articles/peopletemporarilyawayfrompaidworkintheuk/august2020 (accessed 15 November 2020).

package of measures aimed at supporting job retention, keeping businesses afloat and buoying the UK economy. In his summer economic update to Parliament, the Chancellor stated that these measures were introduced because the government 'believe in the nobility of work'; yet this conflicts with years of Conservative rule which has reduced the rights of workers and which, as explored later, undermines a number of the recovery policies.

Workers' rights and employment status under market rule

Before COVID-19, the UK's regulatory labour framework was already problematic. It separates those undertaking work into three categories: employees, workers and independent contractors. Different rights and entitlements attach to each status. Whereas employees are given the highest level of protection, workers are restricted to basic rights. For independent contractors who are in business on their own account, employment protections do not apply. The test for 'employee' requires three components: control, mutuality of obligation and personal service. The test for worker status is less challenging, demanding only that the individual performs work personally for another party whose status is not that of a client or customer of the worker in question.

The distinction between the three groups is elucidated in their historical development. During the era of industrialization, work was *legally* categorized into the binary of employees and the self-employed. Whereas employees are obliged to provide work to the employer as required and remain subject to their control, ideally the self-employed have the freedom to choose how and when to work and can keep the profits of their labour (freedom offset by the risk of market or business failure). However, this rigid categorization failed to accommodate a particular group of individuals who did not fit neatly into either category – because their work was casual, meaning they did not carry the obligatory burdens (or security) of employees; yet, normally because their services were limited to a few (or singular) clients, they also didn't enjoy all the freedoms (or profits) of the self-employed. Notwithstanding a number of earlier exceptions, in 1875 Parliament identified the intermediate category of 'workers' which gave the courts an enlarged and flexible jurisdiction in disputes between employers and 'workmen'.

From 1970 onwards, mainly due to pressure from the European Union, Parliament began to legislate protection for the worker category in recognition that certain self-employed people were so engaged in the business of others that they should be afforded limited protection against certain ills such as discrimination and exploitation. The current definition of 'worker' distinguishes them from employees on grounds that, despite having to provide work personally, they maintain greater control over their work and mutuality of obligation (the obligation to provide and perform work) is less stringent than for employees. In practice, however, the distinction between employee and worker is often blurred and their working arrangements barely distinguishable.

For many workers, the ostensible freedoms are not enjoyed in reality as individuals feel compelled to accept this form of flexible work because there are few other options. Accordingly, as noted in the May 2020 Resolution Foundation Briefing,[4] the majority of workers are low-paid with low levels of education, in occupations such as childcare, waitering, catering, cleaning, that are disproportionately occupied by women and those from minority ethnic backgrounds. The idea that this group deserves lesser rights due to the flexible, or precarious, nature of their work is fanciful and instead needs to be framed within the context of a deregulated labour market which employers and the government consider to be an economic advantage. Freedland (2016) refers to this as the 'paradox of precarity' in that those most in need of protection are the least likely to benefit from it.

The disparity in protection was made even more obvious by the pandemic as numerous businesses were forced to close. Statutory sick and notice pay, redundancy and protection from unfair dismissal are only available to employees, and the latter two are only available to those who have worked continuously for the business for over two years. Accordingly, it is much easier for struggling businesses to dismiss workers, who are then left without recompense and the dismal prospect of having to claim Universal Credit (see Meers, Chapter 13, this volume). In order to alleviate the haemorrhaging of the workforce during lockdown, the Chancellor announced the CJRS; but, it has failed to bridge the existing gap in protection, instead mirroring its existing insecurities.

COVID-19 short-term work schemes

Coronavirus job retention scheme and furlough

The CJRS was introduced by s.76, Coronavirus Act 2020. During June and July 2020, the scheme allowed HMRC to reimburse up to 80 per cent of employees' salaries that had been furloughed, capped at £2,500.00 per employee per month (in addition to pension and national insurance contributions). Employers can 'top up' the salaries of their furloughed

---

[4]   Gardiner, L. and Slaughter, H. (2020) 'The Effects of the Coronavirus Crisis on Workers: Resolution Foundation', https://www.resolutionfoundation.org/publications/the-effects-of-the-coronavirus-crisis-on-workers/ (accessed 15 November 2020).

employees should they choose to do so. Research revealed that 70 per cent of furloughed employees received a discretionary top-up, although men and those with higher incomes were more likely to receive this (Adams–Prassl et al, 2020).

Furlough applies only where there is a cessation of work, yet numerous reports suggested that this restriction was routinely ignored, particularly by male workers who were more easily able to undertake their work tasks at home. Accordingly, only 17 per cent of furloughed employees sampled in that research reported working zero hours. The research also revealed that women were significantly more likely to be furloughed than men with inequality in care responsibilities being a key influencer: mothers were 10 per cent more likely than fathers to initiate the decision to be furloughed (as opposed to it being the employer's decision alone), with no gender gap among workers without children. Women and those on low incomes were also less likely to have their wages topped up by their employers above the scheme's 80 per cent threshold.

Initially, to be eligible for the scheme employees had to be furloughed for at least three weeks out of every four. From 1 July 2020, employers could partially bring furloughed employees back to work, while still claiming from the CJRS for the hours not worked, and from 1 August 2020, employers were required to pay national insurance and pension contributions for each employee. At the time of writing, the government have announced an extension of the CJRS which was initially designed to end on 31 October 2020, to 31 March 2021.

The scheme was sorely needed, as reflected by the current rising unemployment figures which reveal that the UK is now in the worst economic recession since records began, with GDP falling by 20.4 per cent in the three months to June. HMRC statistics reveal that as of 14 June 2020, nine million people (a third of all employees) are reported to have been furloughed at a cost of more than £20 billion to the Treasury.

While the premise of the CJRS is a sound one, there are still fundamental problems with it, primarily because the scheme remains restricted to 'employees' despite extending to 'any type of employment contract, including full-time, part-time, agency, flexible or zero-hour contracts'[5] where individuals are paid via PAYE – PAYE only applies to employees. The language of 'employee' governs the CJRS. Many workers also fall

---

[5]   HMRC (2020) 'Check Which Employees You Can Put on Furlough to Use the Coronavirus Job Retention Scheme', *GOV.UK*, www.gov.uk/guidance/check-which-employees-you-can-put-on-furlough-to-use-the-coronavirus-job-retention-scheme (accessed 24 March 2021).

outside payment arrangements via PAYE as unscrupulous employers seek to categorize workers as being independent contractors responsible for their own tax and national insurance payments in order to minimize the obligations owed.[6] Additionally, the state suffers as a result of these sham arrangements, as it collects less tax, which could be used to fund public schemes such as emergency furlough measures.

In addition to the issues concerning status, the scheme is also discretionary, with no rules obliging employers to furlough their staff. The protection is therefore piecemeal and reliant on an employer's initiative rather than being an enforceable, standardized model of protection for all workers. For example, it is unclear whether agencies would bother to furlough agency workers absent a legal obligation to do so because they have no duty to pay workers if work is unavailable. Similarly, there are no obligations between zero-hours contract workers and employers once their timetabled shifts have ended. Accordingly, the scheme relies on the goodwill of employers to provide for their workforce, which conflicts with the character of the UK labour market. It is unsurprising then that around 300,000 people were away from work without pay because of the pandemic in June 2020.

As reflected by the increased number of mothers on furlough, the CJRS also fails to account for individuals who may be unable to work due to caring responsibilities. There is a serious risk that if furlough measures are withdrawn and childcare options are not put in place as is necessary, these women could be forced out of the labour market. Statutory sick pay in the UK, described as 'manifestly inadequate' by the European Committee of Social Rights in 2017[7] stood at £94.25 per week before 6 April 2020 and £95.85 thereafter. This amount is unlikely to cover the outgoings of the majority of working people in the UK. A further issue with statutory sick pay is that it remains restricted to employees, not workers. Therefore, workers who contract COVID-19 and are forced to take time off suffer a double disadvantage through lack of wages and lack of access to sick pay. Adams-Prassl et al note that workers without sick pay are more likely to continue working when experiencing the symptoms of COVID-19. Inadequate sick pay is thus now not only a social issue but also a public health concern.

To compensate small businesses with under 250 employees which paid employees' sick pay during the pandemic, the government set up the

---

[6] See for example the cases of *Autoclenz Ltd v Belcher & Ors* [2011] UKSC 41 and/or *Uber BV v Aslam* [2019] ICR 845, CA in which the courts rejected the employer's sham contractual arrangements falsifying their worker's employment status for their own capital gain.

[7] European Committee of Social Rights (2017) 'Conclusions: (Art. 12-1) Social Security System United Kingdom'.

Coronavirus Statutory Sick Pay Rebate Scheme[8] which allows employers to claim back two weeks' worth of statutory sick pay per employee forced to take leave. Gaps in this form of protection again exist as it refers to employees.

The self-employment income support scheme

For those self-employed persons negatively impacted by the pandemic, the government established the self-employment income support scheme which gives access to taxable grants based on average trading profits. The first grant, which closed on 13 July 2020, covered 80 per cent of average monthly trading profits and was capped at £7,500.00. The second and final grants will cover 70 per cent of average trading profits capped at £6,570.00 in total. Unlike the process of furlough, independent contractors claiming self-employment grants are able to continue trading or can start a new trade or employment venture.

To apply for these grants, businesses must have been trading for over 12 months to enable calculation of their annual trading profits, which must be no greater than £50,000 per year. Average profits are calculated by adding together trading profits or losses for the last three tax years (or less if the business is only one or two years old). This scheme disadvantages younger businesses which are under 12 months old or have struggled to break even in the first few years of trading, as well as those which are subsidized by a variety of grants and charitable trusts (as this income will not be taken into account in the trading profits calculation).

Reflecting on the COVID-19 short-term work schemes

Data from the ONS reveal that the claimant count for Universal Credit increased by 116.8 per cent between March and July, totalling 2.7 million claimants (see Meers, Chapter 13, this volume). Increased usage of Universal Credit supports the theory that the government's schemes left large swathes of workers without protection. Because the goal of these schemes was to maintain job retention, rather than provide welfare, there is a risk that the money poured into the schemes will have been wasted should it fail to meet its intended objectives of reducing unemployment.

In August 2020, the Bank of England warned that the number of unemployed persons in the UK will spike to 2.5 million by the end of 2020,

---

8   HMRC (2020) 'Check If You Can Claim Back Statutory Sick Pay Paid to Employees Due to Coronavirus (COVID-19)', *GOV.UK*, www.gov.uk/guidance/claim-back-statutory-sick-pay-paid-to-employees-due-to-coronavirus-covid-19 (accessed 24 March 2021).

almost doubling the unemployment rate to 7.5 per cent. This is a higher estimate than data from the ONS and Labour Force Survey have suggested, but this is because many people will not currently be looking for work during the pandemic (which is the threshold for the unemployment calculation). Instead, they are recorded as being inactive, a figure which rose by 301,000 in the months leading up to June. The concern is that, as furlough and self-employment support measures are withdrawn, unemployment figures will rise significantly.

Despite the numerous issues outlined earlier concerning the schemes, both represent an alternative to business closures, job losses and increased claims on unemployment benefit. The advantage of adopting a short-term work scheme is that it preserves the businesses' human capital, reducing inefficient dismissals and redundancies. Short-term work schemes also support businesses in periods of low productivity, allowing business activities to continue, and maintain job ties for workers, as well as preventing deskilling. This is important as many people claiming the unemployment component of Universal Credit end up taking on unsuitable, short-term positions in order to avoid sanctions. This results in high staff turnover and a transitory workforce unable to build upon their skills or plan.

Alternative schemes have been present in several European countries for many years as a means of countering periods of low economic productivity. The German *Kurzarbeit* scheme is one of the oldest and most comprehensive which allows businesses to reduce employees' working hours for a period of up to 12 months. During this period, the government will replace 60 per cent of the employees' net monthly earnings, up to a capped amount. In order to prevent businesses taking advantage and claiming subsidies while getting employees to work from home, payments are only available where firms can prove a downturn in production. In order for these schemes to be truly successful, however, they must extend for the duration of the economic shock, and include as much of the workforce as possible so that substitutions cannot be made between different workers. Increasing unemployment figures in the UK indicate that lessons could be learned from the German model. Removal of the CJRS too early will likely lead to increased unemployment, undermining the goals of both schemes when they were first set out. Indeed, if administered correctly, short-term work schemes could represent an important part of the UK's future socio-economic support programme and buoy our treasured and stretched welfare state.

Undocumented workers

While some workers may slip through the gaps of the existing support framework, there is one group of workers who are explicitly excluded from any form of protection under either the Job Retention or Self-Employment Schemes: those who are undocumented in the UK. The exact number of undocumented workers in the UK is unknown but it is estimated that there are around 1 million people working without the right to work. The pandemic presents particular dangers for this group, primarily because their work is classified as 'illegal'[9] and therefore falling outside of traditional labour regulation. Accordingly, it can be difficult to implement measures such as those relating to health and safety, but it also means that workers cannot access any employment rights such as sick pay or unfair dismissal should their work cease.

Though Bogg (2020) argues that the implied contractual illegality found in s34 of the Immigration Act 2016[10] should be balanced against the weight of protective rights' instruments favouring undocumented workers, I remain sceptical that the courts would adopt this approach (when considering statutory construction and the correct application of s34). Particularly in light of the fact that wages earned by undocumented workers can be confiscated as proceeds of crime. What this means is that undocumented workers are largely disposable and can be dropped by employers with little consequence. Nighoskar (2020) reports that this has been the situation for many undocumented domestic workers since the pandemic hit who have been left without wages or notice pay to keep them afloat. While any downturn in the market will likely lead to job losses, unlike regularized workers, undocumented workers remain excluded from the safety net of the welfare state and the government's job retention and self-employment schemes.

Undocumented workers are also highly unlikely to report instances of abuse on the part of employers in fear that they would be prosecuted for working without the right to work. For those in domestic environments, this could mean little respite from abusive employers during the lockdown period as many workers report being asked to remain or live in their workplaces to avoid the spread of infection. Though the Modern Slavery Act 2015[11] is designed to protect those subjected to slavery, servitude or forced labour in the UK, the criminal law approach used within the Act results in limited protection for those subject to abuse because: individuals are too fearful to come forwards due to the potential risk of prosecution; compensation is only available to victims after criminal conviction of the employer, which relies upon claims being enforced by the authorities; and the number of prosecutions

---

[9]   Section 34, Immigration Act 2016.

[10]   Immigration Act 2016.

[11]   Modern Slavery Act 2015.

is minimal compared to the number of referrals made under the national referral mechanism (in 2015–16 there were 884 modern slavery crimes but 3164 referrals) (Mantouvalou, 2018). The Act also only captures those who are subjected to serious forms of slavery, servitude or forced labour, excluding those who are underpaid or suffering low-level abuse from its remit.

The undocumented remain at the bottom of the hierarchy of rights and entitlements exposing them to greater levels of risk and abuse, as well as the negative impacts of the virus should they become ill with little support to assist them.

Conclusion: Continuing the divide under a global pandemic

It is said that solidarity is often evoked or displayed in the wake of an exceptional event such as armed conflict or natural disaster. In such instances even those that profess their indifference to their communities are likely to discover a sense of collective identity, as their well-being is closely tied to that of society more generally. Without question the UK government's COVID-19 employment support packages were unprecedented. Yet, the measures do not go far enough in protecting low-paid, short-term and precarious workers. One of the most significant issues is that the foundations on which the packages were built remain unstable, weighing on an existing labour framework that is fraught with issues concerning status, regulation and the access and enforcement of rights. It is hoped that in the wake of COVID-19 a collective solidarity is forged to rectify the gaps in worker protection highlighted by the pandemic. Increased protection in both the short and long term is needed, and a radical restructuring of the ways in which we attach value to certain forms of work so that those deemed 'essential' receive the recognition they deserve in terms of pay increases and improved working conditions.

Failure to amend the support packages in line with economic conditions also risks rendering the packages themselves nil and void as removal of the furlough scheme while the country remains in economic shock will likely lead to increased unemployment and claims upon the welfare state. This period of reflection holds the potential to open up a public conversation and policy agenda that could transform the future world of work for the better. However, as the UK moves from massive state stimulus to inevitable austerity, overdue corrections to pay and conditions will not automatically fall into workers' laps. It is only via collective struggle and demands from a position of public support and industrial strength that workers will be able to win the gains they are rightly owed.

References

Adams-Prassl, A., Boneva, T., Golin, M. and Rauh, C. (2020) *Furloughing*, Cambridge-INET Working Paper Series No: 2020/36, 17 August, www.inet.econ.cam.ac.uk/working-paper-pdfs/wp2036.pdf (accessed 5 September 2020).

Autoclenz Ltd v Belcher & Ors [2011] UKSC 41.

Bogg, A. (2020) 'Okedina v Chikale and contract illegality: new dawn or false dawn?', *Industrial Law Journal*, 49(2): 258–83.

Freedland, M. (2016) *The Contract of Employment and the Paradoxes of Precarity*, Oxford Legal Studies Research Paper No. 37/2016, 13 June, https://ssrn.com/abstract=2794877 (accessed 25 August 2020).

Mantouvalou, V. (2018) 'The UK Modern Slavery Act 2015 three years on', *Modern Law Review*, 81(6): 1017–45.

Nighoskar, D. (2020) 'Migrant domestic workers and COVID-19: a call to action', *Futures of Work*, 5 May, https://futuresofwork.co.uk/2020/05/05/migrant-domestic-workers-and-covid-19-a-call-to-action/ (accessed 6 May 2020).

Uber BV v Aslam [2019] ICR 845, CA.

15

From Loss to (Capital) Gains: Reflections on Tax and Spending in the Pandemic Aftermath

Ann Mumford and Kathleen Lahey

Introduction

As 2020 drew to a close, the possibility of a significant expansion of capital gains taxation seemed imminent. The clues were there. In July, after the impact of the pandemic had fundamentally changed daily life, Rishi Sunak, the Chancellor of the Exchequer, requested a review of the tax from the Office of Tax Simplification (OTS, 2020), which is an independent governmental advisory body that has the purpose of advising the Chancellor on ways of simplifying taxation. The report was released in early-mid November, and contained recommendations to increase rates of taxation, and to reconsider certain reliefs. A week later, the Chancellor released a Spending Review, which was, he assured, focused on increasing (and not decreasing) spending (Sunak, 2020). Thus, he enhanced investment in the NHS, and protected it (for the moment) from further cuts. Considering these moments in history together, it is fair to deduce that the Chancellor will need to find the money to pay for a significant increase in spending. Capital gains taxation, given the attention it had received since July 2020, seemed the obvious target.

It is also a moving target, and it is challenging to pin down the exact moment in time that could be designated as safe to pause, and to reflect on the way ahead for taxation in the aftermath of the pandemic. One lesson from recent, trying times is that nothing should be taken for granted. Even more unanticipated events might occur which would prompt the Chancellor to consider trying something else. The risk of waiting for activity to pause, before reflecting, is that assumptions of what should be taken for granted remain unchallenged. At moments of great difficulty, it is perhaps more important than ever that creative solutions should be considered, even if ultimately discarded. This chapter argues that capital gains taxation provides the perfect forum for consideration of basic principles of fairness in taxation, and this is nowhere more evident than in a brief reconsideration of the history of its introduction. A reminder of that history follows, and is then compared with an area of government action (spending) which, during the era of austerity, seemed to operate on a set of very different principles. There is no reason why the principles that underpin taxation, and spending, cannot be considered together. The argument will be advanced that, on the topic of government spending, the possibility of principles seems not really to be entertained – and, especially during an era in which the boundaries of taxation and spending often are blurred, there is no reason that the sort of elegant analyses that supported the introduction of capital gains taxation in the 1960s need not be encouraged in the area of modern spending. There are points of discussion that may be borrowed from the past, in the context of tax, and replicated now, in the context of spending. Given the Chancellor's warning that the economic scars of COVID-19 are likely to be visible at least until 2025, if not longer, it is imperative that the possibility of revisiting successes of the past – and, given that the Chancellor is turning to capital gains tax in a dire time of need, then capital gains tax at least could be described as a tool with some potential – requires consideration.

The shift (in focus) from spending back to taxation

The impact of the pandemic on the economy in the UK has been profound. That the worst economic crisis of a generation follows only 12 years after the last, worst economic crisis of a generation is particularly cruel. The contraction in the UK's economy was described by the Chancellor as the worst for 300 years. The only option available to the Chancellor now is to increase spending – which is a marked shift from the spending cuts of the austerity era. The reason for this move away from spending cuts is clear: without an increase in funding, even more jobs would be lost. Preventing job losses is a key focus of the provisions of the Coronavirus Act 2020 that related to taxation. Section 76 of the Act contained the somewhat remarkable instruction that HM Revenue and Customs should take guidance from the Treasury, directly, on tax measures that might be needed. Notes to the Act make clear that this is for the purpose of deciding upon the direction of the Coronavirus Job

Retention Scheme (CJRS), which offers support both to employees and the self-employed. Saving jobs is the focus of the moment.

It is helpful to consider the CJRS in the context of recent and difficult history. Hope as we entered the summer of 2020 that everything would be back to normal by autumn slowly was replaced by the hope of Christmas 2020 re-openings, which, thanks to the optimism offered by successful vaccine trials, was replaced by hope for Easter 2021. When the CJRS was established, the government will have wished that it would not be needed too much, but also will have feared that it might be needed a very great deal. Thus, section 76 of the Act offers the possibility of flexibility and quick, additional action as needed. The lack of process involved in forwarding the responsibility for further action to HM Treasury may not seem particularly surprising against the background of an act that completed its passage through Parliament in a total of three days. There were a number of specific changes to taxation at the time, but most of these related to VAT, in particular as it applied to the service and entertainment industries that were suffering significant losses in the summer of 2020. The Finance Act 2020 which followed contained a few more changes of significance – for example, the potential of personal liability for directors involved in tax abuse schemes (at Part IV, s100), and the establishment of HMRC as a preferred creditor in insolvency cases (at Part IV, s98), and a bit more – but, ultimately, it was difficult to discern an answer to the question which will have been lingering at least since the furlough scheme began: how will the government be able to repay the enormous debts from the significant borrowing which it certainly will be required to undertake, given that it is spending more than it will be able to collect in tax?

It is within this narrative that the careful steps taken by the Chancellor with regard to capital gains taxation, starting with his approach to the OTS in July 2020, are considered. Capital gains taxation would appear to be one of the ways in which the government may have hoped to begin the long process of recovery. This is very different to the response to the last, worst crisis in 2008: then, the coalition government – admittedly, not in the immediate aftermath, but two years later in 2010, in then Chancellor of the Exchequer, George Osborne's, Budget Speech in June of that year – introduced the period of austerity which is the starting point for this collection. Osborne stated plainly the philosophy for the spending cuts that would follow:

> The coalition Government believes that the bulk of the reduction must come from lower spending rather than higher taxes. The country has overspent; it has not been under-taxed.[1]

---

[1]   HC Deb 22 June 2010 vol 512 c167.

Osborne then proceeded to cite the approval of organizations such as the Organisation for Economic Co-operation and Development (OECD) and the International Monetary Fund (IMF) for post-economic crash 'rebuilding' programmes which focused on cutting spending, as opposed to increasing taxation.

The suffering caused by the decisions made in furtherance of this policy has been described in the chapters in this collection. The fact of this suffering will provide an explanation for Rishi Sunak's efforts to distance himself from any suggestion that he will introduce another period of austerity. The problem with his assurances is that his party adopted an approach of austerity in the past, declared it a success (in 2018, via then Prime Minister Theresa May), and now concedes that it faces an even worse problem than the conditions of 2008. It may be that, as with 2008, it will be necessary to wait two years to find out what happens next.

An important legacy of the era of austerity is a series of cases in which key components of the austerity programme – benefit cap, and Universal Credit – were challenged. A number of themes emerged from the litigation of this era.[2] First, even though women often are the most affected by severe cuts in spending and restructuring of benefits, unless they also have children who also are affected, they will not be able to challenge the impact. Second, the approach that courts often will take is one of attempting to discern whether or not Parliament considered the possibility that a cut to spending might have a painful or damaging impact, and little more – the rights infrastructure available to protect citizens is found to be wanting in this respect. Given the presumed cost of this litigation, the austerity programme appeared, in some ways, to be an exercise in ideology, as opposed to an effort towards economic 'rebuilding'. It is the legacy of this ideology which is considered here.

Back to the 1960s

This chapter puts forward the argument that, although the politics surrounding austerity may have changed, the ideology may not have – and, as capital gains taxation appeared to be a favoured tax for the current rebuilding effort – it makes sense to consider the principles underpinning that tax, and see if they have anything to offer the era following the COVID-19 pandemic. The reason for suggesting that the political context of austerity has changed is that it is difficult to imagine a version of George Osborne's language from 2010 being used today. It is clear that, when the time for repaying the borrowing now being undertaken arrives, the problem will

---

[2]   *R (on the application of SG)*, [2015] UKSC 16; *Humphreys v Crs.*, [2012] UKSC 18.

be seen, as Osborne described then, as one of spending (to mitigate the impact of COVID-19), not of taxation. Clearly, the CJRS, and the additional investment in the NHS, will cost more today than the government currently is able to collect in taxes. The reason why it is difficult to imagine that the language will be replicated, however, can be found in a single word: 'over'. In 2010, Osborne complained that the country had '*over*spent'. In 2020, Sunak seems keen to assure us that he will spend enough to carry us through the crisis. There is no reason to suspect that he will ever be accused of having spent too much on the COVID-19 crisis.

In the Chancellor's consideration of capital gains taxation as a potential way of paying for the debts now being accrued, he is approaching a tax based on an ideology which differs markedly from that which underpins what could be described as the ideology of (or against) spending in 2010. Is it fair to compare spending and taxation policies in this way? The answer is yes, for two important reasons. First, at least since the work of the pioneering American tax scholar Stanley Surrey in the mid-20th century, the argument that it makes sense to treat what might be described as tax breaks differently from benefit payments is difficult to sustain (2013). This is a twist on Dee Cook's *Rich Law, Poor Law* (1988) analysis – where she focused on tax fraud and benefit fraud, Surrey drew attention to tax payments and benefit payments. In both comparisons, the government has less money than it might otherwise. When Osborne highlighted overspending, he was making a clear argument of ideology. Even if it may be stretching his words too much to suggest that he was implying that those who had received the *over*spending did not deserve to be paid, at best, he was suggesting that continuing these payments was a luxury that no longer could be afforded.

'You've never had it so good'

Harold Macmillan's assurance at the end of the 1950s was meant to herald an era of rising living standards, and increasing employment. At the start of the 1960s, the wars were long over, and a period of recovery was slowly being replaced by a time in which families might aim to purchase automobiles, and other modern appliances. Job security seemed strong. Real wages were rising. Five years in to this decade, Chancellor of the Exchequer James Callaghan introduced capital gains taxation, explicitly as a response to tax avoidance, arguing that:

> there is no doubt that the present immunity from tax of capital gains has given a powerful incentive to the skillful manipulator of which he has taken full advantage to avoid tax by various devices

which turn what is really taxable income into tax-free capital gains. (HC Deb 06 April 1965 vol 710 c245)

There were other reasons justifying the introduction of the tax as well, Callaghan explained. He insisted that an increase in the value of capital conferred 'much the same' advantage to the owner as an increase in salary does to a wage earner – but only the latter pays 'tax in full' (HC Deb 06 April 1965 vol 710 c245). The introduction of such a tax would create an environment of 'equity and fair play' for wage earners which would not be possible in a system in which capital gains remain untaxed (HC Deb 06 April 1965 vol 710 c245) In only the third paragraph of his budget speech, Callaghan explains that capital gains taxation will contain a remarkable exemption. Although he expressed the ambition that the disposal of 'all assets, with limited exceptions' will be subject to the tax, the owner-occupied house constitutes the 'most important' exemption.

It is interesting to compare how inequality was addressed in 1965, when capital gains taxation was introduced, with 2020, when the parameters of this tax appeared to be poised for change. First, the tax is based on the presumption of structural inequity. The ability to disguise income as capital will not be available to all (see Bales, Chapter 14, this volume) and, thus, making sure that the system taxed those who are able to disguise income successfully would help to restore faith in its 'fair play and equity'. Second, it was not fair to suggest, Callaghan hints, that those who have enjoyed an increase in the value of an asset have not received a benefit equivalent to an increase in wages. Callaghan indicates that there may be exceptions to this, in particular, in the case of the owner-occupied house, one of the most important features of capital gains taxation in the UK.

A principle of this tax appears to be that it really is only equitable to tax people on the gains realized when they dispose of things they do not need. This is fair because, if they were taxed, then they would not have the money to be able to afford another one. A home is a classic example of something that one needs. A home also, however, need not be a private residence. In this sense, it is possible to make the argument that it is unfair to exempt what is likely to be the most valuable asset that many taxpayers will ever own from the reach of capital gains taxation. Especially given the difficulty that the current generation of younger taxpayers will face in securing the financing to buy their first home, collecting less in tax from a generation which did not begin their careers in the aftermath of the economic devastation caused by a pandemic seems difficult to justify. For example, countries with similar capital gains rules for owner-occupied housing have seen urban housing prices skyrocket, as those with access to their own funding reaped bonus prices when selling and upsizing, while those relying on financing under rules designed to prevent falls in housing prices faced higher mortgage rates. As a result, unexpected pressure has emerged from all groups on adjoining housing markets, driving prices up but leaving those with capital gains exemptions in the best bargaining positions. A good example of this is the Canadian government, which has responded with heightened surveillance of ownership details with significant tax penalties for inaccurately reporting on the facts of owner occupations required to qualify for the 100 per cent capital gains exemption.

This is important, because every current indication is that the economic costs of the pandemic will be borne by generations to come. *Statistics Canada* has now reported that the pandemic has accelerated the movement out of urban centres by those seeking more space and less population density, intensifying the gap between those qualifying for capital gains exemptions versus those whose gains and financial resources are smaller (Verma, 2020). The private residence exemption in capital gains taxation was difficult to justify, in the context of intergenerational equity, before the pandemic, and may be even less easy to justify now as it contributes to the gaps between those who have been able to use this exemption.

It is likely that the reason that Callaghan introduced the exemption in 1965 is similar to the reason why Sunak may be reluctant now to reform it. Perhaps no Chancellor would wish to face the political consequences of introducing a tax which is levied on something as emotionally charged as the family home. Additionally, given the regional differences in house prices, it could be argued that such a tax would fall hardest on the South East of England. It may yet be the case, however, that Sunak treads into territory, if he proceeds with a reform of capital gains taxation, that risks political fallout of a different kind.

One of the recommendations proposed by the OTS is an abolition of the death 'uplift' in the interaction between capital gains taxation and inheritance taxation.[3] Assets that are disposed from one spouse or civil partner to another are free of capital gains taxation. When someone inherits the share of a home from a late spouse or civil partner, they inherit the value of the share as it is at the time of death – not as it was when at the time of purchase. When the house eventually is sold – perhaps after the death of the surviving partner, and when the heirs inherit the estate, the fact that the share that was passed on retains that value may offer a significant savings in tax. The abolition of the uplift, however, while it would be a fair

---

[3]   Office of Tax Simplification (OTS) (2020) *OTS Capital Gains Tax Review: Simplifying by Design.* GOV.UK. 11 November 11, www.gov.uk/government/publications/ots-capital-gains-tax-review-simplifying-by-design, 15.

and proportionate reform in light of the difficult economic times ahead, would tread ever so closely to the notoriously difficult political terrain of inheritance taxation. This patently redistributive, and perennially unpopular, tax – so unpopular that campaigning for its abolition formed a key part of David Cameron's ultimately successful campaign for Prime Minister – bases a great deal of its unpopularity in the supposition that it can prevent people from passing on a much-loved family home. The abolition of the death 'uplift' in capital gains tax might have attracted similar attacks, in a different time, but, in the distracting times of the pandemic, it may be unlikely that it will do so now.

From the 1960s to the 2020s – comparing inequalities

In 1965, James Callaghan introduced capital gains tax to redress inequality between the tax burden borne by the wage earner, and the elite who owned capital. It is in the context of the exemptions that he introduced to this tax, however, that additional inequalities become evident. The interaction between intergenerational inequality and the private residence exemption has been mentioned. The fact of exemptions for spousal transfers has been alluded to, but not probed. On the face of it, an exemption for transfer of assets between spouses seems to make sense. The imposition of a tax consequence in response to a family transfer might feel unduly intrusive. The fact that this exemption is available to married couples and to civil partners, but not to cohabitees, hints at the possibility of yet another intergenerational injustice. Putting to one side the questionable value of offering support through taxation for couples to register their relationship with the state, the current generation of young people is statistically more likely than any generation that precedes it to cohabitate. The spousal exemption for transfer of capital assets is another form of financial support that will not be available to them.

It is interesting to compare how inequality was addressed in Callaghan's budget speech of 1965 (who are we taxing?), with Osborne's budget speech of 2010 (whom is receiving spending?). By shifting the focus away from tax relief (which is the point at which Callaghan starts, with his reference to tax avoidance schemes on the income/capital divide), Osborne engaged in rhetoric which not only invoked the binaries that Cook explored, but also established an ideology of the unfair burden of spending for the decade that followed. In 2020, Sunak has recommitted his party to spending, in an attempt to shift the ideology, but has only hinted at how he is going to fund that spending. In order to ensure that the old ideology of austerity does not emerge – following the pattern after the 2008 economic crash – in a few years after the pandemic ends, it is important to reconsider the possibilities of the tax which attracted him.

Capital gains tax was introduced during a time of increasing economic confidence, even as Callaghan would have been aware that, despite the rise in standards of living, the UK's economic competitiveness with other countries seemed to be waning. Ensuring that wealth does not stagnate is one step towards supporting an economy, and thus capital gains tax had the potential to serve a number of ambitions. Whether the ambitions of decreasing inequality were actually achieved, however, is less clear. The exemptions, and the rates, have hindered the tax from achieving the goals set out for it.

Conclusion

There is a sense that capital gains tax was considered for conscription into an important effort. 'You've never had it so bad' will have occurred to many of the most impacted by COVID-19. These are times of exceptional crisis, and thus the consideration of principles which occurred at the introduction of capital gains taxation might offer the start of a response.

Capital gains tax, as Callaghan's budget speech explained, is firmly based on principles, whereas the focus on spending in Osborne's budget speech of 2010 was based only on reluctance – reluctance to acknowledge human need, and reluctance for the overall project of a welfare state. The tax Callaghan produced is in many ways imperfect, but it continues to offer the possibility of discussion about the boundaries of the tax. For example, the private residence exemption was not smuggled in to the tax in the Finance Bill 1965 – it was declared in the third paragraph of the budget. Does this principle withstand scrutiny today? Similar discussions, in the context of spending, are not really possible, beyond the weak constrictions set up by the courts (that is, it is important to demonstrate that Parliament considered evidence of the harm it might cause when restricting government spending).

The proposals from the OTS do not offer a radical reconfiguration of capital gains taxation – even if rates are doubled, and reliefs are cut. And yet a radical reconfiguration may well be necessary – and, for this, it is necessary to consider the foundations of the tax. Nonetheless, the OTS report is to be welcomed, as is the possibility of increasing the reach of capital gains taxation. The private residence exemption is an obvious target, especially in the context of intergenerational equity. A discussion of an accruals basis (is it really justifiable to continue to assess the tax only when a gain is realized at disposal? Is it not possible to consider different approaches for different types of assets?) may be bound to fail (and to fall at the charge that it will be necessary to sell assets to pay the tax), but it might be worth having anyway, just to recapture a sense of possibility. As the current Chancellor of the

Exchequer warned us, the economic scars of COVID-19 are likely to be experienced for years to come. There is a sense that more needs to be done.

References

Cook, D.M. (1988) 'Rich Law, Poor Law: Differential Response to Tax and Supplementary Benefit Fraud', https://library.lincoln.ac.uk/items/11848 (accessed 20 April 2021).

Office of Tax Simplification (OTS) (2020) *OTS Capital Gains Tax Review: Simplifying by Design*, GOV.UK, 11 November, www.gov.uk/government/publications/ots-capital-gains-tax-review-simplifying-by-design (accessed 20 April 2021).

Sunak, R. (2020) 'Spending Review 2020 speech', www.gov.uk/government/speeches/spending-review-2020-speech (accessed 20 April 2021).

Surrey, S. (2013) *Pathways to Tax Reform: The Concept of Tax Expenditures*, Cambridge: Harvard University Press.

Verma, R. and Hussain, R. (2020) *The resilience and strength of the new housing market during the pandemic*, www150.statcan.gc.ca/n1/pub/45-28-0001/2020001/article/00080-eng.htm (accessed 20 April 2021).

Index

References to figures and photographs appear in *italic* type; those in **bold** type refer to tables.

use of influenza stockpile 97–8

R

*R (DA) v Secretary of State for Work and
    Pensions* [2019] 174
race and racism 65–77
    anti-racist legal education 71–7
    and citizenship 70–1
    concept of race 67–8
    everyday racism 66–7
    front-line workers 188
    impact of COVID-19 65–6, 68–71
    and intersectionality 67–8
    Leicester garment workers 70
    and normativity 69–70, 71, 71–2
    racial state 67–8
    and women 67
    see also BAME communities
Rawnsley, A. 89
recreation rules 82–3, *83*
Reicher, S. 79
relational justice 60
remand prisoners 41, 42, 43, 54, 56, 62–3
Remdesivir 1
remote justice and criminal trials 41–51
    arguments for 47–51
    backlogs 41
    criticisms of 44–6
    dignity of defendant 49–51
    and enhanced sense of engagement 47–9
    impact of poverty 42, 44–6, 57
    latest law and guidance on 43–4
    mixed mode hearings 43, 51
    pre-pandemic 43
    remand prisoners 41, 43
    as response to pandemic 43–4
    technical issues 45
    youth justice 56–7, 61
remote justice and vulnerable litigants 27–39
    and anxiety 30–2
    communication difficulties 34–6
    court interpreters *28*, 32, 34–5, *35*
    and disrespect 34
    and distraction 36–7
    guidance for 38–9
    legal etiquette 28
    maintaining open justice 33
    and mistrust 32–4
    and social security appeals 182
    sources of confusion 28–30
    technical issues 30, 37
    third party access 33–4
remote working 189–90
rent arrears 23, 24, 133, 134
rented housing
    evictions 20–6, 132–5
    as new normal 136
retail trade *see* corporate sector

Rhodes Must Fall movement 72
rights and solidarity in lockdown 79–91
    high profile rule-breaking 88–9, *90*,
        113–14
    loss of liberty 81, 82–6
    public opinion 81–90
    resilience of social solidarity 81
    rights consciousness 82–6
    and rule compliance 87–9, *88*
    seesaw dynamic 90–1
    social solidarity 81, 86–90
rights-oriented social care 127–8
Rolnik, R. 4
rule of six 18
Runnymede Trust 65–6

S

Saini, A. 67
schools *see* education (schools)
Scotland
    Chief Medical Officer 88, 91
    COVID-19 deaths **121**
    discretionary funds 183
Scott, D. 72
Scottish Welfare Fund 183
secondary legislation 17–18
self-employed 190, 194
self-employment income support scheme 194
sexual abuse in adult social care 123–4
Shelter 132, 139
shopping *see* corporate sector
shopping rules 82, *83*
short-term work schemes 191–5, 197, 200–1
Sinclair, A. 17–18
Singh, G. 75
slavery 67, 72, 75–6
    modern slavery 160, 196–7
social care *see* adult social care
social security 2, 171–84
    access to justice 176–7
    algorithmic decision-making 179–81
    appealing decisions 177, 181, 182
    and austerity 172–8, 184
    bedroom tax 4, 178
    benefit cap 174, *175*, 176
    benefit sanctions 171–2
    digital exclusion 177, 181–2
    discretionary funds 182–4
    impact of COVID-19 171–3, 174, 176,
        177, 178, 183–4
    increase in applications 172–4, *173*
    increase in benefit amounts 172–4
    legacy benefits 174, 176
    policy process 177–8
    two-child limit 176
    Universal Credit (UC) 171, 172, *173*, 176,
        178, 180, 194
    virtual courts 182